Th

Three Resolutions

A Philosophy and Handbook

for

Effective Living

For Ty and Sal

who try desperately to keep me honest!

Thank you for your friendship.

Chapter Five – The Third Resolution

Isn't Ambition a Good thing?; The effects of Unbridled Aspiration and Ambition; The Third Resolution; Conscience and the Third Resolution; Talents, Skills, Knowledge and Experience; Applying the Third Resolution – Service; Success –True Success – results from Service; Applying the Third Resolution – Purpose; Stress and the Third Resolution; Exercise; Serving suggestions.

Chapter Six – The Importance of a Mission Statement in Executing The Three Resolutions

What is a Personal Mission Statement; How to prepare your Personal Mission Statement in the context of the **Three Resolutions.**

Chapter Seven – An Academic History of The Three Resolutions

How the **Three Resolutions** developed from a religious tenet into a life philosophy.

Chapter Eight – What Now?

What are you going to do about what you have learned?

Appendix A – Three Resolution Goal Setting

Appendix B – Time Management and the Three Resolutions

Appendix C – Running Programme

Appendix D – Miscellaneous Articles on a Three Resolutions Theme

Bibliography

Preface – A Declaration of Intent

This is a book with several objectives (some of which are quite self-serving).

The purpose of any non-fiction book is to provide knowledge, counsel, instruction or opinion. The purpose of a self-help book is no different, except it is expected, by the reader, to apply to their lives specifically, and to teach them something they have sought out as opposed to something which they have been directed to study.

In some regards this book will probably be no different, except to the degree that in some small way it is intended, in addition to the usual objectives, to be a teeny bit philosophical. Just a teeny bit, mind. Nothing too deep. Bbut just to be clear I would like to express my intentions in a bit more detail. I want to tell you exactly what this book is intended to achieve – for both of us. Yes, I intend to get as much from writing this book as you get from reading and applying it.

This is book focused largely on self-leadership.

It is focused on *self*-leadership because fully and effectively becoming who we want to be, discovering what we want to do and how we want to do it, and finally obtaining what we want to have, is our own responsibility. Being, doing and having. The three key motives to existence.

I use the term Being in the context of how we behave, how we approach life, how we present ourselves to the world, our character. I use the term Doing in the context of our work and personal lives, and in our general activities. And when I say Having, I mean in the sense of our possessions and, in reality, our relationships.

No-one should be expected or directed to make those choices for us if we want to succeed on our own terms. They can make those choices *if we let them* though our own negligence – and I'll deal with that later in the book - but once we make a conscious choice about what we want to be, do or have, other people should only be seen as a source of the support and training we need to get those things.

Having said that, the truth is that in order to be, do or have what we want, we occasionally have to lead or be led by other people, too. That is usually called 'work'. So there will be some observations on leadership from an interpersonal perspective.

But when push comes to shove, at the end of the day, when all is said and done and when the rubber meets the road – I hate clichés.

Seriously, how we lead ourselves is reflected in how we lead and manage others, or how we respond to being led by others, which means self-leadership is foundational to life leadership. Great leaders are great *self*-leaders. Fact.

My intentions are as follows:

- to tell you, the reader, what the **Three Resolutions** are by describing them in intricate detail. My desire is to help you not only understand the concept of the **Three Resolutions** from a theoretical and philosophical perspective but to also consider how the Resolutions might be applied by you to your own circumstances:
- to *encourage* you – either directly 'as written' or as understood and adapted by you – to introduce the material into your own life and to your own individual circumstances. My belief is that the philosophy is sound – the practices might be different for you, but if you read what is written and think 'that's all very well, but in my case......', then provided you actually **do** something about that self-directed analysis, I shall have succeeded. I aim to detail what it is about the **Three Resolutions** that you can take away, adapt and introduce into your own life so that you can reclaim your health, enthusiasm and motivation: and
- to educate you a little by providing a chronological and developmental history of the **Three Resolutions** concept – but not until *after* you've been taught the 'how'.

On reflection, I would suggest that there are essentially two ways books like this tend to be written. There is the more intellectual approach, which is to detail all the theories and science behind any and all of the claims, observations and suggestions made in the text before espousing a practice that will help you to achieve your desired outcome. At the other end of that spectrum is the simple and straightforward 'How to' approach, lacking intellectual substance but telling you, in a simpler, more practical and profound fashion, specific actions you need to take in order to get what you hoped or expected to get from reading it.

In his book, *"How to be Brilliant"*, Michael Heppell described how he presented material like this to a room full of schoolteachers. At that time his approach was mainly motivational and he wanted to teach children so that they could become honest, upright and successful adults. Children didn't need the science, of course. They just needed the 'how-to' and some emotional pressure to do that. Michael had to convince teachers that his material was safe for the kids, and that it worked. After all, he needed to convince the people through whom, one assumes, access to the children would be provided.

He demonstrated his 'stuff' to a room full of professionals, only to be challenged on the scientific basis for his training, and was asked for an explanation of what part of the brain was receptive to it, and how it manifested itself psychologically, etc. etc. He was flummoxed, couldn't answer the questions, and failed in his objective. However, he wouldn't be frustrated so he sought out the information needed to answer that question and was later able achieve his goal.

With the 20/20 hindsight borne about as a result of reading that, I'd have replied, "Did you drive to work this morning, or come on a bus?" Assuming the answer provided was as expected – no-one walks any more, after all - I'd have asked for details of the combustion engine, the order of events in the ignition cycle, the logic behind driving on the left, and a full explanation of under- and oversteer. In the hope that the teacher wasn't an advanced driver and they couldn't answer all the questions, I'd have said, "Sometimes you just have to trust that you know enough to make something *work*." In the same way as knowing how to flick a light switch to help you read in the dark doesn't require an electronics degree.

When it comes to books like these you can approach the content wanting to know the ins and outs of the science, psychology, sociology, physiology and any other 'ologies' behind it – or you can seek out th common sense in what is written, accept that you haven't been applying it, and learn anyway.

My approach has been to aim somewhere in between the two extremes although my focus is, if you like, to the latter, more practical end of the spectrum. My approach is therefore what some may call pseudo-scientific or 'pop-psychology', in that what I am writing is mainly the result of experience and study. other writers. In truth, I discovered my own life philosophies as a result of understanding and applying what I have learned from other writers and speakers, both from the intellectual and motivational camps.

So yes, to a degree this is ~~plagiarism~~ research based material.

The point of this book is to get things across clearly, but briefly. In my mind the subject matter lends itself to that method because so much of it, while it may not be common sense, is so patently and obviously true when you read it that the points made do not have to be laboured. I have tried to avoid overusing sentences with umpteen adjectives in them. It's not as pretty a book as it could be, but it gets the message across. I hope.

Finally and selfishly – I wanted to write the book in such a way as to support my own desire, even my *need* to apply the **Three Resolutions** in my own life. I'll be clear – like you, I (still) have difficulty in living in complete congruence with what I know to be true. Like you, I find living my ideal life is very, very challenging. Writing this book means that I now have to be seen to try harder to live in accordance with what I believe. That's surprisingly hard.

Gandhi said: *"I simply want to tell the story of my numerous experiments with truth, and as my life consists of nothing but those experiments, it is true that the story will take the shape of an autobiography."* I suppose that this, then, is my own experiment.

Without further ado, then, here are **The Three Resolutions.**

First Resolution

"To overcome the restraining forces of appetites and passions, I resolve to exercise self-discipline and self-denial."

Second Resolution

"To overcome the restraining forces of pride and pretension, I resolve to work on character and competence."

Third Resolution

"To overcome the restraining forces of unbridled aspiration and ambition, I resolve to dedicate my talents and resources to noble purposes and to provide service to others."

Foreword

I have been a student of Dr Stephen R Covey and his copious writing since the early 1990s, following the serendipitous 'discovery' of his works while I was conducting my earliest research into the science of time management. I'd read some interesting works on the subject before I came across what was in fact his third mainstream book, entitled 'First Things First' (1994). Up until then I had been enthralled by the concepts and methods of the art of time management as I had tried to improve my productivity in the workplace, which for me was a busy police station in South Wales, UK. Unfortunately, up until my discovery of First Things First, all the books I'd read were essentially vast volumes of methods, how-tos, specific techniques and their numerous applications. But then I found First Things First in my local library and the way I lead my life genuinely changed - although that's an assessment based on hindsight and the experience of the following 20 years.

I want to be absolutely clear – I mean every word of that last sentence. After I read and started to understand this material, things were never the same again in many respects, and not just in terms of productivity. What is more, when I say 'started to understand', I have come to realise that each new reading provides new perspectives on life-leadership and the management of time in the context of 'self', and interpersonal relationships. In fact, even *this* paragraph has been rewritten as a result of that constant change in my levels of understanding.

'First Things First' was my first Covey book and what hit me was that unlike the other famed and expert writers whose books I had studied up until that moment, he explored time (or rather life) management from a far deeper perspective. Time management books had all too often been about self-management, but here was a book that spoke of self-*leadership*, not only in the context of one's use of time but also in the context of relationships with other people, and most importantly in terms of the individual's *whole* life – not just work, but also one's personal life in terms of lifelong goals, life*style*, and the pursuit of a personal legacy. It was deep and profound, but it was also pertinent and easy to follow. Further study over the years has improved my own insights on the subject, and as my vocabulary and my intellect have developed in the broader sense, so has my ability to find new meaning in the content of this classic. Not many books have done that, at least for me.

Many time management books look at the subject only from the individual's point of view, and often only with their management roles in the corporate world in mind. Covey's books dealt not only with an individual's working needs in mind, but also with their private, interpersonal and non-professional personal management needs, a rare perspective. One thing I learned from studying them was that everything we do as an individual is done *for* someone, *because* of someone, or *with* someone else. We are individuals only in a physical sense, but we are part of an interdependent life which relies on and is impacted by others, and where others also rely on or are affected by us.

A prime example of the nature and depth of Covey's thinking is the advice that one should develop and adhere to a Personal Mission Statement, a code of conduct and ultimate life philosophy that should guide your every thought and deed. His emphasis was on the fact that it was YOUR Mission Statement, not one designed, dictated and used as a foundation for judgment *of* you by other people, which might be the justifiable case with corporates. The only entity who can judge you against your Personal Mission Statement should be and shall be YOU, and you alone.

As a result of my understanding and conscious, deliberate application of this concept I wrote many such statements over the following decades, developing them as I myself developed and grew through the discovery and study of the nuances and perspectives of the wider field of personal development. Despite many changes in the precise words, the tenor of the different statement' was always fairly consistent and, in the main, I lived in accordance with the statements that I crafted. But only 'in the main'- in many respects I was not absolutely compliant with the words I had so carefully assembled.

Through my successes and failures to comply with my own ideal, I have discovered the difficulties of writing a mission statement that is powerful enough to make someone 'move' on it, but not one that is nigh on impossible to achieve. The challenges and benefits of the creation of a mission statement will be addressed later.

Covey, to most bookshop visitors, will be known as the author of The Seven Habits of Highly Effective People. In 2020 the 30th Anniversary Edition was published and it reached the bookshelves again. It is usually found in the business section, but whether that is the right place or not I leave to others to decide. However, what you are reading now is the result of my study of his second, less famous mainstream book.

Not as popular in terms of sales as The Seven Habits, it held what was, for me, an absolute golden nugget. That book was entitled *'Principle Centred Leadership'*, and if available, is always to be found in the business section of a bookstore. What I found, however, is that while the latter half of the book relates to leadership in the world of work (corporates, schools, industry, etc.), the whole of its first half described leadership from an individual's perspective – in other words, he invented the concept of self-leadership. He identified how leadership of one's self underpins one's ability to lead others, but could 'just' be a desirable end all of its own.

In this book he explored personal development and self-leadership in the context of a progression from Day 1 (baby steps, new learning) to Day 7 (mastery). He expanded upon important principles and roles like honour, relationships and parenthood.

It is both a sobering and empowering read. It is sobering because it politely and respectfully reminds the reader of their conscience, and helps the reader to see where they are failing to listen to that voice. And it is empowering because it tells the reader that they have the ability to start listening again, if they want to.

The absolute gem in this treasure trove, for me, is a chapter headed "The **Three Resolutions**".

The shortest chapter in the book, it powerfully makes the point that three things get in the way of our becoming principled leaders, whether it be leaders of ourselves or leaders of others. Calling them **Restraining Forces,** Covey describes how they can powerfully influence us to the degree that we allow them to draw us away from what we could become, if we don't fight against them. Like any disruptive force, they need not be applied to us 'head on' to keep us from achieving our objectives. They need only buffet us lightly to create a diversionary effect and take us away from our intended course in life.

To illustrate this concept of buffered diversion, avid cop show viewers will have heard of and seen application of the PIT Manoeuvre, where a pursuing police vehicle gently nudges a fleeing vehicle on the rear corner, causing the target to skid wildly out of control. These officers do not ram the target car. They don't have to. Put simply, they make contact with the back end of the target vehicle, then accelerate hard and steer slightly into the target, pushing the car just slightly out of alignment with the bandit driver's intended direction, and the laws of physics then take over as the back end, pushed, tries to overtake the front end because the police car 'force' is moving just that little bit faster. It is a tiny force, but its effect is visibly dramatic. And very messy.

The Restraining Forces do the same thing as that well-trained law enforcer – they constantly 'nudge' us and we stray from our intended path despite our desire to stay on course. They don't nudge at us from behind, like the cop cruiser, though – they nudge us from the *inside*. We push ourselves off course, but the results can be just as messy.

There is an even more impactive example of how a Restraining Force can take us off course.

Take a compass. Imagine that, for you, North represents the direction you know you should take if you want to live the kind of life you hope reading this book will bring you. Follow that path and you will get to your destination, just as you would if you were lost in a jungle.

Restraining Forces are like a magnet. Put a magnet against that compass and you know, don't you, what will happen. The needle will point at whatever the direction the magnet/Restraining Force dictates. You could, if unaware or uncaring, follow the wrong path if you allowed that magnet to dictate your path.

Like the magnet or the cop, if unaddressed or properly countered you will find that Restraining Forces can and will completely undermine any desire that you may have to live a productive, respected and successful life.

Covey identified and named three Restraining Forces. He called them:

- Appetites and Passions.
- Pride and Pretension.
- Aspiration and Ambition.

On first analysis one could be forgiven for saying that passion, ambition and pride are positive, if not essential values if we are to succeed. Most personal development books would trumpet them as the main characteristics of those who *have* succeeded. In fact, there are probably books written on each individual characteristic as their main focus.

Arguably those characteristics do need to be demonstrated by the successful. It would be hard to maintain a premise that suggested otherwise, but they do became Restraining Forces when they become a primary or sole driver behind our activities, and do so at the expense of more important things like family, society, competence and the conscience-identified 'greater good'. They become Restraining Forces and hold us back when they take over, when their pursuit serves only self-interest, when that pursuit becomes an end in itself. I write more about the definition and application of the Restraining Forces in their particular sections, but for now, please accept that they exist and continue reading.

Anyway, I read that excellent chapter and developed an almost burning desire to discover his expanded views on those very subjects, but while they have probably been dealt with in some tangential fashion in the pages of his many works, there was nothing specific within this chapter to salve my curiosity. I wanted more, but it wasn't right *there*.

Returning to my own story – I had a Personal Mission Statement and in the main it was working for me. But let me tell you about Zig Ziglar.

Ziglar was a writer and speaker who grew up during the Great Depression in the USA, and many of his great stories are a reflection of how he and his family overcame the restrictions and challenges that a Depression can bring to a young family being raised by a relatively young widow. He credited his wise mother with the many great quotes which he later gave to his massive audiences. Joining the US Coastguard during WWII, he completed his service and went into sales, selling cookware. Starting out as an abject failure where he found he was spending more than he was making, he experienced a 'AHA!' moment when his own mentor expressed disappointment that Ziglar wasn't reaching the potential that the mentor saw in him. Reappraising his approach and topping the sales leagues ever after, Ziglar entered the personal development 'field' in the early 1970s.

He started writing a book on personal development. He later stated in that bestselling book 'See You at the Top' that when he started writing it he weighed somewhat more than might have been appropriate for a personal development writer and speaker. He was 30+ pounds overweight, so while he was a successful salesman and philosopher of the science of personal development, he was not 'walking his talk' – and he talked a lot – in some areas of his life. As he put it himself, if he had turned up fat, wobbling and sweaty to sell a philosophy of principled, healthy living, he may have never sold any books at all. In the event he sold millions of copies of that book and established a generation of people who listened to, or read about, character-based personal development. And several years after his death those who knew him still revere the way he walked his talk and tried to live what he promoted (although even he indicated how hard it was).

That's how I approached this project. I knew all this stuff, I'd been studying it for 20 years and for several of those years I'd even been teaching it in one capacity or another. I knew great ways to lose weight and keep it off. I knew ways of managing myself to create excellent results. I had run a half marathon (twice), and while that may not be a spectacular achievement these days, for a non-athlete who at one stage couldn't run for 10 minutes let alone over 10 miles, it was an achievement for me. Particularly when I ran the second one, by which time I weighed 2 stone more than on the first attempt, and detested running! (I couldn't even conceive running twice as far, though.)

But things had changed. Reluctant as I have always been to admit it, it started in 2007 when I was diagnosed with Non-Hodgkins' Lymphoma, a kind of cancer that, to my knowledge, killed three serious athletes in the months leading up to my starting to write this book. (I consider myself incredibly lucky not to have suffered their fate.)

I had just changed jobs and was dragged away from a role for which I had passion onto a project I hated and, while I maintained the sensible diet that had got me to a good weight, the job change to a more sedentary position must have had an effect on my metabolism because from that date to the end of 2013 I gained nearly four stone (56lbs).

I often looked at fat people and thought, "How did you get so fat! Did you wake up one day and realise how fat you are?" But then I realised that two of the four stone had slowly built up, while the last two were probably just me being too lazy and undisciplined – possibly even resigned - to stop it. I watched and actively supported my own efforts to get fatter and fatter! It was all easily rationalised because I could still run – like I said, I ran the second half-marathon 2 stone heavier than the first and only took 6 minutes longer in doing so. Go figure.

As Ziglar himself said, "I chose to get fat. I never accidentally ate anything in my life!"

I was unhappy at work and I felt that although the results I was getting were 'enough' and I was generally getting the respect that I felt I deserved, something was missing 'inside'. I was on the verge of retirement, with no immediate prospect of what I intended to do next. I would sit at my desk uninterested in doing more than my planner allowed: once the list was completed I would wait in vain for an email or telephone call to push me back into action. I would make appointments days in advance for jobs which could easily have been done sooner, just to make sure I had something meaningful to do at a later date. My impending retirement was a situation that did not really lend itself to my taking overall responsibility for new projects because they would easily outlast my employment – as a fraud investigator I knew that any new job could easily take two years to complete, and I only had months left to serve. Furthermore, the organisation's administrative demands in terms of getting the simplest task done, or even obtaining permission to do the simplest of things, were also very wearing. Everything seemed to be so much effort for so little reward. I was so fed up I once punched a fax machine. The kick missed, fortunately.

Oddly, my passion for 'the work' had diminished but my desire to be productive hadn't. I would proudly complete a large job and tick of my to-do list. The more ticks I could get in a day, the better I felt. The world of work was wonderful when I was in control, but when other things controlled me or my activity I could get really, really testy. Ask the fax machine.

I had a couple of side-line activities that engaged my time but which weren't giving me the satisfaction I'd used to get. I was Principal of a professional Institute that was heavily engaged in consultation with government and other departments, but I was doing it for free and it wasn't a constant process; there were large gaps in time when I couldn't do anything in its regard, or at least I felt that way. With hindsight there was probably a lack of initiative on my part that, when I addressed it, made a huge difference.

I'd paid for a licence to train children at a local comprehensive school in the field of personal leadership but there had been some slippage in attendance from my volunteer teenage audience and I was wondering if my personal investment had been injudicious. I enjoyed teaching the students but their other commitments were taking them away from consistent attendance, which was a little demoralising although I was pleased to be able to present 6 young people with certificates at the end of the course of lessons. This training also had highs and lows – one student whose goal was to work for Cirque du Soleil left school for 'circus college' – there is such a thing – and pursued his dreams, while another passed away at the age of 19 from the debilitating after-effects of cancer, the same cancer that I'd fought off. (She faced that challenge with inspirational bravery, starting a blog called "Remission Possible", and her death, post-remission, was hugely unexpected.)

I had been a regular participant in a Speakers Club but having gained the speaking confidence I'd gone there to discover it now seemed an expensive inconvenience as it was 15 miles from my home. I was now doing it to avoid offending the people there, people who worked hard to keep the club as successful as it is.

By July 2014 I weighed 16 stone 10 pounds (234 pounds) at 6' 2" on a sunny day. My measurements were at least 42", 42", and 42", although I could get into a 38" waist pair of trousers. I had been able to run (jog) for 30-35 minutes, but now found 12 minutes a challenge. I'd fought and beaten the cancer but I just wasn't happy with my body image. This was brought home quite dramatically in the workplace.

At one end of our open-plan office was a convex window, placed exactly opposite the end of an office-long central aisle. As people walked towards it, the lighting was such that the window reflected the employee's image right back at him or her. The convex construction mean that the image reflected was a tad wider than reality, meaning that the expanse of a corpulent waistline was exaggerated with comedic effect.

In the end, there was only one truly effective solution to this in-your-face obesity challenge. No, not losing weight, but putting a large piece of paper right over the offending window. Talk about rationalising and denial!

In truth, I was not committed to training my mind and body to do anything to get me back to where I had been in 2004 – 13 stone (182 pounds), fit as a fiddle and happy – *gloriously* happy - in my work.

It was as a result of these experiences that I later decided to write this book. I had concluded that for all the material written and provided in audible form by many personal development authors and speakers - none of which was wasted - the solutions to my own problems could all be found through judicious understanding and application of the **Three Resolutions** (3Rs). In other words, by applying the 3Rs philosophy to what I already knew, I could create or recreate the results I had been missing, and perhaps go on to even greater personal successes.

So I decided that I would start applying the **Three Resolutions** and retake control of my life. And I did.

This book explains the concepts of **the Three Resolutions** and how they can be applied in your life. I would wager that many of the things I cover are things you already 'do', but reading this may make you more aware of why you are doing it, and identify where you might do more of whatever it is you are doing that makes you great - and less of what is getting in your way.

Including doing less of the 'you' that is getting in your *own* way.

Have you ever noticed how people love to tell stories? Going further into that, have you ever noticed how, when someone tells *their* story your first and almost overwhelming desire is to tell *yours*? Your story, the one that: is better/funnier/more tragic than/more interesting than/reinforces theirs? The fact is that we all think we have a story that is either parallels or puts an alternative spin on that experienced by others.

I quoted Gandhi earlier. He wrote: *"I simply want to tell the story of my numerous experiments with truth, and as my life consists of nothing but those experiments, it is true that the story will take the shape of an autobiography."*

In that regard, this book represents my own struggle with the concepts described. I hope you see them as parallels to the problems and challenges you experience in your own life. It was once said that what is most general is most personal – in other words, we all suffer the same challenges to varying degrees or in different ways, but there are similar characteristics to all challenges which, studied deeply, touch a chord deep within us all. That's why I believe this book is worth reading – not because it's about me, but it's about all of us – including you.

In addition, I quote Leo Rosten. He was a teacher and academic, but is best known as a humourist in the fields of scriptwriting, story-writing, and journalism. He said:

"A writer writes not because he is educated, but because he is driven by the need to communicate. Behind the need to communicate is the need to share. Behind the need to share is the need to be understood."

And behind my need to share was not only the need for the **Three Resolutions** to be understood by the reader, but also my need to understand myself. I felt the overwhelming emotional need to be a better person in so many ways, so that I could properly teach others what I knew to be true by living it fully, and to not be seen as someone who talks the talk but does not walk the walk.

Learn from my learning. I hope you enjoy reading this book as much as I enjoyed – and ultimately benefited from – writing it.

Be an active learner

Books such as these occasionally, in fact more often than not, fail in one regard – they don't fully and properly encourage the reader to make the changes they espouse. This is not necessarily a deliberate act – they just don't take the opportunity to ask the reader to pause and reflect on what they are reading.

I would invite you to take a piece of truly profound wisdom to heart – and start a journal. (Oh no, not a journal!)

There is one thing I don't want you to do is get hung up on - terminology. Runners keep a log, as do pilots. Lawyers keep diaries, others a daybook or an occurrence book. Whatever they call their records, they are a chronicle* of what they were doing or thinking at a particular time, and these notes are the lessons we learn and our musings on what to do next. (*I'm running out of synonyms, as you can tell.)

So when I say keep a journal, what I am going to ask you to do as you go through this book is to take the time to think deeply on some questions which occasionally arise as you go through the book (Sorry, nearly said 'journey' – I hate that term as much as you.)

At the end of each chapter, or occasionally within a chapter, you will discover a series of questions designed to make you think deeply about your situation and what you are going to do about it in the context of the **Three Resolutions**. I would counsel you to put the answers into your journal. In the main, my questions will probably be all that you need to make some progressive changes in a positive direction, but if something occurs to you that isn't being asked but which has a deep meaning for you, make sure you write it down because if you thought it while reading this book, it must be important to you. We've all experienced that occasional blinding flash of brilliance and insight, only to ask ourselves 10 minutes later what it was that we were thinking, only for the insight to be lost. Don't make that fatal error: write down what occurs to you, and even put the book down and focus on that new insight if you think it will be of benefit. Heck, if it's that profound you can even throw the book away* and move on in your own direction. I'm not so egotistical to believe that all the answers are here – I hope a lot of the questions are, but the better answers are within you, not me.

Take a diary/planner page/Moleskin notebook/MSWord document and write the answers down as they occur. Write down any thoughts **as** they occur to you, too. Doing this will make the next chapter you read even more revealing as you understand how what you – learned impacts on what you *will* learn, and how that (in turn) can have an effect on what you will *become*.

You are designing your better self, and you know it.

Things to Do

1. Get a notebook, diary or open a Word document upon which you can start writing down your answers to these questions, and questions that arise in your own mind as you read the book.

2. *Maintain it!*

(*Give it to someone else.)

Chapter One – The Why and How of the Three Resolutions

"The moment you stop trying to become a better person, is the moment you start to become worse than what you already are. " Carroll Bryant

We all have a philosophy to life, as may be proved evident from the number of Facebook memes with which we are annoyingly peppered by our friends, friends who are often completely unaware that we have seen said memes numerous times. People circulate those epithets because they believe the content to be true, at least to them. These mottos, tenets, quotes and sayings are a reflection of what they, and/or we, perceive to be truths. Those perceptions, then, are part of our life philosophies.

These pretty and pithy memes are, in essence, the unwritten rules by which the posters live – or wish they did. And by virtue of that posting on social media, they are also the (now) written rules with which they would wish others to comply, even if they are making that wish subconsciously.

For most of us, these rules remain unwritten because it never occurs to us to write them down unless and until we see someone else has written them on a picture of an inspiring sunrise. Despite not having written these rules down, we *communicate* them in the way we behave when we are at the top of our game; but we excuse any failure to comply just as effectively. Not writing them down, or not otherwise making our rules clear to others by stating what they are, makes it easier to justify our occasional (regular?) failure to live by them.

Unconsciously, perhaps, or possibly with total commitment in the moment, when we make or post these statements we are declaring what our ideal is. That statement of the 'ideal' may only relate to a specific circumstance: for example, I am amused about how amateur athletes demonstrate total commitment to training for a triathlon, then spend non-training weekends on the 'deserved' bottle. Their memes will reflect dedication, commitment, power and personal strength, but will only apply to their sport. Not their whole life.

That said, we will go on to discuss how what we are in one circumstance, we are in all circumstances.

Reading this book is the start of the process through which you will first identify what your rules are, and then go on to start living by those rules. Those experiences await as we go through this book, but underpinning your execution upon, and compliance with the rules you are about to make, are the **Three Resolutions.**

Put simply, the **Three Resolutions** are personal commitments that an individual can make with a view to identifying and then implementing personal improvements, regaining self-control, seeking and achieving success, and making those contributions that he or she feels conscience-bound to make.

Read that again. Is that what you want? If so, read on.

'Could I Do Better?'

It may be a bit of an over-generalisation but I would respectfully suggest that we all know where we could do better. We are aware t that some part of our lives is not *quite* what we would like it to be whether, or not, we are the fine, upstanding person we consider ourselves to be . We know, deep inside, that there is a gap between what we are and what we want or pretend to be.

That applies to most of us, but for some the gap is wider than it is for others. But be of good cheer – we are a lot better than we once were. Once upon a time, whether through immaturity, lack of training or even a lack of experience, we were not the ideal that we now see, although in the past we may not have realised what that ideal was. Over time we have met people who we admire, whose character and achievements we respect and wish to emulate. I think this idea is best illustrated using a diagram.

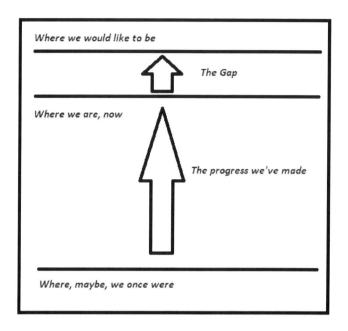

That Gap can be really narrow, but it is there for so many of us. For some, the reason for the gap between their current state and their ideal could be enormously impactive – it could be that they are an athlete with a nasty drink habit, a successful businesswoman with relationship issues, or someone for whom nothing seems to go right whatever they try. It can range from one specific personal issue – weight gain, for example – to a general feeling that nothing in our lives is as we want it to be. It may only be a small gap that you want to close, but it's an important gap to you. That gap represents the distance between who you are today, and who you would like to be tomorrow. To go further, the gap is between where you are and where you want to be as an individual, and as a professional, neighbour, friend, colleague, parent or sibling.

My own experience also suggests that the greater the Gap, the easier it is to close it, but as you approach the ideal and the Gap is at its narrowest, it is often the case that the effort required to close it is all the greater. If you have a number of challenges, as you pick them off one by one the remaining challenges are the greater ones, and they are in the final part of the Gap.

Which might go some way to explaining why people who demonstrate high levels of professional excellence and talent find it so difficult to match that excellence in their personal lives or in the way they treat people. The Gap is still there, but at the top of their game the Restraining Forces appear stronger because they become more attractive and more easily obtained. Pleasure (appetites and passions) dictate lifestyle, rather than service and purpose. Competence may remain high, but character falls away, as we will see.

Don't let all of this put you off, though. Be in no doubt – by the time you get to that level of difficulty, the strides you have made to get to that level of disciplined character and noble purpose mean you have already become someone that deserves respect, and provided you don't dwell on that last bit of Gap, your self-esteem will be high, too.

I have known a number of people who I perceive to be very close to the (my?) ideal, but if you were to really probe them for a deep self-analysis I would imagine there would be something, even if only *one* thing, that they felt could be improved.

For example, I know one person who is exceptionally fit, socially active, a friend and helper. That individual is successful professionally and socially, with a wide circle of friends and a desire to serve others as his (or her) abilities and skills allow, with an incredibly positive work-ethic. He/she supports and is supported by many friends and colleagues. To me, that friend has an amazing life balance and superb relationships. But my friend suffered from very poor self-confidence. I would say that he (or she) is wrong to feel this way, but to my friend this feeling is real and this belief can be supported with evidence as to why it is so. My friend has told me about this 'flaw', but I also know that my friend hasn't done anything meaningful about it.

Like my friend, many people have at least that 'one thing' that *they* consider a personal flaw.

This one thing (or, for some, a wide range of things) is gnawing at us because we know that 'it' or 'they' could be better. And while that lack of confidence is often borne of a lack of training, more often or not there is a quiet, insistent and ultimately truthful inner voice that is telling us not only what is wrong but also that **we aren't doing something about it that we know we ought to be doing**. That inner voice has a name – it is **Conscience**.

Psychologists are a little torn on Conscience. Freud suggested that Conscience is very much developed societally, in that those around us cause and develop it by showing us the societal norms against which the exercise of conscience is measured. We are taught by society what is wrong, and thus tell our conscience what it should remind us is right or wrong when a choice is to be made. Carl Jung, on the other hand, suggested that we have an innate conscience, something we are born with which provides us with the same message as Freud's version, but without the societal input. I suspect the truth lies somewhere in between, and here's my take on it.

I'm not going to get all philosophical here, even though and possibly *because* the subject of conscience could lead to a whole debate on ethics and morality. It is a veritable minefield, but ultimately one thing can be said with a degree of certainty.

All but the most psychologically challenged among us has a conscience which tells us that what we are doing is wrong, when it is a wrong that we are doing.

In a 'cause-effect-cause loop' sort of way, we and/or society have taught ourselves what that wrong is. We know this because we have invented lying. And in the context of this book, the conscience is telling us that we are lying to ourselves.

If you aren't convinced, cast your mind back to when you were a child. One day you did something wrong, but on that day you were not aware that it was wrong. For example, you left the house because a door was open, or you delved deeply into the choccy biscuits without asking, or you took a toy from a shop shelf and opened the packet to play with it. (Let's face it, there are *thousands* of potential examples!)

Immediately you were discovered, there was often a loud, occasionally painful consequence. Mum or Dad yelled at you sharply, making you jump. They may have slapped or smacked you (in the days this was considered acceptable). You learned that what you did was wrong and that there was a negative, emotionally upsetting consequence. At the very least you felt that what you had done resulted in a sudden withdrawal of love.

A short time later – particularly in respect of choccy biscuits – you were tempted again. The jar or toy was in reach and easily accessible. You knew you wanted it and there was no one around to see. So you delved in and suddenly there was a witness. As you looked up and smiled that chocolaty, toothless smile, Mum asked, "Have you been stealing biscuits?'

And in that moment, knowing the consequences of admission – *you lied*. You knew that the truth would hurt so you ignored the voice that told you, "Yes, you've been stealing biscuits" and you denied the theft in an effort to prevent that expected negative consequence.

What you hadn't learned at that stage is the Investigator's Motto – 'Never ask a question to which you don't already know the answer'. Parents are investigators. Remember that.

In our example, your lie failed. Evidence thwarted you.

Now and then, however, a lie succeeded. Unfortunately for us and for society, the lesson we learn as a child is not always "Phew, that was close, I won't do that again', but occasionally "Phew, that was close. I'll try that lie more often." Instead of deciding not to misbehave we start to develop a strategy that mitigates the consequence of the misbehaviour.

And you've probably been using that strategy on and off ever since. Maybe not on others, because you are essentially an honest individual. But you've been lying to yourself as a strategy for a long, long time.

We don't just lie to prevent immediate punishment, as in our calorie-intensive example. We are lying when we say that "cigarettes aren't harmful so I'll be fine", that a soggy meat pasty "won't hurt now and again" (and again and again), that we can give up drinking 'any time I like', that "my husband will never find out so it's okay", and so on.

What about these simple and common lies that we tell ourselves – "I can't be bothered" or "I don't care"? The truth is that you *are* bothered and you *do* care. You just don't *want* to do something about what is bothering you. The list of conscience-arousing lies that we tell ourselves can be quite long.

And we know it.

What are the lies you are routinely telling yourself? What is it that you should be doing, but aren't, because of some personally acceptable yet deceptive falsehood that allows, even justifies your persistent failure to act? Only you and your conscience know the answer for your particular situation.

I would at this point respectfully ask you to thoroughly consider what it is you should be doing that you aren't. And, indeed, to consider anything you *are* doing that you *shouldn't*. I suggest that there must be something of that nature – one way or the other or both – that is bothering you *because you are reading this book* and so you know that something isn't right. I'd even go as far as to say some readers will read on without doing that 'exercise', knowing that they should. That is exactly what I am talking about. Pseudo-psychologists would call that 'denial'. What are you denying?

Conscience and Integrity

That hidden voice we call Conscience is something that we must listen to if we are to successfully achieve the goal of living in accordance with Principles, in keeping with what we know to be right, and in identifying what we feel is wrong. Conscience identifies when there is a gap in our behaviour between what we are or are not doing, and what we should be or should not be doing. And it practically screams at us as the Gap narrows!

What we know to be right can be based on acknowledged, scientific fact at one end of the spectrum, to blind faith at the other. In between there can be many levels of 'knowledge', but the conscience truly recognises only principles – undeniable truths – and our personal values. Using that knowledge, the Conscience identifies and makes known, to us, the existence of the aforementioned gap.

When our conscience is speaking to us it is telling us one of two truths: either that what we are doing is wrong according to unchangeable, undeniable, self-evident principles, or that what we are doing is not in keeping with our personal values (the distinction being that principles are true *whatever* we think, whereas values are true only because we think they are: unless we value the principles).

For example: when we lie, our conscience makes us feel guilty, even if we do not change our behaviour accordingly. We are told we are doing wrong. The conscience knows what is wrong because we, or someone we respect, told it so earlier in our lives.

The Conscience isn't overly chatty and only speaks when necessary. When we are on any weight-loss programme based on our values-driven need to be healthy and slim, our conscience only speaks to us when we are about to reach for a piece of cake. Our conscience is the voice of our integrity. It is the voice that tells us to speak out when something is offensive, or to shut up to stop us being offensive to others. It is the same voice that shouts at us for *not* doing either of those things. It isn't constantly nagging, but when we transgress or intend to do so, it never, ever shuts up – until we listen.

And when we *do* listen – we feel peace.

Helping Our Conscience to Help Us

To establish an effective working conscience, it is prudent to ensure that we are wholly aware of what principles apply to us and what our values are. What is the difference between Principles and Values?

To recap: Principles are defined for our purposes as undeniable truths that apply all the time, everywhere whether we believe in them or not and whether or not we apply them. Just as gravity applies to us while we remain on the planet's surface – and will still apply if the science we use to temporarily overcome it fails in flight – principles such as Truth, Honesty and Integrity will apply all the time. You know when you are dealing with a Principle when you try arguing against a Principle – you always find that your arguments make no sense.

As principles are self-evident I need not touch upon them further except to say that if you act outside of them you do so knowing that the results will not be good. In effect, all principles apply to all of us so thinking otherwise is foolish. Gravity is a principle – you know that so you don't jump out of 30th storey windows. Try arguing against it through demonstration.....

Values, on the other hand, are states of being, possessing, feeling or thinking that are of importance to *you*. You can value happiness, wealth, truth, a nice house or garden, being intellectual, adventure – a value is anything that you consider to be of worth. The potential values range from A-Z and there are a lot of lists of values available to you on the internet, in religious or atheist books, within organisations, etc. – none of which can possibly cover every value or every circumstance precisely because they are usually personal, cultural or societal.

Everyone has values, and it has been suggested that they are like fingerprints – no two people have the same values. That may not be true on first analysis because two people *can* have the same or similar value 'lists', but their personal *definitions* of those values may differ.

Values colour judgement. As a value is something you truly believe in, then any contradictory thought, comment or action angers you to varying degrees. It could be suggested that the stronger the value, the angrier you get when that value is challenged, or isn't met when expected. The strength of feeling might range from outright hostility, through frustration (hasn't happened yet) and on to disappointment (won't happen at all).

When a value is contravened, the behaviour of the person whose value it is will be affected. They may demonstrate quite extraordinary behaviour in such circumstances, or they may just appear miffed. The strength of the feeling in terms of that behaviour usually reflects the strength *of* that value.

The media has begun to show that people are losing control of their emotions over values differences. Political discourse seems no longer done at a tactful, diplomatic level. Now, it is hate-filled, polarised, and occasionally extremely violent. It is no longer enough to disagree over a values system – people seem to think that the only way to express a value system is to use violent and insulting language. This state of affairs demonstrates just how important values are to people, although it is sad that they cannot control their emotions, realise that values are not absolute truths and others are allowed to value different things.

Sidebar: *For on example of the difference between a Principle and a Value, look at morality and how that value affects thinking. You may consider morality to be a principle. One definition of the value of 'morality' is the belief that sex is something to be contained within marriage. Therefore, people who stand by that definition of morality consider sex outside marriage to be immoral. Let's be frank, the Church supported that contention as did the law, whose original definition of rape described the offence as 'unlawful' sexual intercourse, thus meaning that as sex within marriage WAS lawful, a man could not rape his wife. Thinking changes. Therefore, morality, as its definition changes over time and by culture or religion, arguably cannot be a Principle.*

Unlike Principles, values tend to be more personal and even general in nature, although you can value principles like truth and honesty, of course. Examples of values that aren't principles could include valuing money – it's a great system of exchange but tends not to work amongst people who have none, or whose exchange system is one of barter, therefore it is not a principle. You can value the possession of a car, but you could live without one. You could value freedom of the individual but as others believe that the wellbeing of the masses is preferable to the total freedom of the individual to do whatever he or she likes regardless of the 'greater good, unrestrained freedom is not necessarily a principle (even though there is probably a balance between the two extremes that could be).

Whether you value principles or not, you *do* have values. You may not have given them any thought; in which case they've probably been developed by watching others and infusing theirs into your own life. You may value money because you've been impressed by someone who is wealthy. If they are generous, you will be too. If they are greedy, you may follow that characteristic.

Your values, in a nutshell, are influenced first by your parents, then by your friends, then by your workmates. I say influenced because in each case they are the people around whom you spend most of your time, but the power or otherwise of the earlier experiences will influence whether the later experiences will or won't affect your values. If your parents influence you strongly, then your friends will do so to a lesser degree.

But the opposite may happen if (for example) you hated your parents or feel they weren't supportive, and you feel that your friends *are.* This is the rationale for the popularity of gangs. Yes, some young people join them through fear but many join them because they provide a sense of connection that their family did not. And when the gang's values are negative, the 'connection' rationalises the behaviour.

Sidebar: Psychologists have described a process whereby a person adopts values of a greater body. The process is essentially Belong, Believe, Behave. Someone desires connection, a basic human need, so they join a group even though they may not wholly agree with that group's thinking. In time, arguments are made (or other influences applied) and the individual starts to believe the whole ethos of the group. Finally, with that sense of belonging and a newly held belief in the group's ethic, the individual behaves wholly in keeping with the group's behaviour.

Discuss the growth of Nazism ….

There is a direct link between Conscience and Values. Your Conscience knows what your values are, even if you aren't consciously aware of them yourself. It knows when you are acting in keeping with what you value, and what you value is what you believe to be 'right'. I say 'right' not necessarily in the sense that they are legal/ethical/moral, but in the sense that *you* believe them to be true.

This is an important distinction. Principles ARE always ethical and moral, and in the main they are legal – you can't make a principal unlawful. (If you could, we'd save a lot of flight time by making gravity an offence.)

As someone put it, principles aren't out to lie to you, to deceive you into doing something that will have a negative consequence. They just 'are'. We rely on them to be true – when principles apply we can know, without a second thought, what the consequences of any act will be. Try jumping off that cliff and arguing that you can fly.

Values might not necessarily be ethical or moral (or legal) BUT your conscience believes that they, and actions associated with them, are permissible and justifiable because your experience has trained it in that belief.

This is why you know when you are lying but can simultaneously think it is okay to cheat on your partner. A lie breaches a principle, but if you've been brought up to think having multiple sexual partners is okay you will happily 'put it about'. On the other hand, if you then lie to your partner about doing so, then you may have a values conflict…

Here's an important point – whereas you are stuck with Principles, you can choose your Values. You can identify them, choose the ones you want, dispose of the ones you do not, and even amend your preferred definition of the ones upon which you finally settle. You get to choose – if you want to choose.

How do you make that choice? By defining what's important.

Defining Your Values

The advice of all personal development speakers and writers is this – **take the time you need to decide what your values are, and how you want to define them.** You also need to review them a number of times just to make sure that you have them properly set, defined and accepted.

Once you have completed this work – including the occasional review to make sure they are as you want them to be – you will have begun to establish in your own mind what your values-based rules should be, and as a result your conscience will automatically kick in to let you know when you are failing in your efforts to act in keeping with those values.

There is a wealth of material available to you on the internet and in books to help you identify these values, but in a nutshell the process is as follows:

1. **Find a word that describes what you feel truly represents your value, e.g. honesty, wealth, fitness.**

    To illustrate, we'll use **Integrity.**

2. **Turn it into an active statement or phrase, thus giving it life.**

    For example, **"I have personal integrity."** Your integrity is thus made current and not something for the future, a common error made by those who write, "I *will have* personal integrity." That sentence excuses a lack of integrity in the 'now'.

3. **Define what *you* mean when you use the term.**

    It may quite legitimately be different from a dictionary definition (although you are quite able to use that dictionary if you wish). It is my experience that when I suggest Integrity as a value, a room full of people may well define it differently, even if they do so with a degree of similarity. Some restrict it to 'Honesty' (speaking the truth); I prefer the wider definition of 'being' the truth – walking the talk, not just talking it. Think deeply and define your value accurately for **you.** For example, **"I show integrity when I stand up for what I believe in, or act in accordance with that, even when it may not serve me to do so."**

4. **Finally, decide and write down how you will behave in accordance with that value.**

   For example, **"When I am tempted to deny my beliefs I instead affirm them wholly to others, whatever they may think of me as I do so."** Or perhaps **"I act in accordance with my thoughts and my words."**

Having done this work you should reinforce your decision – and it has been YOUR decision – by reading, re-reading and (if necessary) re-writing what you have written until (a) it reads as you want it and (b) you know it to be true. Say it out loud as an affirmation if you are comfortable doing so. Emphasise different words until you create a personal mantra that reflects exactly how you feel about that particular value. Once you have done that your conscience will support your integrity by reminding you of your value every time you consider deciding to act *without* integrity.

For example, if you have chosen the value of Integrity, when someone challenges you (how you look, how you speak, whether you comply with their social convention and ethics, etc.) and you are tempted to change your mind just to avoid confrontation, to avoid being put on the spot or just being tempted to 'fit in', your conscience will help you revert to standing up for that particular belief whatever the social consequence. Again, and I cannot emphasise this enough – *if you listen*.

To provide an example of how this values-identification process should work, here are my own primary values. They are:

I Apply High Levels of Self-Discipline and Self-Denial

I live in the fullest integrity with the values that I have identified and which are as follows:

I Seek Excellent Health

I live a healthy lifestyle, eating carefully and with balanced nutrition for weight control as my primary goal. I am committed to regular aerobic exercise. I stretch for flexibility. I get sufficient sleep - I wake early and I retire early. I am conscious of my posture, weight and breathing.

I Live for and Love My Family

I love them, teach them, play with them, entertain them, treat them, and spend time with them. I never, ever entertain the thought that there is anyone else in this life for me but my beloved, faithful and loving wife.

I Commit to Worthy and Challenging Goals

I plan and commit to worthy goals that are in keeping with these Unifying Principles. I develop challenging goals in my chosen and appointed roles – as an individual, in work, with family, as a trainer and as a writer.

I Demonstrate Professionalism

I know my trade and I carry out all my work with excellence. I investigate allegations diligently and in depth. I am highly productive, filling my time with work as directed by my employers and other stakeholders. I challenge wasteful or unfocused practices.

I Thrive on Intellectual Pursuits

I seek out new and broad knowledge that enhances my professional and private lives. I read broadly. I look out for, fund and use learning opportunities. I maximise the minimal time spent on television as a learning resource and for high quality sport and entertainment. I exercise my mental acuity with challenging activities and I enjoy music – to listen and to sing.

I Use Clear Speech

I avoid invective, and I use intellectually meaningful terminology in speech. I enjoy using illustrative language to make points clearly. I take the time and the opportunity to improve my speaking skills.

The essential purpose of understanding the philosophy behind, and the methodology of the first of the **Three Resolutions** is to use that knowledge in a committed effort to apply the self-discipline and self-denial that empowers compliance with your own set of values. This starts to happen once you have decided, with total clarity, what your intentions actually are, and continues with you making sure that you persistently train your conscience to tell you when you aren't wholly compliant. Then your conscience continues to tell you so until the point at which *either* you listen to your conscience without internal debate *or* you don't need to listen anymore because you are living wholly in keeping with your values.

That is when you get inner peace, by the way. When you don't even have to think about it anymore. When it becomes habit.

Identify your values, know them, commit to them, apply them, listen to your conscience, act in keeping with what you heard – and do so until there is no thought required. That is what the first of the **Three Resolutions** can do for you.

What does your conscience say to you, now? If your answer is 'I don't care', then why, may I ask, are you arguing with your conscience? It is yours, after all, not mine. It is *your* inner voice that is telling you that you are acting out of synch with what you *know* to be right. Of course other people, peers, groups and communities can and will influence what your values are, as outlined in earlier paragraphs – but while such people ***can*** influence you to accept their values, you need not let them ***dictate*** your values to you. **YOU can** decide what your values are, in the end. (Having said that, as we mature we tend to discover a certain amount of truth in what others told us as we grew up, provided they were following principles themselves.)

You carry out this work in an effort to identify where ***you*** will be applying the **Three Resolutions**.

Please don't take this as a criticism without compassion, because I know all too well what it is like to argue with my own conscience. I used to look at fat people and say, "Did they suddenly get fat overnight?" only to gain three stone myself without any conscious thought as to how it was happening and when or how I should stop. At 15 stone I thought I ought to do something about it, and at 16 stone I thought the same. But never did this *conscious* thinking make any difference because I was ignoring my *conscience* every time I went back to the fridge for another slice of bread. It was not that my conscience wasn't talking to me – it was that I was deliberately ignoring it.

We ignore conscience because it suits us in the moment. We tell ourselves little things that justify a failure to act correctly in any challenging situation.

These things are not always lies. Sometimes a failure to act one way can be justified because of a genuine circumstance. These occasions do not apply as 'failures' - we act 'differently' in such times because our conscience tells us that the alternative is the right thing to do at this moment. It may be that you are about to exercise in accordance with your values for fitness when a family member bursts into the room in tears over some crisis. In such circumstances exercise should be abandoned, and your conscience will tell you it is right to change your plan if you have put family first. Your conscience only kicks in if you genuinely value exercise over family.

This is a second facet of values based living. We can have values which create conflicts in how we live. This is a good example, where our desire to exercise conflicts with the need to look after a family member. What do we do?

Values, it is believed, have a hierarchy. When two collide, one will take precedence over another. Sometimes they conflict to the point of confusion, for example when someone values 'adventure' and 'survival' and has to decide whether to do a Grand Canyon bungee jump.

When defining your values, a 5th step (if you want to go that far) is to decide their order of priority. You can decide, for example, whether 'professionalism' – a desire to work hard, do a good job and dedicate yourself to professional results – is more important than Family. An odd example and one that many deny they make, but so many people do put going to work ahead of a family event. Another example may be to place loyalty above honesty – so when the boss you admire tells you to do something mildly unethical you would do it, whereas if you placed honesty above loyalty you would not.

An often used example is when we have a choice between jumping out of a perfectly serviceable aircraft with a parachute and going on a boat trip. If we value adventure above security, we fly, if we value security over adventure, we sail.

To do this, take your list of values and write each on a separate piece of paper. Take each in turn and compare it to another. Decide which of the two is more important and place them in that appropriate order. Do the same for every value, set against every other value, until your hierarchy of values is complete.

If you wish, to can also *amend* that order to see if changing it, changes your attitude towards how you live – to use the earlier example, if you placed security ahead of adventure, experiment with the order and put adventure before security. How would you live, now?

Once you've settled on the final order of values, you should find that decisions are made with that sequence in mind. Family before work, and so on.

That isn't, necessarily, the last time you have to consider that order, however. How do you make a decision when the *same* value applies to *all* available options?

I had an interesting experience on the day my first grandson was born.

At 5.30am that day, I got the call from my wife. My daughter was about to give birth to my second grandchild/first grandson. (All doing fine, by the way) That morning, I was also due to attend a District Meeting of an organisation where I held office as a local President.

Now, as far as the birth was concerned it was over by the time I'd have risen for the meeting, so timing wasn't the issue. The actual issue was threefold.

1.   Although the family support systems for the new baby were ample, I felt as though I had a duty to be present for any and all developments.

2.   I also had a duty to the club to support members in the meeting competitions and to simply represent the club.

3.   I have a dog that wasn't going to be exercised while the rest of the family was focused on the baby.

For many the choice may be clear, but that's how values work – your values won't match mine and you may scoff at my trilemma. But as one of my higher values is duty and all three represented a duty, I found myself anguishing over whether or not to go to the meeting.

In the event, I stayed home, walked the dog, ferried great-Grandma to and from the hospital (and watched the Australian GP in the gap….), but it had been a hard choice.

Which made me think – how to get around such a challenge to one's conscience. In the end, it could be argued that the answer was obvious, but then some answers are. But when it comes to values, you occasionally find yourself blinded by the obvious.

The answer, I feel, is that when faced with a decision between options that appear to match the same values, as I was, *you must look for another value for each option and see where that lies on your* **hierarchy.**

In my example, instead of 'duty' being the value attached to each option, I could have simply put 'family' against the appropriate option – and then my own prioritisation of family over duty would have made the decision easier. Or, if opting for that value did not ease the decision itself, the post-decision emotion would be 'I have done the right thing' and not 'did I do the right thing?' Which is a whole lot less debilitating.

If you find yourself in a dilemma, trilemma or any other kind of emma because all of the proposed actions match a particular personal value, instead of sweating over the whole shebang, look for the higher value that you can associate with one of the options, and choose that.

When it comes down to it, a values-trained conscience is key to a successful and effective life.

If you are gaining weight and reach for a chocolate éclair, your conscience now shouts, "NO!" at the top of its voice. Your "one won't hurt" response is a lie, because you say it in the knowledge that it may be one, now, but the next 'one' won't hurt either. But added up, all the ones *will* hurt – and you know it. You have just rationalised a conscience-contradicting decision. You have told yourself a 'Rational Lie'. Or, put simply and accurately, you have made an excuse for stupid behaviour. Strangely, this is the kind of excuse you wouldn't accept from other people. In fact, the kind of excuse which you would consider justified your pointedly remarking upon when other people use them. Hypocrisy abounds when we ignore our own conscience.

To return to the subject at hand: application of the **Three Resolutions** is the most effective response to the conscience-defying Restraining Forces that stop us acting properly. The **Three Resolutions** are, as indicated in the opening paragraphs in this chapter, Resolutions that you make to empower personal change in three specific areas of life.

These are the areas of **self-discipline** (getting things done, living sensibly, seeking levels of good health and fitness, living 'right'); **work and relationships** (getting the right things done properly, being a good person/friend/colleague/citizen); **and contribution** (service to others, ultimate contribution and being all you can be so that others remember you).

If you think about it deeply, I think you'll find that these three areas cover your whole existence. Self-discipline is about you and your personal life, your relationship with yourself; work and relationships cover how you relate to others (employers, colleagues, customers, family); and contribution can cover those relationships and how you feel about what you are giving to others through your work, voluntary activities, willingness to teach others or do charitable work, etc. There is, I would suggest, no part of your life that is not covered by one or more of the areas mentioned above and which cannot, therefore, be improved by application of one or the other, or even more than one, of the **Three Resolutions**.

These three terms therefore cover all the areas that your conscience *may* suggest to you are not being properly dealt with. You may have issues with only one area, but as we live a life as one indivisible whole (as Gandhi put it) it is my contention that if we lack in one area then that lack has an effect on all three.

For example, and an example with which I am all too familiar and, I suspect, so are many of those seeking advice of this type: Weight gain.

If you are overweight to any serious degree, and by that I mean that your clothes no longer fit, or you are breathless when you shouldn't be, or you suffer from any number of such symptoms, then do you find you are short with people occasionally? Or do you find that, now and then, your willingness to do something normally quite easy (like walking to another room in your house) feels like too much bother? Or that 'one more cake won't matter because of how fat I already am'? Does someone asking you to do them a favour make you think 'why me'?

How do others see you – or perhaps more importantly, how do you *think* they see you, and how does that perception of what you think they think of you affect your relationships? And to be extremely blunt – when you say you are perfectly happy being obese, as many do – are you lying to yourself and to everyone else? Can *they* see your rational lie?

To be blunt, if you are overweight, does your weight have an effect on the other areas in your life? If you don't think so, look more deeply and see if it truly does. Are you more inclined to drink? Are you less inclined to exercise your mind as well as your body? Is your work suffering? Are you less charitable, and do you contribute less on a community level that your conscience tells you is the right amount?

*Sidebar: You can be happy **despite** being obese, but as you lumber breathlessly about living a life restricted by that obesity, can you be happy **that** you are obese? It's a subtle distinction. Think carefully.*

How about alcoholism, adultery/infidelity, drug addiction, even exercise addiction? Do any of these situations apply to you and have a negative effect upon your capabilities and contribution? Is there something that takes up space in your psyche that (your conscience tells you) ought to be spent somewhere else?

How do the Three Resolutions help?

Counselling tends to take an age. A counsellor focuses on discovery of the cause of a problem, and the deepest understanding of the consequences of the problem. This is great in many cases, but it reinforces the memory of the problem, and this may not be the solution – it keeps the subject mired in the cause and effect, rather than on what to do to get away from it. The alternative we now call 'coaching', which is about the future – "never mind what *happened*, let's do something about what you *want,* instead." It is solution- rather than problem-orientated. All that said, the 'problems' do cause the conscience to talk loudly to us, and so the 'problems' are the focus of the mind when that conversation takes place. There is an almost inextricable link between the cause and the solution. No cause, no problem, and therefore no possible solution.

Something always causes us to want to be better. That problem initiates the conscience to talk to us. The conscience tells us what is wrong, and that we should be doing something about it. The 'wrong' is very often mired in one of the three **Restraining Forces**, and I believe that the **Three Resolutions** will help any reader to overcome most conscience-identified personal development, productivity, health or other issues that affect them.

The **Three Resolutions** are, as I have stated, personal Resolutions that you apply with the intention of building the conscience 'muscle' to the point at which it drives you to achieve the things you consider to be important, to do them consistently and to the highest possible standard, for you and for the people you love, respect or wish to help.

As the values which underpin them are your own, then committing to the **Three Resolutions** will – not could, *will* – support and influence you to create the change you seek, *if you apply them fully.* The **Three Resolutions** simultaneously provide you with a mental framework for progressive development towards better behaviour. **The Three Resolutions**, properly considered and then applied, will both initiate and then facilitate your desired success.

What are the Restraining Forces?

Taking into account that the three areas already described (self-discipline, work and relationships, contribution) encompass all that we are and all that we do, then it seems reasonable that anything that challenges our Resolution to act properly in those areas can be considered to be a **Restraining Force**.

Let me use the analogy of a car, which is under-performing in the moment. The question is, when your feet are on the both the accelerator and the brake, which will get you moving more quickly in the right direction? Do you apply more power and expect to move? Or do you take your foot off the brake and discover, miraculously, that you don't need as much power as you thought to make effective progress?

This illustrates what is meant by the term **Restraining Forces (RFs)**. They are obstacles that stop us moving forward despite all our 'accelerator' efforts. They are obstacles we voluntarily or involuntarily apply , the removal of which will empower us to progress properly and with far less effort.

Situations that develop wholly outside our control, as opposed to those we *let* develop, are excluded from this definition. In such cases, it is application of RFs to our potential *solutions* that hold us back.

Restraining Forces are forces over which we *can* have some control, and are therefore those which we can overcome to a lesser or greater degree. Some examples may assist in explaining how they affect us.

What stops us from exercising self-discipline? It is usually the immediacy of a perceived pleasure or avoidance of anticipated pain. We set aside what conscience tells us is in our long term interests because what we see immediately in front of us looks so attractive. If the immediacy of the pleasure is plain, then we are inclined to seek it. If we anticipate that exercising a conscience-compliant choice will cause us discomfort, we are inclined to avoid compliance. That is human nature, and the human curse. This describes the first Restraining Force.

What stops us from working well with colleagues and in the interests of those we serve? Occasionally it is the immediacy of quick results, which lead us to think about how wonderful we are so much that we believe it, and so we keep on doing what got us that immediate psychological reward, at the expense of what we ought to be doing. This is urgency versus importance, self-interest vs greater good.

As a result of acting that way and getting some great short-term results, we become what others have come to expect us to be or have designed us to be, rather than us being what we *are*. Rather than being true to ourselves and being congruent with our own principles, values and beliefs, we become what others have designed us to be - which in time serves only them, not us or those about whom we should care. We essentially go on to respond to such ego-building stimuli by becoming two-faced, pretending to be something we are not, and justifying it despite what we know we should be saying and doing. This exemplifies the second Restraining Force.

Sidebar: A good example of this in action is 'noble cause corruption', a term initially applied to the police force when they bent the rules to ensure a bad guy got convicted, to the point at which they'd make up evidence because the end justified the means. To fit in, otherwise ethical officers slowly and inexorably took the lower path because it was socially expedient. And look at the consequences – a society that easily believes that all coppers are bad, when in reality it is very few.

And what Restraining Force stops us from contributing? Self-interest. We look to see only what we can get from a situation, how it can serve us. We apply the same selfish focus when dealing with people, asking ourselves what we can get from them or out of them, and in doing so we reduce them to the status of things. They become resources to our needs, rather than part of a greater, synergistic, co-operative good. This is how the third Restraining Force affects us.

The Restraining Forces (RFs), therefore, are the antitheses of the **Three Resolutions**; the 3Rs are the arch enemies of the RFs, and the descriptions and effects of these restraining forces are profound.

The RFs against self-discipline are Appetites and Passions, things we want now despite the better things that can serve us for longer. The pleasure of immediate satisfaction: the deferral of the pain of having to make a long-term commitment; or the avoidance of short term discomfort; all weighed against the benefits of applied self-discipline and self-denial in order to get what you need.

The RFs that challenge our success in work and relationships are Pride and Pretension, where we consider how people see us to be much more important than being ourselves, and therefore we change to suit our egos (as served by their praise) rather than stay steadfast and true to ourselves. The pleasure of being liked now; the avoidance of the pain of being perceived as not enough ; the inconvenience of having to work longer and harder at being competent in our work; all weighed against making the effort to learn in order to be highly competent, and of living a life of good character.

Here are some of the more common Restraining Forces that affect people's ability to live in a way that serves them, and the ones they live/serve/work for, etc. you may find it interesting to look at these and explore the extent to which they affect your life. Naturally, I open the table with the originally identified Restraining Forces but then move on to other examples, both obvious and surprising. An astute reader will probably notice the occasional overlap.

Feel free to identify and define your own Restraining Forces, but I challenge you to find any that aren't included in this list in some way.

Appetites and Passions	Our tendency to find something we like doing and keep doing it despite the need to be doing something else or something better. This does not mean you should avoid being passionate about the right things, only about the wrong things.
Ambition and Aspiration	Our need to be, do or have something, whether a 'thing' or a position. This only becomes a Restraining Force when it gets in the way of better things and is self-focused to the detriment of yourself, and others.
Pride	Our tendency to believe in ourselves to such an extent that we believe we can do no wrong, can never *be* wrong and that anyone suggesting otherwise is less than us. This is not self-esteem - it is self-importance. Nor is it to be read as a justified and temporary sense of personal satisfaction in a job well done – in this context, it means smugness.
Pretension	Our tendency to avoid the reality that we are not necessarily all that we can be, and instead of addressing our potential we pretend that we are something we have not yet earned the right to be.
Comfort Zones	Our tendency to stay where we are, physically or psychologically, in order to remain secure that what is, will remain so.
Social Mirror	Our tendency to only act in a fashion which those around us, whose opinions we respect (rightly or wrongly).
Procrastination	Linked to the Comfort Zone, procrastination is our tendency not to do things because they represent change. But we also procrastinate because we don't know what to do, we fear the consequences, we don't want to risk something we have.
Routine	While routine serves us very well indeed, it can become the enemy if it stops us changing approaches, using our initiative, or developing positively as individuals. Routine can keep things moving smoothly, or it can keep us in a rut.

Internal Dialogue	How we talk to ourselves has a massive effect on how we behave and, therefore, the results we experience.
Addiction	There is a tendency in all of us to succumb to things we love to do to the exclusion of other things which, if we gave it sufficient thought, would be preferable and better for us.

The primary RFs against contribution are Aspiration and Ambition, where what we want is considered far more important than what others need or want and, and this includes where what *we* want is considered to be even more important than what we *need*. The pleasure of immediate personal gain, or the avoidance of the pain of inconvenience, all weighed against the longer term benefits of a lifelong legacy of contribution and genuine acknowledgement for a job well done.

And so we move on from here to a more detailed discussion of the **Three Resolutions** as they are applied to the Restraining Forces, with a view to understanding how *committed* application of the 3Rs can help us become who we want and were meant to be.

How important is this? Let me conclude this part with a quote from Stephen Covey.

The ability to make and keep Resolutions to ourselves is a direct reflection of our personal integrity. Talk can be cheap, but the value of 'walking your talk' defines the richness of your character. (From The Seven Habits of Highly Effective People.)

How the Three Resolutions Fit Together

Management and personal development books routinely and usefully use diagrams to illustrate how concepts fit together. It therefore seemed logical to me that the **Three Resolutions** should be treated in the same way, provided that doing so serves to improve understanding of the concept. And this is the result.

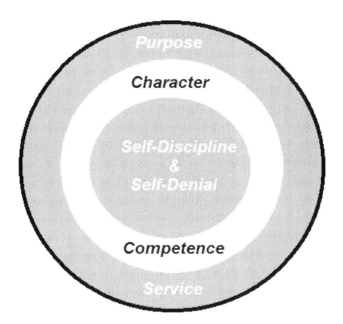

This illustration shows a progressive relationship between the Three Resolutions. It looks like a progression of circles, but I would ask that you consider it to be a sphere, instead.

Here, it is succinctly shown that the core of the sphere contains the objectives of the First Resolutions, specifically self-discipline and self-denial. The core lies within and therefore underpins the layer containing the objectives of the Second Resolution, namely character and competence, and outside that layer lie the Third Resolution 'fruits' of the application of the first resolutions, - purpose and service. This diagram clearly indicates how the application of Resolution 1 is foundational to success in Resolution 2, and the first two Resolutions support the discovery and execution of the third.

I believe that the First Resolution relating to self-discipline and self-denial is foundational, and always has been. Without it, the other two layers of the sphere cannot effectively exist: it is difficult to see how the higher two Resolutions can be effectively applied without at least some small measure of self-discipline. The two outer Resolutions rely on the sound, solid core of the

First Resolution. How can I be remotely competent without some self-discipline – I have to learn a trade, don't I? I have to have something in which I am competent in order to serve in some capacity, after all. Can I contribute and serve completely randomly, without some sense of direction or competence borne of discipline?

Consistent application of the First Resolution creates a strong sense of personal self-esteem, which is a confidence in oneself from which our character and capabilities flow, develop and improve. It is the central foundation to our ability to exist, produce and serve and is arguably the most important part of the **Three Resolutions**. The First Resolution 'base' is the core of success in any profession, service – and life. If our application of self-discipline and self-denial remains firm, it creates stability. Imagine the absence of a firm centre – the whole sphere collapses in on itself if the central core is absent.

Supported by that core comes the next level, Resolution 2. Competence and character are the fruits of self-discipline and self-denial either deeply or in part, either by design or accident. The root of Resolution 2 lies within Resolution 1. The fruits of Resolution1 are the foundations of character and competence.

Great competence and a strong character still require and stand upon discipline. A hollow sphere is never as strong as one that is solid. Nevertheless, a hollow sphere can still possess an element of stability. If you like, it's where most professionals exist – competent, with some character, but perhaps (occasionally) their character and competence are not deeply supported by the elements of Resolution 1. They are, to varying degrees, faking it. And this kind of sphere, if pricked by the needle of discovery, deflates quite quickly.

Finally, we see the Third Resolution as a further extension of the layers beneath, of the two earlier Resolutions. We are better able to serve noble causes, and to contribute, if those activities are the result of a disciplined lifestyle that supports and feeds our character and our ability to do what it is we seek to do, our competence. The fruits that come about through our sense of purpose and from our contribution rely upon the roots of our character, competence, and discipline.

Ask yourself the question *"Serving a noble purpose without discipline, character and competence will bring results – but will they be the best?"*

The answer is obvious. Discipline is a prerequisite to the greatest possible results. Competence is better used in the service of others. Character is also of use to others – people trust the trustworthy, and trustworthiness is the effective combination of character and competence. Trustworthiness is a reflection of an ability to do an excellent job, allied to humility and good character. No matter how good a doctor you are, if you are arrogant and demeaning towards others, you will never be truly respected. At the same time, if you are an incompetent, no-one will use your services no matter how nice you are. The two characteristics are inextricably interwoven if success – true success – is sought.

If the inner cores are missing, something of the outer rings can still exist, but will the results be as positive, creative, well-executed or successful? Will the results be consistent? If they are good, will they remain so or will some external force puncture our objectives in some way? I suggest not.

Sidebar: Given time and inclination, how many examples of highly competent but flawed politicians, celebrities and other notables could you come up with? If a focus on money, an inflated ego, or the prospect of fame push at a noble cause/contribution that is not based in character, competence and self-discipline, what happens? Amy Winehouse? Janis Joplin? John Belushi? Disgraced politicians? In fact, you could probably use, as an example, any of the mighty who have fallen.

Imagine the passion of a person of strong, principled character and excellent competence who *does* serve a valuable, noble purpose, who contributes his or her time and talents to a worthy end – which can include formal, paid employment. (I see no reason why someone should not be rewarded for their contribution.) Allied to all-encompassing and underlying self-discipline and self-denial, incredible results are almost a given.

There are, historically, great illustrations of this process in action - Lincoln, Florence Nightingale, Thatcher, Gandhi, Andrew Carnegie, Mother Teresa and Ben Franklin are all prime examples of men and women who had cores of self-discipline underlying their competence and character, and whose purpose, service and contribution are now plainly evident.

Could *you* sit comfortably at a table occupied by such people? Yes, if you were willing to apply yourself. You may not become famous and serve in a public, visible fashion. You may not get a mention in the Queen's Honours List, but you could sit alongside those greats if you lived and behaved as they did, in your own circumstance.

Those who execute all **Three Resolutions** are people who have integrity, the self-discipline to demonstrate, through living, the truth of what they are saying, and the ability and willingness to use their character and competence to serve a noble purpose.

In other words, this illustration shows how *effective* execution on a noble cause through personal and interpersonal contribution *requires* self-discipline, character and competence – they are not merely desirable, they are *essential*. As you read the chapters on the **Three Resolutions**, I hope that you will come to see the overlaps between each. You will see how service and purpose influence, and are also influenced by the need for character and competence, for self-discipline and occasionally self-denial?

Character BEFORE Discipline?

In his foreword to the 25th Anniversary Edition of the Seven Habits of Highly Effective People® Jim Collins, (author of Good to Great and Built to Last), opined that "There is no success without discipline, and there is no discipline without character". This would suggest that character comes before self-discipline and to an extent I would agree, but with a caveat. (Who am I to contradict or qualify an industry great?)

Self-discipline does require character, unquestionably. To apply self-discipline and to exercise self-control does require inner strength. But many people have 'enough' character and do nothing with it. They are the people fun to be with, a laugh and a joke, and even generally 'good' people exist at that level of character. We know these people, and we know them to be flighty, adulterous, occasionally dishonest (and able to justify that dishonesty with the phrase 'everyone does it') and essentially not the people a reader of a book like this would choose to emulate. That is not to say we dislike them, disrespect them or treat them with derision – I'm only suggesting that we would not like to BE them, because we don't like what we truly know they are.

My caveat with Collins' quote is the addition of the word 'some' into the quote so that it reads, "There is no success without discipline, and there is no discipline without *some* character". And essential as that 'some' character strength is, it does not compare with the character strengths that derive and develop from the exercise of the First Resolution through the application of self-discipline and self-denial.

Who we become is as important as what we achieve, to paraphrase Jim Rohn. When we use that 'little' character strength to start proactively exercising our self-discipline and our self-control to any effective degree, who we become in terms of personal character is superior – *vastly* superior – to the character strength we were able to demonstrate before. To an immense degree.

Returning to my diagram: while it flies in the face of Jim Collin's quote in terms of progression from Resolution 1 through to Resolution 3, could I suggest that in the core of this sphere there lies an 'atom' of character which supports the whole shebang? People who read books like this, and who accept the validity of the arguments put forward within them, are invariably people who have character - but who acknowledge that their character has not been strong enough, until now, to act as they know they should .

The challenge, therefore, is to nurture that seed of character and to exercise it in making, living and keeping the **Three Resolutions**. That is much, much easier said than done. And therefore so worth the effort.

An Alternative Approach

While reviewing this book for the updated second edition it occurred to me in a moment of clarity that the sphere could also be looked at academically from the reverse perspective. That's not to say that the progression from self-discipline, through character and competence to service is not valid, however. To my mind that is really the only *practical* way that The **Three Resolutions** can be applied. Like most projects there is a need to start at the beginning in terms of execution of a progressive plan. Each part builds upon the part before it.

However, while I believe that the **Three Resolutions** can only be *applied* in an inside-to-outside fashion, I now believe that from a longer-term perspective it can be *designed* the other way, i.e. *planned* by taking the route from service, through character and competence and towards self-discipline and self-denial.

This alternative approach complements the suggestion that one should develop a personal mission statement. Taking the view that a Personal Mission

Statement is a plan on how you intend to live your life and what legacy you want to leave by its end, then approaching **The Three Resolutions** *from* the end, rather than the beginning, makes sense.

Consider for a moment that you have some sort of idea of what you want to have achieved by the end of your life, or even just your career. At least a small element of that plan would likely involve some kind of service to others – it would be difficult to see how it would not, given the fact that financial rewards require the provision of a service. Even if your plan to make millions was self-serving you'd have to provide some kind of service in order to do it, unless you plan to win a lottery.

Through the creation of such a life plan you would first look at your Third Resolution and decide on the service you intend to provide. In doing this you would in turn discover and define the character traits and competencies that you would need to seek out and nurture in order to carry out that service. And, having decided on those traits and skills, you would discover what disciplines and self-denial would be required to obtain them.

This perspective turns the sphere inside out at the design stage, but it remains 'as is' – worked from the inside-out – for application.

Whichever approach you choose, it is understanding and complying with the **Three Resolutions** that matters. But the question now arises – apply it to *what?*

Chapter Two – Where are you now?

When people pick up a book of this type it is usually because they are sat on a curve, a continuum that runs from their having a nagging feeling that something is missing in their lives, to a place where they know that they have an almost desperate need to improve themselves in some way. Whatever your own motive, I invite you to complete an exercise in self-analysis, by looking at what was, what is, and then (eventually) what could be.

The final test of those three – your future – I would ask you to work on later, as you go through the pages of this book. Don't wait until the end – you may forget something. Don't make the plan now – you may find something more important as you read. Just focus on what was and what is – discover whether you are improving or declining. If you are declining this book is an opportunity to reverse the process. If you are improving, it's a chance to start moving even faster.

Take the time to look deeply. If you go to my website http://threeResolutionsguy.com you can cut and paste onto a Word document so that you can do it digitally, if you prefer.

First Exercise – what is the TRUTH?

1.   Why did I pick up this book? What am I looking to achieve?

You know in your head and your heart – and your conscience – where you don't feel 'right'. Write it down.

2.   Alternatively, what is it that I am trying to avoid?

Occasionally it's not what you want that is clear – it's what you don't want. If answering this question is easier than answering question 1, don't be concerned because the ultimate result is likely to be the same – you'll discover what it is you need to do, or stop doing, and find a way forward.

3.   What is it that I am NOT doing that I should start?

Rest assured there will be something that your conscience tells you that you ought to be doing, but make sure that whatever it is telling you is coming from you and not from someone else's perception of who you should be.

4.   What am I doing that I know I should stop?

It's a similar question, isn't it? Your conscience will guide you again.

5.   What excuses have I used?

What frightens you, even a little bit, about making the change that you know you must make? Don't worry if the list is long – they often are.

6.   What GOOD am I doing that I should continue doing?

This question is an opportunity to celebrate the greatness in what you already are, have, and are doing. Take that opportunity to realise there is potential in you to achieve what you have identified as the ideal.

7.   What am I known for?

We all have a reputation. If you don't know the answer to this, find someone you trust and ask them for the truth as they see it. Their response will still be flavoured by their own perceptions, but less so than someone who you do not trust. Your friend's thoughts can then be tempered by what your conscience tells you is true, and as a result you'll better understand yourself from another perspective.

8.   What do I believe in?

The answer to this question could be faith-related but does not have to be. Some of the answers were found during the exercise on discovery of your personal values.

9.   What am I capable of?

Look around for the people who you believe have what you want. There's your answer, or at least part of it.

History Exercise

1.   What have I done in the past that served me?

You are where you are because of your past. If you have a job, then that is a success, even if it isn't the career you want, yet. Certificates, qualifications, awards – these are representations of what you are capable of no matter how petty they may initially seem to you, or to others (whose opinion of these achievements is irrelevant anyway).

2.   What have I done in the past that served others?

You can think as wide or as narrow as you wish with this one. Routinely opening the door for an OAP is as valid as 'giving one of my millions of pounds to a beggar', if not more so. Your situation often dictates your ability to give. Hopefully you'll have done more volunteer work than you can immediately think of, so think about it for a while.

3.   What was I good at?

My own experience is that, over time as my roles and situations changed, what I was good at changed as well. For example, I once wrote a book on tracing wanted persons and at that time was exercising that skill regularly. Now I don't do so, so I'd have to look up my own book to start again. What did you do well that you don't do any more, and what skills did you use then that you can transfer to the present?

4.   Who did I admire?

Who made you better when you were young? Who guided you for your sake rather than their own? What lessons did they teach you that you can still look back on and say, 'they taught me that'? Whose character did you admire because you knew it to be genuine – there was no duplicity?

5.   Who DO I admire, now?

In 21st century living many people look to 'celebrities' for their role models. If the celebrity you admire has got where s/he has through real talent, hard work and a little bit of luck, good. Identify those talents and attitudes and let the luck take care of itself. If the celebrity was in a reality programme based solely on geographical or body stereotype, then you are truly lost.

6.   If that has changed, what brought about the change?

For me, it was a change of perspective. What I used to look for in people changed from professionalism to people skills. These are not independent of each other but as I grew I noticed the latter – character - just that little bit more. Do you look for, or see differently than you did before?

7.   Was that a positive or negative change?

If it was positive, well done for seeing it. If it was negative, now is a time to go back and redress the error.

8.   If that has NOT changed, what lesson is there in that?

Think deeply. If the truth is that you have always been an admirer of 'good character', then it is not a surprise that you still recognise that.

Keep your answers in mind as you read the book so that you can make personal sense of what you read – make the experience your own. Read this book in your own context, not that of someone else.

Chapter Three – The First Resolution - Self-Discipline and Self Denial

"To overcome the restraining forces of appetites and passions, I resolve to exercise self-discipline and self-denial." S R Covey

I believe that many people, having scanned the contents of this book, have quickly turned to this page to see what it is about, and I would surmise that their motive is based firmly upon one piece of self-knowledge they all possess but one which they would dearly love to deny or to explain away – that if they applied some self-discipline or improved their self-control, their lives would be better. I believe this to be true because it has been my own experience. I know I have failings and I know when I am not doing something about them. So do you.

It has been said that "what is most personal is most general", and this is why we absolutely know when others are failing, why we take a moment to gently remind them that they are failing, and all the time do so knowing that we are prone to failure as well. When attacking the flaws in others we're often just getting our defence in first.

It really hurts when I realise that my failings are down to the inconvenient truth that despite years of study in the field of personal development, I still have great difficulty adhering to the standards I repeatedly set for myself.

Is this your experience? Is there a part of your life where you aren't doing what you know you should be doing? *Is that why you're reading this book?*

I recently read of a 54 country, 118,000-person survey where people were asked to 'rate' leadership qualities in leaders they liked or respected. They were also asked to rank in the order in which the surveyed participants perceived those chosen leaders *demonstrated* those chosen characteristics. To recap – choose a leader; choose leadership characteristics; rate the former on their performance in the latter. Or, in other words, they were asked 'how well does your chosen leader execute on leadership qualities?'

It was interesting to note that 'self-regulation' – or self-discipline – was considered by participants to be one of a number of *essential* leadership characteristics, yet was seen by the participants to be one of the three *least* evident characteristics shown by their chosen leadership models. In other words, even if liked or at least respected, the leader they admired was 'known' by those surveyed to lack self-discipline.

Is this true for you, dear reader? Are you a person acknowledged by others to be a good person who regulates themselves in a disciplined fashion, but who knows, deep inside, that you aren't? That you are, in fact, faking it? If so, read on.

This Resolution comes First

I have already shown in the opening chapters that the **Three Resolutions** apply first to self, then to your relationships, and finally to your levels of contribution. I demonstrated how self-discipline and self-denial are foundational to success at the higher levels of character, competence and contribution. In other words, you now know how self-discipline is foundational to a happy life.

In *The Seven Habits of Highly Effective People* Stephen Covey explained how those Habits work on a continuum, where self-mastery comes before interpersonal mastery because, frankly and concisely, one cannot master relationships until one has mastered oneself. You cannot truly be an effective part of a team/club/organisation/family until you have identified your part to be played in that structure, and you have prepared yourself to enact that role to the best of your ability.

An effective individual contributes, provides advice and is able to consider the rights and wrongs of any action taken in respect of things which affect the 'team'. An effective person knows what's what and how things are done and does things well. An ineffective person is one who has not mastered self to any practical degree and is therefore a 'people-pleaser' who has no sense of self except to the degree that others define it for them. They tend to act in accordance with whatever the group supports, regardless of the rights and wrongs, because they want to be seen by that group as one of them. Lack of a proper sense of self means that others dictate their attitudes and actions. Ergo, self-mastery is a precursor to, and positively affects optimum interpersonal effectiveness.

Furthermore, if I am feckless and unquestionably blow in the wind with public opinion, there is no reason why anyone should listen to me because I have no alternative view to give. If I am resolute and disciplined, my opinion will be seen to be of value.

Therefore, to the degree that self-mastery is a pre-cursor to interpersonal effectiveness I would argue that of the **Three Resolutions**, this first one is a precursor or prerequisite to mastery of all three, and without it there can be no true mastery of any of them. In fact, commitment to the Second and Third Resolutions requires application of the First Resolution because self-discipline and self-denial serve one's character, competence, and the ability to serve other people and noble causes.

Without self-discipline one cannot be a true master of self, and this should be borne in mind by anyone seeking to ignore the benefits, strengths and challenges of self-discipline and self-denial.

To be historically accurate, the original sources for the **Three Resolutions** suggest, from their tone and initial interpretation, to refer only to self-discipline in terms of the physical self – control over one's physical appetites in terms of eating, drinking, rest and exercise. My research would suggest that the source material argued that proper respect of the body is essential because the body is the temple through which God's work is done; therefore, treating it accordingly is a required discipline.

I, on the other hand, believe that the First Resolution can be interpreted more widely than simple 'purity of the body', and can be applied to our entire existence – physically, yes, but also mentally in terms of our application to education, relationships, work and personal lives. Application of the First Resolution is important in the physical dimension, certainly, but that is only part of the equation. It can apply to all four of the human dimensions whose existence has been supported in various ways by other respected writers in the fields of sociology and psychology. There have been many observations on the precise number and nature of human needs but I have accepted Stephen Covey's Four Human Needs as all-encompassing and therefore use them to illustrate where you may consider self-discipline needs to be applied; they are the **physical, mental, social** and **spiritual** dimensions.

Taking each in turn:

Physically – do you exercise? Are you flexible or stiff? Are your eating habits sustainable or are they killing you? Are you a slave to your stomach or to any other physical vices, e.g. sugar, alcohol or drugs?

Mentally – are you a reader? Do you read pulp fiction or is your focus on non-fiction/quality fiction? Are you up to date professionally? How about current affairs – do you understand them or do you focus on 'Okay' and 'Hello' magazines? Can you debate at an intellectual level or is your argument prone to emotional outburst and interruption, rather than objectivity and consideration? Are you considered and deliberate, or loud and abusive? (See Twitter.)

Socially – do you spend all your time alone or do you mingle? Are you nice to people or do you detest company? Do you like yourself or not? Are you a conversation facilitator, or silent until called upon to provide input?

Spiritually – is your life filled with purpose or are you an example of Zig Ziglar's 'wandering generality' – someone who goes with the flow as their current emotional state dictates? Are you happy in the moment but then wonder what's the point?

In all of these areas, are you exactly where and what you wish to be? If not, why might that be?

Is it because you aren't doing what you know you should be doing?

This question frequently arises in all of us and, for each of us, in all four areas: Where do you find yourself unable to apply self-discipline and self-denial to the degree is having an effect on personal effectiveness in any area of *your* life? (Clue: ask your conscience.)

At this juncture it is routine for the average student to pass on to another section, one that is more egotistically 'convenient', one where you aren't going to read what you wish you didn't have to read. As a result, the opportunity to effectively use the information and observations that come next, is lost.

This philosophy doesn't work in a vacuum. A philosophy needs something to work *on*. It must be applied to something to be of any benefit. In this case, that something is a someone. That someone is *you*.

The potential for this book to work requires a context that YOU, the reader, can provide. That context is your situation, the situation that caused you to buy the book and to read it. The objective is for you to apply it to your life – your life is the context within which this philosophy will work.

So stop here, grab a pencil and paper, briefly note the areas in which you find yourself under-performing, and then consider those jottings as you read the advice and observations that follow. Better still, get absolutely clear on identification of the areas where you are not performing as well as you know you can, by specifically stating where you are failing and why you think that is. For example:

I am failing in the area of organising my work. The amount of work I have is enormous, so I don't keep it organised because just as I finish one task the next pops up and I start on that. By the end of the day I have a list of disorganised but completed tasks, which sounds great but then I can't demonstrate how well I've done or quantify my success because I can't find the completed paperwork! And by the end of the day the sheer size of the organising task is so great that I just let it ride until the next day – and the next, and the next..........

I eat too much. I know I eat too much but in the moment, as I open the fridge door because I am peckish, I reach into the gargantuan white Narnian cabinet that is my destiny and I remove some treasure for instant gratification. Even as I eat it I feel guilt, but that doesn't stop me.

I don't exercise. I breathe like a straining steam train as I climb even one flight of stairs, I wilt at the thought of jogging, and I grunt as I get out of a chair. I'm not even 40, yet! I want to be fit, but the effort needed in the part between Fat and Fit is too onerous to think about.

I procrastinate. I'll tell you about it later......

Do the exercise now and make a note of your self-identified, conscience-highlighted indisciplines – perhaps using the questions at the end of this chapter to guide your deliberations. Or just write down your one word answers, truthful jottings about where you are not as you want to be. Choose to exercise self-discipline from RIGHT NOW.

What are Appetites and Passions?

The First Resolution is intended to lead the individual in overcoming the Restraining Forces of Appetites and Passions through self-discipline and self-denial. So what exactly are they?

Appetites and Passions are things which draw us forward when carefully identified, observed, and managed. We need to eat, so our hunger is an appetite that serves us. We pursue work that we love, so our passions direct our efforts for good.

Unfortunately, when our Appetites and Passions are unspecified or unknown, or when they *are* known but are allowed to drive us without thought or control because they are not properly managed or even eradicated, then they direct us away from what we love and know to be right for us. They drive us towards gaining more than we need at the *expense* of those very needs, and ultimately towards self-destruction. Worse still, they often provide what we *think* we want, when what we want is not what we *need*.

By unspecified appetites and passions, I refer to those appetites, desires or wants that creep up on us psychologically and without thought. Often these needs and appetites have been introduced to us by others, others who have no interest in our wellbeing but are wholly focused on their own. It is a parallel to the actions of drug dealers who will let you have one free sample and then take money off you as you destroy your life trying to repeat what that first hit gave you.

It is the same with a lot of our destructive habits. Suddenly you find you are being driven by an unconscious force, driven not towards something your body and mind need to function at their optimum, but instead towards something which will seriously affect their efficiency at best, or even worse, destroy them.

Sometimes the activity is not so obviously or immediately destructive but the same principles apply – temptation of the new iPhone, followed by an overwhelming desire to get one, followed by another urge to get the next model even though the one you have serves you more than adequately. This is often the power of advertising – creation of a sense of 'must have' rather than 'truly need'. Something outside of you creates either a self-destructive, or certainly diverted focus.

More often than not, when you look at your behaviour in terms of what you spend your time pursuing, you will discover some sense of what I am writing about. When you find that you are not achieving an outcome which serves you or those about whom you care, there is a very good likelihood that you are doing something else, instead; something that provides you pleasure in the short term by providing an emotional benefit, but which you know in your conscience is not really serving your long term needs at all.

Or it could be something which merely replaces the pain of doing something which serves you, but which you know will mean discomfort of some kind. Most of us would rather go down the pub than exercise.

Whether it is seeking a short term pleasure or avoiding a short term pain, something is getting in the way of your better self.

If there *is* something like that in your life then that is, for our purposes, an appetite or a passion.

Examples – perhaps obvious ones – are food (emotional binge eating), alcohol, drugs, smoking, sleep, television, the internet, and pornography. They all divert you from what you are supposed to be doing – something that is important to you, to those about whom you care, or to those you serve – into instead carrying out an activity that does *not* serve you or others and which on, occasion, can be self-destructive. These destructive activities, when taken to the extreme (either in kind or in time taken), we call Addictions.

Why we fail - Addictions as a Restraining Force

For many, this deflective activity, this 'other thing that results in our failure to perform at our best, can often be slotted into the Addictions pigeon-hole.

Don't be put off by that word – I'm not suggesting that any 'addictions' you may have identified or which you may come to identify within yourself relate to illegal, immoral or unethical practices (although for some it would). To restate, for our purposes we are defining addictions as those unproductive avoidance activities towards which we gravitate when not applying conscious thought about the consequences, and which divert us from the things upon which we should be focussing our time and efforts. Avoidance activities, for example, like binge eating, alcohol, television, the internet, pornography, procrastination and even exercise, all of which can become restraining addictions. How so?

The generic signs of an addiction have been dexcribed thus:

(*The addictive behaviour ...*)

- Creates predictable, reliable sensations;
- Becomes the primary focus and absorbs attention;
- Temporarily eradicates pain and other negative sensations;

- Provides artificial sense of worth, power, control, security, intimacy and accomplishment;
- Exacerbates the problems and feelings it sought to remedy; and
- Worsens functioning and creates potential loss of relationships.

* quoted from First Things First by Stephen R Covey, A. Roger and Rebecca Merrill. Adapted by them from S. Peele: 'Diseasing of America: Addiction Treatment Out of Control', Lexington Books 1989, P.47)

Consider the list of activities listed earlier and review them within the framework of these accepted definitions of addictive behaviour. Ask yourself if any of those activities have become addictive to you, even if only to a small degree. Do those activities provide any of the 'benefits' listed within the box? Do they provide *all* of them? Think deeply – sometimes the effects are invisible, or we pretend that they aren't there at all. I suspect that if you look deeply within yourself, then if you find that you are overdoing the activities the signs will all be there, at least to some degree. Be honest.

Take excessive eating: it has been well established that 'emotional eating' is a challenge to the overweight. But even the happy and slim can fall victim. How so?

Eating creates predictable sensations – sugar, savoury flavours, satisfaction, satiety, and so on. As a society, and even across cultures, we still use eating as a central event in celebration. We even call many holidays 'the feast of' - so there is a social impulse to consider. We feel good when we are being sociable and being sociable requires that we eat – and eat well. (Not to mention drinking!) There is a loop. We eat when we celebrate, so we then *seek* happiness by eating. And for some reason this has now extended into the ever-present Facebook post of a meal yet to be eaten. Society unconsciously recognises the importance of food not just as fuel, but also as a source of connection and of emotional contentment.

It can become the primary focus – I know from my own experience that 'where/when am I going to eat' can take my attention, particularly when I am on a diet! And don't forget the aforementioned social imperative.

It eradicates pain – disregarding the obvious and biologically necessary reduction in hunger that comes from eating, those who have suffered weight problems know exactly how this symptom of addiction feels. Seeing themselves in the mirror they feel that they are failing, and so go straight to the fridge to make themselves feel better. The pain is replaced by the sweet, sweet sensation of taste.

Provides self-worth – incredibly, someone who is overweight can feel a sense of significance for a brief moment when someone focuses their attention on them, asking 'who ate all the pies?' Attention implies importance, albeit in this case an attention of a self-defeating kind.

Exacerbates the problem – emotional eating to overcome a weight problem? Need more be said?

Worsens function (etc.) – If you take all the above into account, do 'eaters' focus better or not? How will they apply themselves to their goals? If they feel bloated, how will they perform? If the overweight individuals feel bad about themselves, how will they feel about those who call them names, or who try to 'help' by bringing attention to their fat issues? Never mind the 'real' bullying from others – how about the 'bullying' that their low self-image's imagination invents all on its own?

Apply these symptoms to the other behaviours mentioned above (*alcohol, television, the internet, pornography, procrastination and exercise*). Are they not self-evidently potential, if not actual addictions? And is it not self-evident that these addictive behaviours are therefore restraining forces, stopping us from being at our best?

Sidebar: *I love that expression people use in times of stress. They come home frazzled, and declare, "I need a drink." Then they go to a bottle of alcohol, pour themselves a miniscule amount of (say) whisky, then they knock it back in one fell swoop and state, "Aaah, that's better!" What an amazing lie. A brief mouthful of nice-tasting liquid has just solved all your problems – or you've just fallen victim to a societal 'truth'. No, when you come home and 'need a drink' because you're stressed what you really mean is, "I've got to get drunk!" because that's the only way you'll forget those challenges – by getting too chemically confused to see them anymore. And that is a road down which you might not want to travel.*

I cannot emphasise this enough; we are not talking only about the accepted, illegal or unacceptable addictions. We are talking about over-emphasis on ANY self-selected activity, peccadillo, intrusion or other deflection from what we should be doing. And by self-selected I also mean when we choose to follow someone who has selected a diversion for us.

Furthermore, and this might just blow a mind-fuse, we can include in this paragraph things which DO serve us but still get in the way of *more important* things when they become the focus of our attention just a bit too often. For example, exercise is good for you, but if you regularly and freely go for a run when you should be doing the accounts, then that is, potentially, a Restraining Force in action.

Addictions – and if you can't accept that term just continue to use Appetites and Passions - of any level or depth are Restraining Forces because they deflect us, like the traffic officer in the car chase, from our intended or best direction. They push us off course or even magnetically drag us backwards by taking up valuable time, metaphorically obstructing our path and creating further reliance on the vice, occasionally until the vice itself inadvertently becomes our purpose. Our purpose is no longer what we originally intended it would be. We have sabotaged ourselves – perhaps unwittingly and without intent, but effectively, nevertheless. The purpose of this section of the book is to make sure that you don't unwittingly become addicted, by identifying how easily it can happen.

Look at these Restraining Forces and addictions from another perspective. In his book "The Success Principles", author Jack Canfield suggests that we sonetimes don't do the things we know we should be doing *"because they involve risks. You run the risk of being unemployed, left alone or ridiculed and judged by others. You run the risk of failure, confrontation or being wrong. You run the risk of your mother, neighbours or your spouse disapproving of you. Making a change might take effort, money and time. It might be uncomfortable, difficult or confusing. And so, to avoid any of those uncomfortable feelings and experiences, you stay put and complain about it."*

Put more simply, just 'doing nothing but complaining' is a Restraining Force and can be, in our minds, the explanation and even the justification for our failure – even though we decline every opportunity to do something about it. We can also become addicted to, or at least have an appetite or even a passion for the status quo, for the reasons Canfield suggests. We can become addicted to the security of not trying, because (in turn) we are addicted to:

- being loved, under the condition that we don't rock the boat;
- being safely employed, money regularly available without having to try too hard;
- being right, approved or even just tolerated;
- being 'safe' with the situation as it is;
- being confident because we aren't threatening that confidence with new situations or the need to learn new things;
- liking what we are doing, and so being reluctant to change things.

Looking at that list, can you see how the addiction benefits can be found by these influences? Just to remind you, an addiction:

- *Creates predictable, reliable sensations;*
- *Becomes the primary focus and absorbs attention;*
- *Temporarily eradicates pain and other negative sensations;*
- *Provides artificial sense of worth, power, control, security, intimacy and accomplishment;*
- *Exacerbates the problems and feelings it sought to remedy; and*
- *Worsens functioning and creates potential loss of relationships.*

As I read this with both lists to hand, it is plain – addiction to the status quo is as much a Restraining Force (and obstacle to our success) as the more obvious and sinister, accepted and derided addictions – and for *exactly* the same reasons.

(People generally don't like change, while paradoxically seeking it out. But they are happy seeking change provided they choose it, not when it is chosen for them. Ask anyone whose job is threatened by cost-cutting managers. Make a note – this book is about you deciding on the changes you want to make, and the status quo is no longer an option!)

Appetites and Passions are the things we do that we like to do 'now', but which don't serve us in the long term. Like drugs which feed a 'high', addictions are something we have an appetite for because it makes us feel good or simply helps us to avoid 'pain' – indeed the word 'appetite' is appropriate because we need to feed that addiction. Even if you cannot accept the term 'addiction' you can at least acknowledge that you like something because it makes you feel good or prevents you from feeling bad, and you therefore become passionate about it – whether 'only just' or to the point of obsession.

Is an addiction one of your Restraining Forces? If you have understood the hypothesis the answer is obvious – it is holding you back to some degree, whether it is an 'accepted' addiction, a 'vice', or simply an addiction to the status quo.

Appetites and Passions are not necessarily the only addictions. Most obvious 'addiction' circumstances mean that you are 'doing' something which directs you away from your chosen or (reasonably) imposed path. Those words imply that an appetite/passion/addiction is the *active* pursuit of something, but there is an alternative addiction which can be just as destructive, which is better described as IN-action.

I mean inaction as in doing nothing at all, as distinct from the earlier unwillingness to take *required* action, This kind of 'doing nothing' happens when you are literally giving no thought to anything other than just 'doing nothing' – not only 'in the moment' but 'ever'. This can be the result of disinterest in finding something to do, but even more insidious is the situation that arises when you have no vision or purpose – in other words you are doing nothing because you have not identified *anything* towards which you want to direct your efforts.

This also describes a life that lacks purpose, which is where applying the Third Resolution will help but such a life is also the result of an addiction to surrender.

Century 21 – Social Media and other Addictions

There is one relatively new potential addiction that can be debilitating, and that relates to modern communications technology. On the one hand Information and Communications Technology (ICT) is an amazing modern tool without which we could not work and communicate as effectively as we do. Television is an informative and entertaining medium which we are privileged to possess and which we frequently use to make us happy. The Internet is a vast and occasionally reliable source of information, entertainment, amusement and interconnectedness, even more so because we can interact with it in a way that until recently we could not do with other forms of entertainment. Social media is a good way of staying connected with friends, and with making new connections. As a tool for business, social media has had a tremendous impact.

On the other hand, I am fed up as I sit there paying £46 a month to watch Friends for the millionth time ("Oh look, it's in a 'special', that makes it different"). And have you noticed that all the commercial channels very much show adverts at the same time, so channel hopping those channels is no longer the escape you'd like it to be. (I even saw a quite amusing advert where they tell you they're doing it!)

My wife constantly invades my Facebook page with video drivel of puppies and weddings intended to make her friends go 'Aaahhh', past which I have to navigate to get to MY far more insightful and important entries. Not to mention those quizzes and puzzles, the only aim of which is to sell stuff or obtain your account details so that they can defraud you, later.

I am constantly interrupted by the digital buzz of an automated telephone call trying to tell me I have compensation coming despite the fact I know I have no cause for any such reward.

And doesn't the fact that you notice that the various media *do* these things indicate that, perhaps, you spend too long voluntarily being subjected to them – like me?

Like any addiction/restraining force, overuse or overemphasis on technology, as an escape rather than as a tool, stops you from doing those things which your conscience tells you would be better. Worse still, those things become so addictive and we rely on them so much that we forget that there *are* alternatives, or we stop using our initiative and intellect to solve problems. For example, in the police force I have genuinely known people who, if they can't solve a crime on the internet or force systems, do not realise you can go and knock doors to find the answers using the old technique of 'talking to people'.

If you find yourself overusing social media or becoming over-reliant for your amusement on the computer – recognise your addition and look to modify your behaviour.

Read a book. (Oh, you are. Sorry.)

The consequences of ill-discipline

Allowing ourselves to be victim to appetites and passions, and even worse addictions, is the antithesis of discipline – it is *ill*-discipline.

For ourselves to be ill-disciplined is one thing, and for many people they can excuse that lack of will because they perceive that it only affects them. If I live alone and have no job I can probably get away with having no self-discipline, but that is the route to self-hate and suicide. No hyperbole. if you have no reason to live *properly*, you may find yourself with no reason to live *at all*.

Self-esteem *requires* some self-discipline, because if you have none you have nothing to feed your ego. You start by telling yourself 'it isn't worth the effort' and eventually conclude that *you* are not worth the effort. In fact, there would be some scientific basis for concluding that people who 'think' that way eventually conclude that they 'are' that way – their ill-discipline becomes an element of their identity. You might think that this is harmless – it only affects the individual. Tell that to their families and colleagues, the ones who pick up the pieces when it all goes wrong, particularly when tragically so.

And make no mistake – a lack of self-discipline often communicates to others that you don't consider them important, either.

Two common examples of how a lack of self-discipline communicates disinterest towards others are a lack of punctuality, and phone etiquette. Being on time communicates that what the person being visited is doing, and being present at the appropriate time to do it, are important to you. As most of what we need to be punctual about involves other people, they are reliant upon us to be there on time, as promised – in part because they have often made their own plans around that same appointment. Ergo, us being late impacts on their needs, and therefore implies that their needs aren't important – and therefore that they aren't important, either. In a similar sense, answering a telephone when engaged in a meeting with someone else sends the same message (unless clearly explained and agreed in advance). The message is "This (potentially unknown) caller is more important than you.".

Sidebar: I was once in a meeting with a senior colleague who answered two calls during a meeting we'd arranged beforehand. I decided that if he answered a third I was going to excuse myself, go next door and ring him myself. And advice for professionals – if you make an appointment with customers for 9 am and leave them outside in the street until 9.20 am while you have a 'team meeting', don't be surprised if the customer never comes back.

Another sociological phenomenon I have noticed, connected to but oddly the flip side of the above example, is this: just as we are now expected to answer a ringing phone, people expect us to divert attention from one person to them when they feel like it. I was in a supermarket and saw two staff talking. One was evidently a supervisor, talking to another staff member stacking a shelf. At the far end of the aisle, with a clear view of this conversation, was a second staff member – who kept shouting the name of one of the first two, regardless of the fact they were already talking. In this case they ignored him, but so often I have seen people turn to the interruption and engage with them, thus being rude to the original party. People have turned into phones!

In general, however, ill-discipline leads to the failure to create any results other than the maintenance of a poor status quo, at best, or destructive results at worst. The rule of nature is 'if you don't grow, you die' and this is a clear description of what happens if you don't 'act', which can itself require self-discipline. If you do not create results you will not be paid for your work or rewarded for your effort – because you haven't made any. If you do not demonstrate any self-discipline the message is "I cannot or will not provide you with what *you* want because I am not willing to put the effort in myself."

Self-discipline is an absolute requirement of any life worth living, to any relationship worth having, and in any situation where there is a sense that something important must be done.

You may nevertheless think that an awful lot of people out there have the ability to exercise self-discipline and self-denial in spades, in that they seem to be prosperous and to have succeeded in the very areas that we see ourselves failing. As you read this book you will realise firstly that they, too, have their issues – ask Amy Winehouse (oh, too late). You will also find that what they are successful at, they enjoy doing, so while they ARE disciplined in the accepted sense, it's a kind of 'easy' self-discipline fed by desire. But such people are so often ill-disciplined in other ways, often morally, so this philosophy is as applicable to the 'success' as it is to any of us. This book is aimed at those of us who do find difficulty with Restraining Forces of one kind or another.

It is, therefore, aimed at all of us.

The Solution is in Application of the First Resolution

I hope that, by now, you have concluded that the arguments against appetites, passions and addictions have been made out. In all honesty, we know that there is only one way to overcome addiction. The logical next step in your thinking should surely be that to overcome those restraining forces, we must commit ourselves to better behaviour; we must commit to application of some level of self-discipline and self-denial, and some of us need to do so in more than one life area. If our appetites and passions are holding us back, the *only* effective response is to apply self-discipline and self-denial.

It's been said that to prove the logic of any contention, one must explore its opposite. If the opposite is ridiculous, then the original contention is, by definition, accurate. We've already gone some way to show that, but just to labour the point:

Eating badly will never make us slimmer;
Sitting on our butts won't make us fitter;
One more cigarette won't assuage the addiction to nicotine; and
Being 'comfortable' with our addictions won't cure us of their impact.

We absolutely, unarguably, intellectually and unconsciously know that. And equally, we know that for those of us already subjected to the tyranny of the restraining forces hitherto mentioned, the answer only lies in one response: the application of self-discipline and self-denial.

Both phrases imply an expectation or anticipation of some kind of hardship. These terms immediately cause us to feel as though we have to do something uncomfortable or deny ourselves something pleasurable. It suggests that in order for us to get something we need or want, we must do something unpleasant, and/or deny ourselves some kind of pleasure. Or to put it in a nicely profound way;

Self-discipline means doing the things we don't want to do because doing so serves us; and self-denial means not doing the things we do want to do, because doing them does not serve us.

But this imposition is not necessarily wholly negative. It is not a case that we apply the First Resolution and immediately make life hard for ourselves; its application only really means that an *easier* option is occasionally denied to us.

What does that mean, in practice?

Consider the blurbs cited on the cover of most, if not all diet books. What is promised? What do we see?

"The Easy Way to Lose Weight."

"The Quickest Way to Weight Loss."

"Weight Loss Made Easy."

Each phrase offers us a weight-loss method that doesn't task us. It implies that we can lose weight with no application of thought, effort or inconvenience. No one in their right mind would try to sell a book using these blurbs:

"The Hard but Effective Weight Loss Method."

"Lose a Stone in 5 Months!"

"Sweat and Deprive Yourself Slim!"

I ask you this: when you read these examples, you knew, didn't you? You just knew that the 'easy' options were drivel, and the 'hard' options were an accurate reflection of reality. <u>You know that to be true.</u> Even though you'd rather it wasn't. Yet this is where the problem lies. In truth, the most effective ways to lose weight and thereafter maintain a healthy weight is to apply those harder methods. That is, through the application of discipline and self-denial.

People who pay their money to the popular weight loss programmes (Weight Watchers, Slimming World, Jenny Craig, etc.) would have noticed that their weight loss is gentle, even slow, but generally healthy and successful *if the diet is adhered to*. On the other hand, crash dieters frequently find that they regain their weight, and this is usually because they revert to type on completion of the diet.

This may be because the disciplined 'slow' dieters apply their new levels of discipline for a longer time, and thus develop eating habits that take over to the degree that the practitioners stay on the path, while the crash dieters apply much stricter discipline *only as long as needed to get the result*, and then reward themselves. In their case they may have not applied the discipline long enough to change that discipline into a new habit, or maybe they didn't realise it was the self-discipline that supported the weight loss. The diet worked as they expected, but the internal discipline didn't have time to fully develop.

If the application of 'truth' is more effective and rewarding in the longer term, why do we prefer to try the quick and easy way? One possible reason may be because 'Discipline' is a dirty word.

What IS discipline?

The Oxford English Dictionary (on-line edition) defines discipline thus:

Discipline: (noun):

- *The practice of training people to obey rules or a code of behaviour, using punishment to correct disobedience.*
- *The controlled behaviour resulting from such training.*
- *Activity that provides mental or physical training.*
- *A system of rules of conduct.*

Given some of the terms used in this definition it is hardly surprising that discipline holds such negative connotations. However, remove terms such as 'punishment' and 'disobedience', and focus instead upon the last definition - *a system of rules of conduct* – and immediately 'discipline' starts to appear more attractive – or at least less onerous.

When they train soldiers they are taught to march up and down, press their trousers, shine their shoes and say 'Yes, sir' on demand, amongst other things. It is called Discipline and it is forced upon the trainees. The majority hate it, and probably always will.

But like we suggested earlier, when looking at discipline objectively we can best reinforce its value by looking at its opposite. Without discipline, what would we have?

Using the examples from the above paragraph, indiscipline wouldn't be that much of a problem – would it? Soldiers would have scruffy looking shoes and trousers, but "smartness isn't as important as being able to do a good job fighting". And they would not be able to march in time around a parade ground, but "it's all a bit 'regimental' and we won't do it when we leave the Training Camp".

That is the effect of purely 'how' training. "Do as you are told and don't question the instruction." And you resent and question that training, or the need for it, for ever more.

But without discipline, we'd also have no trust in those around us to do what we needed them to do, when it had to be done, in the way it had to be done.

Take the principle of punctuality, not often directly equated with or described as a 'discipline'. Suppose the police force organised a 9 AM briefing for a major operation, and people started wandering in when they felt like it? Not too late, but 5 minutes here, 15 minutes there, perhaps a half hour late at most? All these latecomers relying on the fact briefings always start late, anyway?

And presumably they would also be relying on the fact that the briefing won't start until they get there, or someone else can concisely and effectively summarise what was said, that the target will himself be reliable and still be where he is expected to be even when the police are late? Or that the security van they anticipate is a robbery target will be a bit delayed? That the robbers will wait for them? Or that the Judge won't cite them for contempt because they're late for Court? Or the boss didn't really want that report for the meeting that finished before we managed to deliver it?

Or to use the Army example, the soldiers would meander to the battlefield, arriving in dribs and drabs with their kit unprepared for combat. How would that work? What would happen in battle when the sergeant shouted, "GET DOWN!" and GI Joe responded, "Why should I?"

Discipline is a key principle of effectiveness. Without it, life becomes a non-stop round of adaptation to circumstances rather than a smooth execution of priorities and essential activities. With discipline things get done. Without it, things get passing attention and results are indifferent at best, impossible at worst. Referring back to the examples I spoke of (shoes, trousers, marching), the observant reader may suggest that they were bad examples of discipline as an essential element of effectiveness. Shiny shoes aren't a measure of discipline, surely?

Let me let you into a little secret. I felt the same when I was in the Forces and during the early days of my policing career. It was after about 15 years of work that I realised that the imposition of discipline in the forces (both armed and police) was not intended to inconvenience me at all. It was intended to instil within ME a sense of SELF discipline!

The problem was, and probably still is, that no one ever took the time to tell me that I was having self-discipline instilled within me. Certainly not in a way I heard, anyway – they focused more on the fear of non-compliance than the personal and universal benefit of application of what is being taught. But the truth is that the imposed discipline was a good method of identifying a way of living and working that raised my standards for the best in terms of work, but also for me and those around me.

The omitted information was the 'why' discipline was important – to me. If only they'd taught me the philosophies of Gray and Emerson. (See a bit later....)

Sidebar: As an aside, do you notice that when **we** are undisciplined it's easily justifiable, but if someone else is undisciplined and their indiscipline impacts on us, we describe them in unflattering terms? Isn't that called hypocrisy?

Properly understanding the 'why' brings a whole new – and occasionally even motivating - comprehension of the 'what'. The objective of the theory, if properly explained, is to instil within you the motivation to practice the discipline as a precursor to effective performance, and this can only happen if the why has been dealt with. Knowing the rationale behind and the benefits of discipline will help you to raise your standards and will assist you in improving your ability to execute your work (and life) to a higher standard.

Discipline requires *only* the committed observance of a set of rules. And use of the term _Self_-Discipline means that we can choose to set and then those rules for ourselves.

Sidebar: I have a good friend who tells a story that I believe makes the point very poignantly. His father was a 'mere' postman. When someone pointed that out to his father, the man responded, "I deliver the Queen's mail to people who *need to receive it. How is that NOT important?" But that's just an indication of his character and perspective. The story I want to use as the illustration is about when my friend noticed his father polishing the soles of his boots – the soles, mind.*

"Dad, don't waste your time doing the soles. No-one will know."

The old man paused, looked up, and said, "I'll know, son. I'll know."

That's the point. You'll 'know', too.

What can discipline get you?

Common wisdom suggests that 10,000 hours, or ten years learning and application of a skill, can turn a complete newcomer into an expert.

Malcolm Gladwell's book 'Outliers', Geoff Colvin's 'Talent is Over-rated' and 'The Talent Code' by Daniel Coyle all reveal to their readers the idea that 10,000 hours is the 'magic number' of hours required to create a talented exponent in any art, science or other field of endeavour.

Another writer, Ben Carter, wrote *"The 10,000-hours concept can be traced back to a 1993 paper written by Anders Ericsson, a Professor at the University of Colorado, called The Role of Deliberate Practice in the Acquisition of Expert Performance. It highlighted the work of a group of psychologists in Berlin, who had studied the practice habits of violin students in childhood, adolescence and adulthood.*

All had begun playing at roughly five years of age with similar practice times. However, at age eight, practice times began to diverge. By age 20, the elite performers had averaged more than 10,000 hours of practice each, while the less able performers had only done 4,000 hours of practice."

(Source: Ben Carter, BBC News article 'Can 10,000 hours of practice make you an expert?')

If you were to accept that number as being accurate – and why not, it's as good a number as any – then that means to become an expert in your field you need to apply 250 working weeks, or (allowing for holidays) roughly six and a half years, to your preferred field. That is six and a half years of constant practice, not just evening classes, or an hour or two of attention every day after earning your daily crust. Given that we need to live, and to earn money in order to do that, it is inevitable that the 6½ year period for most of us extends into decades, often two or three. It is common for expertise, or at least publicly acknowledged expertise, to take up to 30 years to accumulate. Such is the reality of existence, particularly in the academic field. That said, things are changing as we realise that expertise is not the sole domain of the middle-aged and we develop new ways of imparting knowledge.

But if we were able to dedicate more of our efforts towards the study, development and application of any skill it is almost undeniably true that our 'expertise' will blossom faster. That suggestion applies not only to academic, external knowledge – but also to our knowledge and understanding of ourselves. It's amazing, when you think of it, how 10,000 hours after being born, or leaving school, or starting work – many of us aren't even experts on how 'we' work, mentally or physically. This is why I put some questions to you prior to this chapter – I wanted you to really think about 'you' as you are today, and about the 'you' that you are capable of becoming if you apply the **Three Resolutions**. I wanted you to reflect on where you are, and are not, disciplined.

When is it best to apply discipline?

The beauty of the principle of self-discipline is that it pretty much exists in the 'now'. Or to put it differently:

> *Proactive compliance with our self-discipline can occur at any moment, and all of the time. But the time when it is most effective – is Now.*

The 'now' is the only point over which we can have and take any control. The Past is gone and is set in concrete. The future is outside our control – we can try to affect it but, in the end, those things that lie outside our control (like other people) influence it to a degree that we often cannot.

The hours required for the learning of many of the life skills that underpin all our desired character traits and competencies can start accumulating the minute we get out of bed, and that new learning can keep being considered and applied right up until the minute we retire at night. And it can be learned both consciously and subliminally.

We can choose, every morning, to start acting in a disciplined fashion on ourselves, on our work and on our relationships. Each decision to apply self-denial or self-discipline takes only a moment to make, if we want it to. It can also take hours, but an immediate decision to act in accordance with your ultimate objective is much more effective. Think about things too long and you inject doubt, fear, laziness and other obstacles (excuses) into your development. And no-one like injections.

I know from my own experience that the longer I think about exercise, the worse I feel – until I do it, then I feel great. I propose cutting out the middle bit, where you can.

I suggest that a little self-discipline can potentially empower any individual to make incredible gains in terms of life skills, career skills, relationship skills and general 'living'. Once you set your mind to the achievement of a new skill, either technical or 'soft', the next stage is the disciplined application of study towards that end with a view to becoming at least competent.

Principles as a Resource

That said, Principles Apply! As indicated earlier, principles are universal laws that apply whether we like it or not. We cannot overcome them. We can choose to commit any act, but the consequences are dictated by principles. The consequence may be delayed, or it may not be as expected, but they will come to pass. A criminal may not get caught, but he will engender distrust and dislike in others, and reap the rewards accordingly. An adulterer may avoid detection for a while, but rarely forever. And the guilt that eats away at the psyche never goes away. The point is that a principle always brings about an anticipated result, because it is universally, eternally and externally true. They apply everywhere, all the time, regardless of whether or not we believe in them. And the truth is we know that, even though we sometimes pretend otherwise.

They apply, therefore, when we are setting rules for self-discipline.

You must realise and ultimately accept that you cannot ignore the potential consequences of any decision. You can be unaware what they may be if you give them little or no thought, or if experience has not taught you what they may be. That is life.

But more often than not you can reasonably know what the consequences will be when you make your plan - which is remarkably convenient. When you drive, you do so knowing your destination, of course, but you also drive there safe in the knowledge that (in the main) everyone else will be driving on the same side of the road as you. They will act in certain ways – even the poor drivers – and, as a result, you can be fairly confident of arriving in one piece. (Even in India!) When you approach a door, the nature and positioning of the handle will tell you whether to push or pull – and when this 'rule' is not observed by the door maker it can be amusing to watch pullers push and pushers pull.

There is an amusing demonstration of this at Techniquest, a science-orientated exhibition and activity centre in Cardiff, UK. There is a gate, and attendees are invited to open it. They fiddle with the latch, they push it down, they pull it up, they heave, they sweat, they attack it and, eventually, they discover that the way to open it – is to push the *gatepost* down. That illustrates how 'norms' (principles) can be both used and *ab*used.

The same 'principles' apply to how we make and execute on our self-discipline orientated decisions and plans.

- You know that if you overeat you will gain weight.
- If you don't exercise you will lose physical freedom.
- If you turn up late for work you may miss an important call or opportunity, or you may get sacked.
- If you cheat on your partner, the consequences of discovery will be emotionally and financially huge.
- If you commit the 'perfect' crime, you still spend the rest of your life looking over your shoulder.
- And so on.

Principles apply. Knowing the potential consequence of a decision allows you to make the right one. But the power to make that decision remains yours.

To conclude this input on Principles, I recently heard an interview between Anthony Robbins (author of Awaken the Giant Within, and Unlimited Power) and Stephen Covey, where Covey described how, at the end of his courses, participants were invited to write their mission statements. By that time, they had explored the concepts of values, roles and goals. What Covey found was that while the vision part of the mission statement varied according to what the student sought to do with his or her life, the values section – the rules they set on how they would achieve that vision – varied very little.

Participants would choose words like honesty, industry, persistence and so on to describe the characteristics they felt they needed to implement; those that they knew they must and would apply in order to attain what they were committed to achieving in the future. This, Covey suggests, is social proof that we all know, when allowed time and space to properly consider the question, what the 'right things' are in life.

In his book 'Moral Courage', Rushworth M. Kidder, wrote of a 1996 values survey conducted by the Gallup Organisation, which was distributed at a 'State of the World Forum'. This event, chaired by Mikhail Gorbachev and other statesmen and women, asked attendees to identify their top 5 important values or virtues. The top 10 were

- Truth
- Compassion
- Responsibility
- Freedom
- Reverence for Life.
- Fairness
- Self-respect
- Preservation of nature
- Tolerance
- Generosity

What was unexpected was that the varying cultures, nationalities and religious 'groups' all agreed, in broad terms, on the top 10. Whatever their noticeable differences – and there are many – they *all agreed the same top 10 principles.* They merely chose to *apply* them differently, and to ascribe compliance or priority differently.

In any event, the survey showed that people 'know' which principles are real, and which are fake. And self-discipline is real.

In a final effort to reinforce the importance and benefits of the application of self- discipline and self-denial we again turn to an example experienced by

Robbins. In one of his many audio recordings he describes how he was asked to coach US Marines on leadership and motivation, and in doing so he was told that the men and women present were at the peak of their performance 'lives' in terms of both physical ability and in self-discipline. His source then added that when these Marines left the Forces their standards almost invariably slipped.

When Robbins tells the story, he opined that the reason their standards slip is because the expectations of the veterans' post-service peer groups – new colleagues, friends, communities and society in general – are lower, and so the new standards displayed by those veterans are a reflection of the lowered expectations of the new peer group. Expectations and levels of discipline were very high in the Marines, and objectives and methods were routinely clear. Outside, they became more about 'whatever works in the moment' and 'whoever I have to impress – or not': whether the impressing is done on a personal or professional basis, the standards changed accordingly. Once in a peer group with lower expectations, they elected to adopt different standards. If the shoes didn't need to be shiny, they weren't polished. If they could start to talk back to authority, to 'get by' with their productivity, or to lack punctuality – they routinely did exactly that.

I agree with this hypothesis – that people's standards are a reflection of their peer group - as I see it all around me in terms of fashion and societal norms, but I also ask the question whether the discipline imposed, acknowledged, accepted by and required of those Marines is not the whole part of the equation. In other words, I wonder which came first, the chicken (system imposed-discipline) or the egg (self-discipline)?

In this story the suggestion is that it is the chicken, but what if you applied the 'egg theory' in your situation, instead? Surely the average Marine recruit already has some elements of productive self-discipline within himself or herself, before they join the Marines and have some more imposed upon them?

So, too, do you. You have 'some' self-discipline as a foundation for more. Perhaps not in terms of strength, technical skills and 'fighting fitness', but at least in terms of your own capacity to do what your work/life/purpose requires of you? What if you identified the ideal characteristics that were required of you if you are to be your best, and then applied strict self-discipline to learn, develop, perfect and display them? What if you created your own, high self-expectations and disciplined yourself to make them happen?

You already know the answer - because Principles apply.

Self-Denial is Self-Discipline.

The First Resolution refers to self-denial as well as self-discipline. Self-denial, put simply, is to deny yourself something that may appear attractive (or be addictive) in recognition that it is (a) pleasurable only in the short term and (b) self-destructive in the longer term.

Looking at the second phrase another way, the failure recognises that what they consider denying themselves is damaging – but if they act on that whim they rationalise that they can address that damage if and when it happens. It isn't 'now' enough to worry about. The successful individual exercises self-denial and avoids the negative consequence. Pertinent examples would include:

- sweetly addictive foods,
- all narcotics,
- alcohol,
- pornography,
- and so on.

Disciplining yourself to avoid these potentially damaging intrusions into your otherwise ethical lifestyle is always beneficial. Denying yourself these fleeting pleasures allows time for better activity, results in more personal and ethical productivity, prevents the guilt associated with their indulgence and quickly makes for emotional freedom.

The only difference I see between self-discipline and self-denial is - self-discipline drives you towards certain empowering behaviours through creation of a set of rules that you apply to yourself and your situation, while self-denial is intended to drive you *away* from any ultimately destructive behaviours that prevent you getting what you want. I repeat:

> *Self-discipline means doing the things we don't want to do because doing so serves us; and self-denial means not doing the things we do want to do, because doing them does not serve us.*

Easy Discipline?

There are a number of ways to look at discipline, each of which has a consequence that may help or hinder the application of discipline in your own life.

First of all, have you noticed how *easy* it is to be disciplined about something you *like doing?* People who love running get up early and trog the cold streets without a second thought, while those running 'because they have to' procrastinate and find the easiest excuse not to do it, or they run grudgingly and hate every step. I have a colleague who rises at 5AM most days of the week to take his children to the pool to train, after which he comes to work quite early – he does this because he loves his children and loves swimming himself. However, his girth suggests to me that if he had no self-discipline at all we'd be lucky to see him at work at all.

Sidebar: For my part, I can get up at 5am if I have something meaningful to do, but not as a matter of routine. When I wrote a book that became the Manual for Professional Investigators I was on a training course in Bristol, and slamming out 1,000 words before breakfast was easy – I enjoyed doing it. Not only that, but I would rise at 6am, go for a 30-40 minute run on a treadmill, have breakfast and then do that writing. I was out of my home comfort zone and the desire to do it was assisted by the environment change. I therefore suggest that when 'it' is enjoyable and/or there are no distractions, 'it' does not require much discipline at all.

Second, it is easier to overcome indiscipline when the ultimate objective is something you look forward to and know you *will* enjoy, even if you don't enjoy the interim discomfort. Looking ahead to your intended success diminishes the pain of the applied discipline as you prepare. If you have decided to run a marathon, for example, consider how happy you will feel when that medal appears in your hand, how fit you will be, how good you will look and how proud you will feel. If it is weight loss, think about your new wardrobe. If it is writing, think about how your book will look on the pages of the Amazon website.

Please note, though – self-discipline applied to what you love is *easier,* not necessarily e*asy.*

Next, discipline is easier to apply if you minimise the opportunity for indiscipline. If you manage your surroundings in such a fashion as to minimise temptation while facilitating an easier way to execute your plan, discipline is easier to apply. For example, emptying the cupboards of bad foods and refusing to buy any more will make dieting a lot easier, even if environments outside your control still threaten your efforts. Charles Hobbs opines that when we are feeling stressed we long to or actually return to our comfort zones (usually home or the pantry), where we feel safe, or at least familiar with things. If we can't go to that place we create it, mentally. In doing so we relax and create a space for our excuses.

Another way to make self-discipline 'easier' is to immerse yourself fully in the desired discipline by joining with other people who are seeking or have achieved the same end. It is said that we are the average of the 5 people with whom we spend most of our time. If you spend your time with the lazy, then you tend to adopt their attitudes and become lazy as well. The counter to that is to spend time with people whose attitudes match the ones you are seeking to apply to yourself, making the 'self-discipline' more of a desired 'group-discipline'. If such a group does not exist or is not conveniently nearby, reading books and articles written by the kind of people whose discipline you respect can also be of benefit. (Even the laziest Marine is a lot fitter and more productive than the average Joe.)

An example of the popularity of this idea is the international Park Run phenomenon, where thousands of people gather at 9am on a Saturday at a suitable spot to go for a timed 3-mile run. While many participants are evidently fit, active and annoyingly slim there is a large contingent of the less physically athletic who go there to get fit or improve on their capacity to 'be' disciplined about something that is, to them, ordinarily uncomfortable. The presence of a group enables them to apply self-discipline and to perform better.

How about utilising the art and science of time management? The advice given in all quality time management books is simple – once you have decided what is important, plan it into your day or week. Creating a values-driven, discipline-related 'to do list' in a planning system, whether electronic or paper-based, influences you to earn the 'tick' that you use to cross out a completed task. I have found that while this is not an infallible method, it does have some power. (See also Appendix B for a short, practical course in time management.)

Finally, the least favourable attitude to discipline needs to be addressed, which is use of the phrase 'I have to' or, even worse, '*Do* I have to?'

I suggest that this is the place where failure is most likely, and where the particularly disciplined should be celebrated. Something imposed, as I suggested earlier in this chapter, is frequently something that is resisted *because* it is imposed.

The first comment – I have to - is a statement and implies that what we are doing is something we would otherwise resist but will be doing it anyway. We resist because we want to be in charge, and imposed discipline is imposed by something or someone outside of ourselves – we are no longer in charge. There is only one answer to this imposition, and I again refer back to earlier comments about recognition of the 'why' so often neglected with imposed disciplines.

We are responsible for deciding our response to that imposition – so we accept it and recognise it for what it is, namely an imposition that is intended in some way to serve us as much as it serves the person or system that is imposing it upon us. In other words, and to use an Americanism – suck it up and Do It Now!

The second example – the question, '*Do* I have to? – is potentially more harmful than the acceptance comment, because a question allows for alternative responses, whereas the statement is accepted as a fact and *must* be acted upon. A question promotes choice, and all too often that choice will be the easier option of those available. The three answers are 'Yes' (good); 'No' (bad) and 'Yes, but' (worse). 'Yes, but' is the worst answer because it requires the making of an excuse, a justification and even a rationalisation as to why we won't do what we have simultaneously stated we should. And this excuse, once made and accepted, creates a tendency to adapt it to other disciplines we don't want to apply.

The way to make discipline easier to execute in this circumstance is to make sure that 'Yes' is the only answer you are willing to accept. It may be 'Yes', followed by reluctant action, but action must follow.

Applied self-discipline lies on a continuum between easy at the one end, where we like what we are doing or are sufficiently focused on a longer-term objective; and nigh impossibility at the other, where wild horses *may* get you to do it – but probably not.

It is relatively easy to apply self-discipline for mundane tasks, for example – cleaning your teeth, mowing a small garden lawn, walking a dog after work, and so on. As tasks get more onerous, so does the will-power required for their completion. And when the task to be done is particularly challenging, then the application of self-discipline becomes harder – and even more essential. And this paragraph excludes the influence of the other 'fun' things (or values-driven activities, to be specific) that we might rather be doing.

Having already discussed how the Restraining Forces of addiction slow us down in our objective to be better individuals, now we can look at the Restraining Force of **Avoidance**. Avoidance not so much as a distaste for the new effort, when we avoid because we simply don't *want* to do it, but more about avoidance of losing something we had before we started, or avoidance of losing out on something which is an attractive alternative.

Avoidance is the selection of a psychologically rational alternative to what may cause perceived discomfort or perceived loss. Avoidance arises when we are comfortable and don't want to change that. It is avoidance of leaving our comfort zone.

With comfort comes complacency, however; the deeply held feeling that change is unnecessary if we are to maintain the safety, security and even sanctity of what 'is'. In other words, when the change we seek is not *definitely* going to give us what we want, then the possibility of failure, or (even worse) the possibility of getting something we *don't* want, pushes us into avoidance. We are hard-wired as human beings to avoid risking a negative consequence to our security. If we stay where we are, we have the confidence of knowing what we'll get (principles). If we change, we risk compromising that sense of personal security.

That is probably what makes the application of self-discipline so uncomfortable in the mental dimension. The pain involved in application of discipline in the physical sense is temporary; if we can just get over the sweat/inconvenience in the moment, all will be well. We face the dentist's needle knowing it will be but a fleeting discomfort. But the emotional 'pain' of change cannot be accurately estimated in advance, only during and after the process. In advance, we tend to over-estimate it – and thus engender inaction.

In the final analysis there may only be one solution: get over it. Acknowledge that the pain is temporary if inestimable; accept that it will happen regardless of whether we want it to, or not. Try, wherever possible, to remember that it IS always temporary because we know from experience that we can deal with change – we do so every day of our lives but forget just how resilient and adaptable we can be.

Consider commuting as an example of familiar change. Most of those who travel any distance to work will recognise that travel is paved with inconvenience – traffic jams, train delays, blocked routes, and so on. Yet each day we set out again to make our way to our places of work. We are familiar with, and ultimately resigned to the possibility that something might obstruct our journey, but we set out secure in the belief that even if it does so we will either (a) get around it or (b) be late for work, which is no big deal if it can be fairly justified. Yes, we may miss an appointment but this has rarely been fatal, after all. We become accustomed to non-threatening, even routine 'change'. It holds no fear.

So ask yourself – how will I feel about this tomorrow? The truth is often that you will have forgotten that it was inconvenient at all. (I *really* wish I'd figured this out in my teens.)

So it can be with self-discipline. It will be inconvenient, we may encounter challenges, and we may not enjoy the trip – but we know we have an ultimate destination and we intend to get there somehow, even if we get there later than planned.

A proven rule is to just get started, lean into it and within no time at all the flow begins and it is not quite the monster it was before you began. A sound time management principle has always been to look at a task either as multiple 5-minute taskettes ("You can do it for 5 minutes, can't you?"), or as a Swiss Cheese into which you, by taking action, can make the holes. Or use the example of a Salami Sausage off which you can cut slices which move you from the start towards the finish.

But in the end, getting started is the key. Each time you consider taking an action towards a self-discipline 'rule' that you have set yourself, begin it. Momentum is magic.

This approach is not so easy with self-denial, though. You have to consider the opposite mind-set to 'ACT' when it comes to it, as the default for denial must be 'STOP'. That said, you don't have to say 'ACT' for 5 minutes, or on and off, or now and then – you have to say it only once, but you need to *mean* it and then 'ACT' on that instruction. Self-denial, on the other hand, means stopping yourself from doing something. That's easy when the opportunity to do something you want to deny yourself is fleeting, as in absolutely 'now' or never. But it is a lot harder when you are surrounded by, immersed in or unable to avoid the physical presence of whatever represents that temptation.

The 100% Rule

When it comes to self-denial you will probably discover that unless you have already and successfully applied the following rule, you will have to repeatedly say 'STOP' as long as the temptation is present.

In his book 'The Success Principles', Jack Canfield wrote about a principle he called '**99% is a Bitch, 100% is a Breeze**'. The idea was that once you make a self-growth (denial or discipline) decision you act on it 100% of the time. This is because acting in accordance with your decision 100% is easier than doing so for 99% of the time for a simple reason that is both philosophical, and surprisingly logical .

With 100% there is no need to apply any further mental or emotional effort to the decision and its subsequent consequence. There is no doubt, reconsideration, angst or time wasted. With 99% you have to reconsider that decision every time a circumstance arises in respect of which you have to decide whether or not you should apply your standards/discipline/denial/values/principles 'this time'.

For example, if I decide I will write 500 words a day (like Ernest Hemingway, apparently), then if I am taking the 100% route, that's it– I *will* write 500 words a day, come what may. I'll make sure I have my laptop with me, or I will write longhand on paper and transcribe it later along with the 500 words for that day, too. If I go '99%', then I have to decide, each day, if I am going to bother. That's when the easy excuse will be 'I have to go shopping, instead'. Or 'I don't have a pen'. Or 'my laptop's battery is a bit low and I'll never make it'. Or 'just one packet of crisps/pie/cigarette won't hurt'.

The same applies to *not* doing something (self-denial). If I decide that I will no longer eat chocolate eclairs, then application of the 100% principle means just that – never.

You can set your own rules for applying this principle. You can, if you wish, go 'never' – or you can include justified exceptions to 'never'. You can decide not to eat chocolate eclairs ever again, or you can add an exception – but it must be a specific exception, and it must be observed. In the case of the eclairs you may elect to eat one on a new moon, your birthday, the 1st of the month, or whatever exclusionary rule suits you provided that it does not *excuse* you. That's the material distinction. If you have a rule it must be specific and it must not undermine the original intention. Nor can it allow for or provide excuses for non-compliance. 99% or less doesn't cut it.

99% doesn't work because it allows for mistakes, errors and, most of all, excuses. 100% not only does not allow for excuse or failure but it also demands creativity, imagination and discipline. If you 'cannot' execute on your disciplined objective for some external reason, the 100% rule demands of you that you find a way to overcome that temporary barrier/obstruction. Wayne Dyer, famed writer on metaphysics and life philosophies, reportedly overcame a 'cannot go for a daily run' when flying by running up and down an aircraft's aisles. (BTW – *not* recommended!)

When fully applied 100%, this concept covers the appropriate application of both self-discipline AND self-denial. The only caveat I have to add here is this – don't commit to 100% compliance until you are absolutely certain that you want to. This is because without that certainty of commitment you will make excuses almost as soon as the first decision whether to comply or not comes up. And as soon as you make the decision *not* to comply that 'one time' you are already on the path to failure and guilt. It's already 99%, or even less. And the next time that decision arises it will be even harder to make the right choice and the downward spiral speeds up. Momentum works both ways.

Only commit 100% when you are truly ready.

Do it so often it becomes easier

Here's another piece of profound wisdom that is well placed in this section. Ralph Waldo Emerson once wrote *"That which we persist in doing becomes easier to do, not that the nature of the thing has changed but that our power to do has increased."* In other words, the more we do something the easier it gets both technically *and* psychologically. We become conditioned to do something to the point at which it becomes unconscious – we arguably become 'unconsciously competent' and at the same time 'unconsciously *willing*' to do that which started out to be hard, and which was once an unwelcome imposition upon us.

An obvious example is the development of skills in driving a car. I remember my first lesson – having to look at the gearstick when changing gear resulted in an unplanned drive along a footpath. Now I am an observer for trainee advanced drivers. In the same way, making a decision to do or not do something becomes easier the more we do it. It's *incredibly* hard to say 'No' the first time, but according to the author Gretchen Rubin in her book, Better than Before' it isn't that long before a part-time denier becomes an absolute abstainer. Imagine being able to completely give up sweets, all because for a few days you overcame the urge to have 'just one more' chocolate almond?

Starting today, think of something you should be denying yourself. Alcohol, coffee, sugary foods, an afternoon power nap that is really work-avoidance kip – I'm sure you can think of just one thing that fits the Restraining Force 'bill', which you know in your conscience you should be denying yourself. And 'start stopping' that from today. In a couple of months you'll forget you ever allowed yourself that lapse.

Utilising what I have written in the last few paragraphs, therefore, and in order to help you in your application of self-discipline and self-denial, I therefore respectfully suggest that you can consider the following strategies:

1. Decide what enjoyment you can find in your application of discipline.
2. Recognise the ultimate, post-discipline objective for what it is and focus on that whilst applying the discipline.
3. Redesign your environment by choosing your places and peers in order to facilitate your self-discipline.
4. Use Time Management to great personal effect.

5. Be strong in the hard moments and lean into the task just to get started.
6. Apply the 100% rule once you have identified whatever it is to which you need and intend to apply self-discipline or self-denial, but *only* once you have decided that you are willing to do so.

Disciplined about WHAT?

Having something about which you *can* be, *want* to be, or *need* to be disciplined is, of course, essential. It is difficult to be disciplined in a vacuum. The suggestions provided above (health and fitness) may provide you with a starting point, but at the end of this chapter there are some other questions that may help you to focus your mind on other life areas within which new disciplines may be identified and then applied. Consider them and establish, in your own mind, what your new 'discipline and denial' objectives and behaviours might be.

Suggestions – How Resolution 1 can apply to YOU

Where aren't you as disciplined as you could be, and how can you apply this philosophy to your situation? Only you know the answer to that question and it is your conscience that's loudly helping you to identify it . But let me take some areas of our lives that are fairly common to anyone reading this book. They are: Personal Life, Work, Home, Family and Friends, and Community.

Personal Life – The Physical Aspect

This heading pertains to the physical disciplines, particularly diet, exercise and personal hygiene, but it also applies to certain standards of moral and ethical behaviour. The original texts on those things that undermine good intent were specific about self-discipline and self-denial being directed towards physical appetites. I believe these ideas can be applied more widely, but the 'physiological restraining forces' are as good a place to start when looking at how **The Three Resolutions** can be applied to your benefit.

In order to perform at its best, a car must be used at its optimum efficiency. It must be topped up with oil, water, fuel and other lubricants (food). Its parts must be maintained at a high level of effectiveness (care). And the vehicle must be used properly and regularly (exercise). If any of the above elements are missing, a car won't work properly, and it may not work at all. If the standard of 'food' and parts fall (due to cost considerations), the level of performance may falter. If it is not taken care of, it will deteriorate over time. For example, in 2012 it was reported that an estate agent had purchased a Jaguar V8 car, only to discover it was faulty. It transpired that he was driving this monster to and from work – 2 miles away in a 30mph limit. It never warmed up properly and so declined in its performance.

The same applies to your body, which I have seen described as the only means through which we can turn our thoughts into our achievements. The three elementary disciplines that apply to maintenance of our physical body are – rest, nutrition and exercise.

First, we'll address rest. The human body requires a period of regular rest if it is to perform at its best. Experience (and I mean everyone's experience in this context) shows us that too little sleep affects our levels of personal performance – but so does too much sleep. Not being an expert I will not presume to explain the science of sleep. You know from your own experience what is, for you, too much or too little. You know what affects the quality of your sleep (late eating and alcohol absorption), how you feel when you wake up or whether and by how much you challenge your body's need to rest when socialising.

So let's keep it simple. The human (like most animals) sleeps best during the hours of darkness. It seeks to sleep almost from the point at which twilight approaches and starts to prepare for rest. It is we civilised peoples that try to fight this. Ideally, it could be suggested that you align your sleeping hours with the darkest hours – say 11pm to 7am. You can adjust this as your fitness, career, personal preferences or even your geography and environment dictate. You may elect or be able to sleep less than the 'recommended' 8 hours a day. (Some researchers suggest 6-8 hours is enough, allowing for more adjustment.) In fact, application of the nutrition/exercise element of self-discipline will help you in reducing the length and increasing the quality of that period.

Sidebar: There is a scientifically proven theory that as we sleep in 90 minute rhythms it may be prudent to set your alarm to wake you at a time 7½ hours after you anticipate falling asleep. I tend to go to bed at 10pm, and I find that if

I wake at 7am (9 hours, exactly on 6 x 1 ½ periods) I awake without alarm and feel fine. If I wake at a point 30 minutes earlier or later as a result of an alarm, I feel awful. So there might be something in it. Or not.

If your situation is like mine, you may have experienced how what was a 9-5 work life has become an 8-4 work life. You may also have started to notice how that is creeping towards a 7-3 work life. My own experience suggests that this is for environmental reasons, namely the levels of commuter traffic after 8 AM and the subsequent inability to find a parking place if your arrival is later. A few years ago the enlightened 9-5ers thought "if I work earlier there'll be less traffic and I'll get a space (nearer the front door!)". So they changed their hours to start earlier. Soon enough, society caught on and now we are having the same experience an hour earlier, and the early risers are rising even earlier! And they arrive tired because they haven't rested properly. (At my place of work they also have a tendency to breakfast when they are supposed to be working, instead of eating it at home.)

I would invite you to at least consider (and this may be subject to your workplace requirements, anyway) starting work later and starting the day in a less frenetic fashion. Rise at a sensible time. Have a light breakfast, and travel in to work gently. If doing that results in your having to park further away from your place of work when you arrive – bonus! You get to exercise a little, too! But make the decision yours – and discipline yourself to abide by that decision.

Sidebar: I am amazed by the number of people so desperate to get to work that they drive like maniacs, stressed out as they drive, spending vast amounts of money on extra fuel and risking prosecution in the process. Leave earlier, arrive calm.

Next comes nutrition.

I suggest we all overeat. Some obviously so, some by a far lesser degree. Those who overeat least tend to be slim while those who overindulge regularly are easy to spot. I say this because people who fast or go on hunger strikes don't tend to die quickly.

I was overweight, and I was overweight because I ate badly, too often and too much. By badly, I mean the wrong foods. By too often, I mean a combination of more often than I needed or when I simply didn't need to. And by too much – well, you've been there.

As an intelligent race we discovered how to grow our own food, then how to grow it on an industrial scale – and then how to make it sweeter, tastier and even prettier so that we could sell more of it. Until that last stage we were doing pretty well as a race but that's when it went a bit wrong. It is not that sweet foods are wrong *per se,* only that we now tend to gravitate towards eating fatty, sweet, easily obtained, chemically laden foods. Not to mention that we are being encouraged to do so by advertisers who make it sound and look pretty, and by manufacturers who accidentally or by design make their foods addictive. In addition, the hectic pace of life – or should I suggest the *perceived* hectic pace of life, has caused us to move more towards the convenient rather than the good, and to the good in preference for the best. And as many have suggested, the enemy of the Best is the Good.

Any study of 'eating' advice, or at least well-informed eating advice, is that fresh salads and vegetables are the staple content of any good diet. They are what our bodies were intended to eat, and all things being equal they do us good. We *were* designed with canine teeth so we are capable of eating meat, but we were meant to eat meat only when the other (better) foods were scarce, e.g. winter. Ask any ape. I'm not suggesting readers should go vegetarian – that is a matter of personal choice, and I am not a vegetarian myself. I *am* suggesting that you consider favouring the 'live' foods over the 'dead' ones as much as possible.

Sidebar: I have twice followed what is known as the Natural Hygiene Diet for a period of two weeks, and each time I lost a stone in weight. In a nutshell the diet regime is - eat nothing from midnight to midday, giving the body time to properly digest a day's food. Don't mix proteins (meats and dairy) and carbohydrates, have either one or the other with a salad or vegetables. For those familiar with Slimming World's method it is very similar but without the 'sins'.

Over time, for me, my initial religious adherence to that diet was overcome by environmental issues (shift work and an admitted failure to continue with that self-discipline) but it did prove the point in my case that when we eat as we were designed to eat, our body uses the food better and we do not gain weight. We also move back to what our weight is meant to be. That, incidentally, was with minimal exercise and a reasonably active working environment.

Next, that devil called Exercise.

The body is meant to move. It is structurally designed to walk upright on two legs, with a pulley system intended to make it able to lever great strength where appropriate and in keeping with its design, and a fuel distribution system of incredible efficiency when used properly.

Remember the car analogy, earlier. A car, if it left standing, will atrophy and not work effectively again unless and until carefully restored. Sure, it will work at a level of effectiveness if we pay passing attention to its maintenance, but if we truly want it to perform at its best we must treat it properly. And that means giving your V8 Jaguar a decent run, pushing it hard occasionally, and regularly.

I am not suggesting you now leave the book and go for a sprint – that may be self-defeating. I *am* suggesting that you consider and then design a sensible exercise regimen that serves your own ability to perform at your optimum, ideally with professional or authoritative input.

Research suggests that 3 hours a week, or 30 minutes a day of sensible exercise will be enough to maintain a healthy lifestyle (if the other two physical elements of rest and nutrition have also been carefully monitored, of course). If you wish to be fitter, fine – start and maintain a healthy exercise programme that provides you with that outcome. Aerobic (with oxygen) exercise is preferred – the body works better when using oxygen, with a healthy heart that can only be exercised effectively in that fashion. If you wish to be strong, exercise with weights. If you want to be healthy, focus on running, swimming and cycling. And by all means combine them as you see fit. The Triathlon is an option, not obligatory.

Do not confuse fitness with health. Fitness is an athletic capability and is desirable, but health is the state of being where all of the body's systems (organs, structure, musculature and senses) are working at their best. I would rather have the latter, served by the former, than the former without the latter. Remember the founder of 'jogging', Jim Fixx? Fit as a fiddle, reportedly died from chronic heart disease. Health is preferable. We have seen many 'strong' people who dropped dead because their systems failed through drug, steroid or alcohol abuse, or by simply overstretching the capabilities of improperly served systems.

I therefore suggest the adoption of the following disciplines in terms of your body:

- Sufficient rest.
- A sensible diet.
- Sufficient exercise.

Reducing the 'convenience' food intake dramatically, disciplining yourself to eat the 'natural' foods a lot more, moving about a lot and placing gentle, incremental but greater demands upon your body will result in your body being better able to serve you at work and at play. It will NOT be a bloated, sluggish, stiff and unresponsive machine when called upon to perform. Your body, properly treated (fuelled, rested, serviced) will be flexible, far more energetic, hugely fitter and much more ready for action!

The First Resolution, applied to 'you', will make applying it to the following areas a lot easier.

Home

Is your home clean and tidy, with all systems working to their fullest efficiency? Or is it something to be embarrassed about? And if the answers are not what you wanted them to be, what is the reason?

The *real* reason? You want to do the fun things, not the cleaning things. But you know that a house remains operating at its best and cleanest when someone within it takes the time to do the tasks that cause those results! If you live alone, that is YOU.

Self-discipline. Put things away as soon as they are finished with, not 'later' - which occasionally means 'never'. Fix things as they break, don't tolerate their inefficiency. Wash up after the meal, don't utilise the draining board as a shelf for dirty dishes.

Self-Denial. You fear you might miss a fun opportunity. But you know that if you carry out these tasks instead of wasting time in other pursuits like surfing the 'net, watching television and playing computer games, then you will have the environment you desire. You also know that if you spend money in the area of your home instead of passing fancy, you and your loved ones will all benefit.

Make a plan to apply the First Resolution to the care and pride you take in respect of your home environment.

Family and Friends

Are your familial and social relationships mutually rewarding or are people just interference to your goals? Do you show respect to other people from the outset, or do you require them to respect you before you consider them worthy of the same courtesy? Do you take time for people – because people serve us, as we must serve them, for anything to get done?

What is the right thing to do?

Self-Discipline. You have to stop and pause when tempted to dismiss or disrespect people. You have to discipline yourself to listen before decisions can be properly made, or advice given. Make allowances, without making excuses. Let people make mistakes and be aware that errors are often not the result of attitude but the consequences of a lack of understanding, training or communication.

Self-Denial. Start putting other peoples' needs before your own, just occasionally and when doing so does not undermine your own goals. Be compassionate and put them first, just now and then.

Make a plan to apply the First Resolution to your relationships.

Community

Do you serve within your community, or do you rely on it to serve you without you pulling your own weight? Are you someone who thinks that people are not only there to serve you, but they must be *made* to do so – for example, you litter in the expectation that someone will clear it up, it's their job. Is it your view that one-way systems in a car park are advisory, it's getting a space before anyone else that matters? Rules are for the observance of others, but only guidance for you? Politicians for the 'other side' are always wrong, and your side is always right?

How *should* you treat the world around you?

Self-Discipline. Follow the rules, because they apply for a system to work for everyone's benefit. Work with a system long enough to understand it before deciding what could be improved. Listen to viewpoints objectively, wait for explanation before judging.

Self-Denial. Wait your turn, it will come. Be mindful that rules have a purpose, they aren't simply invented and applied through malice. And observance of rules keeps us safe from legal punishment, negative results, and other time-consuming and mentally wearing consequences.

Make a plan to apply the First Resolution to your community.

Work

Your working life is largely a reflection of your character and competence, so this will be addressed in more detail in part 2, "Pride and Pretension". However, punctuality is the first discipline you may choose to reflect upon, and another self-discipline may be found by you making sure all the details are always properly dealt with and inappropriate shortcuts are no longer taken.

Make a plan to apply the First Resolution to your work.

Can Self-Discipline and Self-Denial Be Self-Defeating?

During the early part of my implementation of the 3 Resolutions as a self-transformation 'project I was suffering a little from a lack of expected results in the weight-loss goal I had set. I had been eating a baked potato and salad/vegetables based diet for a month and while the first two weeks' weight loss had been spectacular these losses had not continued during the second fortnight. The reason may have simply been that I was *over*-dieting and my body was retaining fat because the body tends to do that when under-fed, as a defence mechanism in times of famine. That's just the way the body is designed.

Given that possibility, even likelihood, I needed to adjust my approach, it seemed. Or I could carry on regardless and see if things changed.

But the question still remained. If I 'carried on regardless' and things *didn't* change, was I applying self-discipline and self-denial to my detriment? Was I being bloody-minded, saying "It WILL work, I'll MAKE it work!" (The Administrator's Creed!)

Ultimately, the answer to whether self-discipline and self-denial can be self-defeating is probably 'Yes' – you can deny yourself and apply discipline to the point at which you spoil not so much the objective you seek, which almost *must* come about because of the discipline, but something else gets spoiled. For example, one example is that of a man who swore he would make a million in sales, come what may. He succeeded – being disciplined – but in doing so he ruined his relationships with his family, suffered a divorce, lost everything and ultimately killed himself. An extreme example, but what about the dedicated athlete who trains himself to breaking point, then finds he cannot perform at the crux moment because the strain was too much? How about the dedicated working wife who works 60-80 hours a week 'making a great life for her children' and can't understand why her children see her as a stranger?

In his book 'The Speed of Trust', Stephen M R Covey wrote that any strength taken to the extreme can become a weakness. For example, you've probably all seen celebrity authors and journalists on panel shows whose opinions are sought on matters. They are experts and are usually exceptionally talented – in their chosen fields. But when they start to espouse about things outside that area of expertise they are usually often talking about that things they have read about in the press, which is an exceptionally risky thing to do, or, in the case of some celebrities who can't read or string a sentence together, what they've heard from equally vapid opinionists.

This is an example of how a strength – celebrity and occupational intellect – can become a weakness; the mistaken belief that they are the font of all knowledge because of their experience and status, a characteristic also known as egotism. This is called Hubris – the belief that they are above reproach because of what they are rather than what they know, and there'll be more on that very subject in the next chapter.

Mental health aside, you *can* take positive traits to a negative extreme – to addiction, perhaps? – and you therefore have to be careful that when planning your ultimate aim you also consider what principles can be applied so that you will get you the result you want, without inadvertently sabotaging either that result, or something else that you are enjoying. In other words, be aware of the potential consequences of your self-discipline and self-denial – ALL of the consequences. Including the negative ones. Don't let self-discipline and self-denial become so much the centre of your life that they become addictions, and therefore become the very appetites and passions you were trying to control.

The Negatives of Success

The negative consequences of failure are usually plain to see, as are the majority of the positive consequences. The latter we know already because when we decided on our objective we were seeking exactly those results, and I only added the qualifier 'majority' because the Law of Unintended Consequences can produce good results as well as bad. But we should also consider some oddly 'negative' positive consequences of our success. Before you think I've gone mad, consider this. When we succeed we occasionally not only get what we originally expected – fame, money, self-esteem, nicer friends, and so on – but we also get an unexpected Bonus Box.

This Box contains Newer Expectations and Responsibilities.

These can be drags on our time if they are not carefully managed. As the newly promoted partner in a professional services firm you suddenly find that you are expected to attend more social gatherings because they are networking opportunities. You may also be expected to take over responsibilities that senior partners want to dump on someone who, they know, has to be seen to be willing and enthusiastic. You discover that a professional association is now courting your active involvement and you find it hard to decline their interest politely, so you volunteer. Now you have extra work that you have to do, and for free. (Which is not necessarily a bad thing – see the Third Resolution – but the point here is that you have to be *prepared* for this contingency.)

There are many examples in many life areas, and this book can't possibly identify all of them. The intention is only to enlighten you to the fact that when you decide what your success is going to look like, you should widen your considerations by asking not only what will happen when you get the result you seek, but also what *could* happen afterwards, just in case it tempers your desire. In fact, you need to do this to see if it actually *increases* your desire – they might be consequences that pull you forward and drive you towards making greater efforts and providing higher levels of service. This analysis should not be used as an excuse to stop you striving for your outcome, it is only suggested that you should decide, well in advance, what you will or will not be willing to sacrifice now and in the future, and how you will identify and deal with any new expectations and demands if and when they are made.

Stopping Yourself from Succeeding

In his audio-programme *'Personal Power II"* Anthony Robbins speaks of self-sabotage, when you psychologically and inadvertently sabotage your own goals by willingly or unwittingly doing something that prevents your success. I would suspect that the term unwittingly caused no eyebrow to be raised, but 'wittingly'? Why would anyone sabotage themselves *willingly?*

Turning up late for an exam, talking yourself into under-performing, shouting at someone you love so that they leave you exactly as your lack of self-confidence told you they would, and so on. At first glance these seem unwitting behaviours, don't they? But if you take the view that we are (or at least can be) the masters of our own choices, we are frequently taking actions (or NOT taking actions) which cause those very results. As I occasionally think as I butter another thick slice of crusty bread, I shouldn't be doing this – but I do so, nevertheless. This is willing self-sabotage and we all do it, sometimes. Self-sabotage is often a failure of self-denial. It is usually a failure to say 'No' to something that ultimately won't serve our interests. It is the ignoring of Conscience.

Just as we do negative things willingly such as over-eat, we occasionally have a tendency to willingly over-train, or apply rigorous self-discipline that physically *hurts*. Consider the extreme discipline of self-flagellation, made famous in the film '*The Da Vinci Code*' where an adherent to the Opus Dei sect tortures himself repeatedly to atone for 'sins' he himself has never committed. Self-sabotage can have a positive motive, too.

The anti-thesis of such self-destructive discipline is often described using the term 'the Ecology of Goal Setting', where our goals are be checked to see if they 'fit in' with a principled, moral or ethical reality, e.g. hurts or offends no-one, including us. But it is also the Ecology of the First Resolution. Self-Discipline and Self-Denial must be applied in a way that serves you. Make the plan and then test the plan for any traps that may restrict your success.

Having done that, execute the plan but be willing to change tactics if the plan isn't working; be willing to alter the way you're applying that discipline in order to achieve the goal. There is no point being disciplined if you don't arrive at your objective. And this way, you'll get there sooner.

Part One - Conclusion.

Why address self-discipline and self-denial first? To my mind, it is because they are so foundational to effective success.

In any text book the writer seeks to take a reader from ignorance of anything to understanding of everything, and this is done by laying a foundation upon which the right bricks are laid at the appropriate time, and in the best fashion possible for the objective sought. That's why you learn to count before you learn to add, subtract, *then* multiply and divide, *then* algebra and *then* calculus. Can you imagine the amusement as you watched someone trying to teach or learn that process backwards?

In the same vein, being self-disciplined and denying ourselves our wants in order to get our true, principled needs satisfied is foundational to being capable of making and executing on the latter two Resolutions. If we are not disciplined, how long can we be competent, or serve noble purposes? We may do those things fleetingly without discipline, but for how long? Or we may do them for a long time – but how well? In order to do those things well, and for a longer period, we must carry through on our commitment to the First Resolution.

One word of warning.

The application of self-discipline will be hard enough without imposing levels of discipline upon yourself *which have not been set or accepted by you.*

Let me illustrate by way of example. Almost every personal development writer I have studied suggests that getting up at stupid-o'clock in the morning and going for a (long) run is beneficial. I do, sincerely, believe them when they say that. However, having tried it myself my own experience is that for me, the two don't mix. I can get up early. I can go for a run. But for me the one cannot, as a rule, immediately follow the other. (However, I admit that I have done this successfully when away on residential training courses, where the change in environment has made it easier because I don't sleep long in a strange bed and breakfast is always prepared by someone else! And the run is always on a treadmill in the dry, windless and half empty gym.)

If you commit to a discipline solely because someone else has proposed it – and you are not really committed *in yourself* - then failure awaits, with an associated but misplaced sense of guilt. Writers on goal setting agree – selecting your own goals based on someone else's value system and vision is a path to self-delusion and failure.

In the 18th century, statesman-to-be Benjamin Franklin selected twelve personal values with a view to living fully in accordance with them, as we have described in these pages. Seeking validation for his choice, or perhaps merely input, he approached a Quaker friend, who looked at Franklin's list and suggested the addition of Humility because, he said, Franklin tended to be a bit sure of himself.

Over the years, Franklin found it hard to apply that peer-imposed value of Humility. He wrote that every time he felt he had achieved humility, he felt proud. The paradox overwhelmed him, and in the end he realised that the adoption of a value that was not his, did not serve him. In the same way, adoption of someone else's ideas for self-discipline will defeat you. That's not to say that other peoples' ideals are not worthy of adoption, just that you should only take on someone else's values or behaviours as your own after proper self-analysis and objective thought.

Sidebar: I think this is what happens when morale drops in any organisation. An employee joins an organisation because they see that what they want to achieve can be achieved through their employer's work. They join the workforce and things go great until a situation arises when what is being asked of them conflicts with the individual's values, and/or their perception of what the organisational values meant to them. This happens most often when, for example, someone is treated preferentially. In my own experience this happened when 'treat everyone fairly and without fear or favour' became 'unless they are senior local authority staff, or they complain and we have to treat them with kid gloves', which in the case in mind compromised the professionalism and integrity of the staff involved in the criminal investigations concerned, and definitely compromised the results of the investigations. It also occurred when we suddenly started letting off criminals with a 'caution' despite their having had several already. In other words, and in my own experience, when we stopped doing what the organisation did when I joined it. The rules were relaxed, the results suffered – and so did my commitment. Or when police forces started supplying clean needles to intravenous drug users – whose mere possession of the drugs going into the needles was illegal.

That is what I mean when I write about deluding yourself that someone else's goals should be accepted as your own. It's something you see when even your boss sounds unconvinced when dutifully extolling the virtues of some new policy. You know the publicity blurb. 'I am really excited to be offered this poison chalice......'

So make sure that when you decide on your rules of conduct, and the self-denial and self-discipline that you want to apply, they are *your* choices. By all means improve upon them, adjust them and implement those fully considered changes as time goes by. But don't go from couch potato to athlete in one day, because that's just about how long that method lasts.

Sidebar: This doesn't apply if you join the Armed Forces or Police Service, but on the assumption that you have not been drafted and therefore chose to join a disciplined organisation, then if you accept the imposed discipline as your own and keep it up when it is not imposed upon you I assure you that you will reap the benefit, in time. It is a matter of personal regret that I did not do so when I had that opportunity. Learn from my error.

And remember to consider the Principle of Progression in your efforts, as I described earlier with the maths metaphor. Don't rush out and plan for or expect to achieve a massive self-discipline or self-denial result 'just like that' – the application of this First Resolution has to be fairly gentle if it is to work. Temper your efforts to your capacities – start with some smaller actions or withdrawals and see how you feel. If they weren't hard enough, step up higher. If they were too hard, ease off and see what you can do instead. Don't spoil things by over-promising to yourself or to others that you're about to become Usain Bolt tomorrow – you'll fail, and you will do so publicly.

If you decide to enter the London Marathon, say so the previous May, not the previous December. Start training towards next year's April London Marathon a full year before and you produce an achievable objective with the time available to develop your ability to carry through on that promise. Start training three months before and you'll disappoint yourself and your sponsors.

The same applies to everything to which you will apply self-discipline and self-denial – your pace matters.

Let me finish on a quote from the aforementioned Benjamin Franklin, a man whose own self-discipline and self-denial made him a magnificent example of what can be done with very little – he was a statesman, inventor, diplomat, philosopher and philanthropist at a time when modern facilities meant a printing press. His example raises questions about our own achievements in an age where 'we don't have the time', yet we have so much more available to us than he could possibly have dreamed of. He said, "Those things that hurt, instruct."

Yes, discipline can occasionally seem painful – but what amazing things we can do when we learn from its application!

One final thought before I set you some work. In his book, 'The Road to Character', author David Brooks wrote, "(and) if we habitually fall for those temptations and do not struggle against the weaknesses in ourselves, then we gradually spoil some core piece of ourselves. We will not be as good, internally, as we want to be. We will fail in some profound way."

That applies throughout the **Three Resolutions**, but perhaps this was the place to remind ourselves of just how foundational the First Resolution *is*..

Now to your exercise in self-discovery in respect of your own levels of self-discipline and self-denial.

Discipline/Control Exercise

1.   Where am I undisciplined?

Here are a few clues that seem to cover most people: weight, exercise, punctuality, productivity, consistency in ...X...., fidelity, living in accordance with value statements. (Herewith my own confessions! Except fidelity, I'm doing that!)

2.   What characteristics do I demonstrate when undisciplined?

Do you find yourself irritable, disappointed, angry and short with other people? These are signs that you have recognised that your failures are your own. This is 'good'. Now knowing that, if you are still blaming other people or circumstances for feeling the way you do when you act in an undisciplined fashion, then you have much still to learn, Padawan.

3.   How do I FEEL when I am undisciplined?

Guilty? Ashamed? Disappointed with yourself? These are good signs because it means the values 'congruency model' is working and your conscience is trying to tell you something. If you felt fine, I'd question whether you've accurately identified your values. That's not necessarily a bad thing unless you want to change.

4.   Where am I disciplined?

If you have kept a job, have friends and remain faithful to your partner then you are demonstrating a level of self-discipline. Make a note of that – you CAN do it.

5. What character traits apply when I am disciplined?

This exercise can be quite hard because self-praise is something we tend to avoid – we're great at self-criticism and nagging, but self-praise has been weaned out of us as soon as we thought we could sing and our parents told us to shut up. Be generous.

6. How do I feel when I am disciplined?

Compliment yourself by all means, but be accurate.

7. In comparing my feelings when I am disciplined and when I am undisciplined – which would I prefer to feel, and why?

Duh! To the first part. The second part of the question is the more important so take your time and focus on that.

8. What do I need to be disciplined about? (Pick THREE areas where self-discipline can be applied.)

Here are a few clues that seem to cover most people: weight, exercise, punctuality, productivity, consistency in ...X...., fidelity, living in accordance with value statements. Yes, that's the same as question 1, above!

9. How am I going to demonstrate that discipline?

You're about to set some goals, in outline at least. That being so, be careful with the promises you are about to make to yourself and to 'the world'. Ensure they are values- and conscience-driven, and your own.

10. What do I possess that helps me in that discipline?

Not just character traits – what physical, financial and technical resources do you have that will help? Include Apps for your phone if necessary.

11. What do I NEED in order to help me in that discipline?

The theoretical part of the previous question – what do you NOT have that you need?

12. How am I going to get that?

And once you've answered this question, execute the plan.

Chapter Four – The Second Resolution – Character and Competence

"To overcome the restraining forces of pride and pretension, I resolve to work on character and competence." S R Covey

Having established that self-discipline and self-denial are the cornerstones of positive achievement we can move 'through the sphere' and start using that knowledge, and the results of our application of that knowledge, to move towards becoming two things – people of character, and people of competence.

The Second Resolution is about relationships, teamwork and learning to create results. As can be implied from the wording of the Resolution, it is about 'our' part in all of those things. It is not about the 'others' in the team except to the degree that *their* execution on the Second Resolution can complement our own. We when we are the best we can be, and when we do the best we can do, those we serve truly benefit. When *everyone* in the relationship is and does their best, we can create tremendous, positive results.

The blunt truth, however, is that in the main it is for us to role model competence and character before we can encourage others. No-one listens to a fat bloke about diets, so no-one will listen to a duplicitous incompetent about there being no 'I' in team. It is *our* responsibility to be the best 'we' that we can be.

We are, as Popeye might say, who we are. Psychologists have been discussing the question of 'nature vs nurture' for a long time, now. Are we who we are because of what went before, or are we what we are because of our choices? Notwithstanding the influence of genetic determinism (we are tall because our parents were tall, we have a predisposition to a nasty disease because they did, etc.), the general feeling in the scientific community is that *in the main* we are a product of our experiences, values and training. Psychologists say that when we are children we experience 'psychic determinism' because we adopt our parents' characteristics, use of language and belief systems because we spend a lot of time being subject to them, either by design (teaching) or accident (seeing it manifested). Proof? How about language, accents, terminology and beliefs?

Then one day we leave the closeness of the parent-child relationship and we enter a new societal phenomenon – first school, and later, work – where we are exposed to alternative values, experiences, training, belief systems and so on. Proof? Fashion sense, the spread of the gap word 'like' amongst, like, the population, and pronunciation of 'th' as 'v' outside Essex because of television, as in 'vis, vat and vee ovver' (aka 'this, that and the other'). This influence is identified as 'environmental determinism'. The latter two kinds of 'determinism' show how experiential influence is the 'nurture' part of the original question.

And it is an absolute fact that psychic and environmental determinism will influence who we are and what we do – *IF WE LET THAT HAPPEN*. It can nudge us towards becoming a certain kind of person, or even dictate our character. You can let it happen deliberately, or by inaction. Either way, it's your 'fault' if you become what your environment makes of you. You can let life design you, or you can design your life.

Put another way, as we grow old we learn to conform. We learn that being different is something to be feared, while conformity brings connection. Ask any child who wears the 'wrong' top to school how they were treated. Ask another how their wearing of the 'right' trainers results in friendship with an 'in-crowd'. Isn't this the core 'reality' of many a college-based teenage angst movie?

As a species, individuals want connection with their peer group and so tend to comply with that group's beliefs and values. If they conflict with our own beliefs and values, then the strength of our need for connection will dictate whether or not we adopt the group's norms or stand up for our own.

This is a psychological 'proof', supported by the experiments of Ruth Berenda. Berenda conducted an experiment whereby a 'patsy' was introduced into a group that was aware of the experiment. A question would be asked of the group, the answer to which was obvious. Those in the know were told to provide a wrong answer, while the patsy would be unaware of that plan.

What Berenda discovered was that as the group deliberately provided the 'wrong' answer, the 'patsy' would change their answer to that of the group. Hesitant at first, as if wondering what was going on, eventually the patsy would enthusiastically agree with the wrong answer.

The self-doubt created by the response of the larger group was enough to cause the single party to change their response to the stimulus – in this case, to the 'easy' question. Societal norms influence, and they can do so to our detriment as much as to our benefit.

Sidebar: Do you think the Germans were anti-Semitic and prone to invasion before they were conditioned by the Nazis into believing that this was their birth right? And do you think that WWII would have happened if Hitler's massively effective and co-ordinated 'inclusion' policy of encouraging everyone to join his club, speak and dress alike hadn't worked?

For an amusing but illustrative take on Berenda's discovery, see the opening scenes to the 6th Episode of the BBC programme 'Red Dwarf X'.

Would you change your answer to comply with that of the crowd? If the question was asked of you, would you give the right answer regardless of the number of hands raised in contradiction of your preferred answer?

This, in essence, is what the Character Question is asking. Are you willing to stand up for what you believe, even when all about you are suggesting that what you believe is wrong? Are you willing to walk your talk? Or do you capitulate and surrender so as not to be different?

Let's face it, your Character is what you *are*. It is how you see yourself and how you behave in light of that perception. It is also, to a very large extent, how others see you, too.

Character

We are not speaking here of 'characters' in the sense of personality, of people who are funny, amusing and entertaining – although that could be their character, of course. We speak here of someone's basic self, their identity, their value systems, what they believe in and how they behave. It is the element of their personality by which we know them. It is also an element of their personality by which we *judge* them, by which we decide how we should behave towards them and how we anticipate they will behave towards us and towards others. It is what we know them to be. And also what we know them *not* to be.

Sidebar: We often decide what we know people to be just by listening to other peoples' descriptions of them, which is disturbing but true. I have often *discovered that I have been judged by people based on what they have been told by third parties, and the reason I know this is because when the 'judges' have actually met me and we have spent time together, they have told me that they have discovered that what they have been told by the third parties was – wrong. Imagine that – we decide about a person's character without even meeting them. And that often influences our first contact, which is a poor state of affairs. But all is not lost because reading on will prevent you from ever doing that again!*

Character, in an accepted and wholly understood sense, is a demonstration that a person holds true to principles or values they know or believe to be true – not *only* because they believe them intellectually, but also because their conscience tells them that those values and principles are true. They demonstrate this character by act, omission or simply 'being'. They do the right thing, they don't do the wrong thing, or they are simply and consistently seen to live in accordance with the conscience/principle-based rules they set themselves.

A person with little conscience, or one who deliberately ignores conscience out of self-interest, can *be* a character, but can never be truly considered to *have* character. Yes, they can act in accordance with their own standards – but they do so knowing that their conscience is shouting at them and that they are ignoring it. And people around them know it. Even bad guys complain about things that 'ain't fair' when it suits them.

It is easy to criticise another person's character. If they do not play by our rules, if they are two-faced, dishonest or self-absorbed then we conclude that they have no character, in part because 'we don't do that' but also because of the innate knowledge of what 'should be'.

Paradoxically, they think exactly the same way about us because we aren't the same as, or we think differently to, them. They distrust us because we are honest, always speak the truth, always behave on a consistent fashion, and don't play by *their* rules! That doesn't only apply to more obvious character flaws – people can make the same negative assessment even if they only disagree with another's personal values. Ask any politician.

This is why people can be so judgemental. *"We judge others by their behaviour, and ourselves by our intent"*. (Covey) In other words, if you do something which I would never do, you must be wrong. If I then do the same thing, however, my intention must have been different, the background circumstances must have changed. I can justify why I did it – you can't.

Character is one of the reasons we make such assessments.

Let me provide an example; I have a reputation for being a bit of an impatient driver. That judgement has some substance, because I have been known to express an overtly sharp and occasionally profane opinion about other drivers. I tend to undertake those who hog a lane if it is safe (in my judgement) to do so. I am the same with people who pull out of junctions in a way that is either wholly dangerous or which, contrary to the Highway Code and Rules of the Road, cause me to have to change direction or speed. In my mind, having been trained to an advanced level, those who fail to abide by the rules – particularly the simple ones they had to know to pass their driving test – are the enemy.

One day, I approached an industrial estate entrance gate at the 60mph speed limit that applied. Visibility from that gate was good in either direction, although hampered a little by illegally parked cars just outside the gate. This should have meant that those emerging from the estate should take care in the knowledge that visibility was poor and the aforesaid speed limit meant that cars would be approaching at speed.

Knowing this, I drive along that main road at that speed, being aware of the potential for tentative emergence and being able to either slow/stop in time if a car appeared.

This one day I approached the gate and could see that 'chummy' was going to pull out in front of me. I anticipated what he was going to do. Based on my training and experience, and familiarity with that gate and the surrounding road layout, and having already looked further down the road to see if anything was approaching, I had already assessed and even planned what I could do about it when he pulled out.

So as he did so I simply went around the back of him without breaking pace and I completed my overtake as safely as I would have if he had already been in the carriageway and had just been driving slower than me. Just as in any other clear stretch of road.

A friend of mine saw this while she drove towards the junction from the direction he had emerged, and later said to me "That was aggressive!"

So, because

- She possibly hadn't had the same training (actually, she had) OR wasn't as analytical as me when driving, OR hadn't experienced that kind of event,
- She only considered the option of braking hard; and therefore
- She decided that I shouldn't do what I did;
- She assessed that because she wouldn't have done it I was wrong;
- And she further assessed that in doing so I must therefore have been angry/aggressive.

She had judged my behaviour based on her value system and experience. She concluded that if she had been driving and had done that, she would only have done so because she was angry and aggressive. In her eyes, if she had done such a thing she would only have done so through anger or aggression. Therefore, I must have been similarly agitated.

Now let me clear – she wasn't *wrong* to think any of those things. In her value system and from where she was sitting, she was right. If my values system matched hers, I'd have agreed with her, or not completed the manoeuvre in the first place. Her values, applied to that incident, were just different. Not wrong.

Had she been in the car she would have seen nothing physical or visible to underpin her assessment of my act - just a smooth operation of my car. Indeed, had I been commentating as I did so, she would have understood what I did and seen just how calm, unfazed and well-organised my driving actually was.

(Don't assume I am an angel – I judge others by their behaviour all the time!)

Another example: in his book "The Good Psychopath's Guide to Success" ex-SAS soldier Andy McNab and psychologist Kevin Dutton discussed the nature of psychopaths, and in summary what psychologists found was that in a crisis some people panic and other people – the psychopaths – don't. They analyse the information and the situation and they respond in a fashion that the panicky type may not understand. This is an example of a proactive response to stimulus. Something happens, we 'psychopaths' consider our response rather than just instinctively reacting, and we choose a different response to the 'norm' considered by the individual who saw only one option.

Years ago I was driving home from my work as a detective when a disqualified driver rammed me because he was driving too fast in a country lane. After a brief foot pursuit I caught and arrested him. My colleagues arrived and saw firstly my battered sports car, then the non-battered prisoner, and finally my calm demeanour. One of them expressed that she couldn't understand why I was so calm. In other words, because she would have been livid and/or upset, she could not understand why I *wasn't*.

The truth – at least I hope it was the truth – was that in both examples I was being who I truly am, or at least that I was acting in accordance with my beliefs, a way of acting that I am trying to communicate within these pages. Not that you have to act as I did: you have to act in a way that is in compliance with what you believe to be true.

In those moments I was acting as my 'best self' and showing great(er) personal character. But others looking on couldn't understand it because, in the same situations, they expected they would have behaved differently, perhaps expressing in a clear verbal and physical fashion what they thought of the individual who had just tried to kill them and had trashed their beloved car.

We all have personalities, and they differ. These differences cause confusion, arguments and disagreements because we occasionally fail to realise this.

Fred Luskin, the Stanford psychotherapist, defined 'rules' thus: "A rule is any expectation you have for how something *should* turn out or how someone *should* think or behave… We all make rules for how WE should act and think, how *other people* should act and think and how life should turn out."

Some rules are just 'ours', based entirely on our values system, and which are rarely set down. The rules include societal norms and expectations, and when someone fails to observe the rules, we want something done.

Those rules – or more accurately our willingness to observe them - really do define our character, and as implied earlier, our 'Character' is 'who we are'. If you don't believe me, here's a quote from C.S. Lewis (author of The Chronicles of Narnia).

*"We begin to notice, besides our particular sinful acts, our sinfulness; begin to be alarmed not only about what we do, but about **what we are**. This may sound rather difficult, so I will try to make it clear from my own case. When I come to my evening prayers and try to reckon up the sins of the day, nine times out of ten the most obvious one is some sin against charity; I have sulked or snapped or sneered or snubbed or stormed. And the excuse that immediately springs to my mind is that the provocation was so sudden and unexpected: I was caught off my guard, I had not time to collect myself. Now that may be an extenuating*

circumstance as regards those particular acts: they would obviously be worse if they had been deliberate and premeditated. On the other hand, surely what a man does when he is taken off his guard is the best evidence for what sort of a man he is? Surely what pops out before the man has time to put on a disguise is the truth? If there are rats in a cellar you are most likely to see them if you go in very suddenly. But the suddenness does not create the rats: it only prevents them from hiding. In the same way the suddenness of the provocation does not make me an ill-tempered man: it only shows me what an ill-tempered man I am. The rats are always there in the cellar, but if you go in shouting and noisily they will have taken cover before you switch on the light."

What he was trying to communicate was that who we are, and in particular the *kind* of person we are (our character) eventually shines through whether or not we wish to hide it. We are our character and when we are put to the test it is that 'true' character that comes out. If we are argumentative, we will argue; if we are violent we will fight; if we are thoughtless we will appear to be selfish. And most of the time we will try to explain away these flaws with excuses such as the old favourite 'He made me do it!', as Lewis suggested, because we know that we are seeking to excuse the flaws in our character - and we do not want to admit to being flawed.

Personality is not necessarily character, although there can be an overlap. Coaches routinely use the metaphor of an iceberg, which as you all know hides most of its bulk, some ¾ in fact, below the surface of the sea. It is proposed that the tip, the visible part of the iceberg, represents the personality, that part of us that is there for all to see. But lying hidden is the bulk of the 'berg, which makes up most of what the iceberg is, and metaphorically most of what 'we' are. The character supports the personality, and the personality would not exist without it − if the ¾ iceberg/character disappeared then the ¼ iceberg/personality would sink and we would be less. We are our character no matter how we purport to show otherwise by showy, false or deceptive personalities (deliberate or accidental). If the character is bad, then whatever the personality we present to the outer world, the truth of the expanse and depth of our character will always, at some time, show out.

But there is hope. With some effort over time, and with productive usage of the gap between stimulus and response in the key-clutch, cellar-rat-scaring moments, we can choose to become people of good − or better − character.

What is 'Good character'?

If you wrote down the characteristics of a 'good person', what would they be?

Few would disagree with terms such as honest, trustworthy, fair, generous, helpful, productive, courageous, considerate, compassionate, faithful, and so on. Good people, people like you who are reading this book, desire and routinely exercise the ability to demonstrate those traits. We probably all know people who act with good, even great character nearly all the time. I have two particular friends who are generous, active, productive, selfless and giving and annoyingly perfect (although not quite!). I am actually jealous about how nice they are.

Some people, including me, are not quite acting wholly, 100%, all of the time in accordance with those known and accepted traits of 'good character', although most of us desire the ability to do so – that desire in itself shows an element of good character.

We may be 'being good' most of the time; it may just be that our conscience is telling us that we could be 'good' a lot more of the time, and we aren't willing (sometimes) or able (more often) to do that. It could be telling us that there is a 'better self' just waiting to come forth.

As I write this part I am conscious that I should be writing about good character by providing examples of good character, but I find it difficult to expand upon something that we already know. A book on Advanced Mathematics does not start with an explanation of how 2 and 2 make 4. A novel doesn't start with lessons on how to read 'big words', or on English comprehension. Such tomes acknowledge or at least rely upon the likelihood that the reader is already partially aware of what is needed in order to understand what is to follow. It is, for me, the same with Character.

You already 'know' in your own hearts and minds what Good Character is. You just perceive and believe that in your case, there is a gap between your having that knowledge and your performance in light of that knowledge. So listing good character traits becomes academic and risks omission by accident.

You already know what I am talking about if you completed the Values Exercises, because you defined good character traits as you did so. I hope.

What is 'Bad character'?

"One way to see if a principle is true is to try to argue the opposite and see if it makes sense." Take that into account and test it against those examples of characteristics that we decided and agreed were 'good', namely honest, trustworthy, fair, generous, helpful, productive, courageous, considerate, compassionate and faithful. We now identify the opposite terms dishonest, untrustworthy, selfish, biased, ignorant, lazy, cowardly, inconsiderate, thoughtless and adulterous.

How many of you would enjoy being referred to in those terms? Nobody reading a book like this, I suspect. Even the people who know that they *are* all of those things don't like the truth. Which is why they lie about it.

And that reinforces the point. We KNOW what good character looks like, and we KNOW what bad character looks like. Occasionally, as C.S. Lewis suggested and explained earlier, we justify our bad character.

For example:

Dishonesty

We even have an expression for the justification of dishonesty – 'little white lies'. You know, the ones that don't really offend, or which keep the peace, or which avoid people being concerned and worried. From the ones we tell ourselves (one choc won't matter) to the ones we tell others (no-one will know, it's only wrong if you get caught, she did it first, etc.)

The renowned speaker Gary King (www.thepoweroftruth.com) proposes that you try and live for 24 hours without telling one lie, not even to yourself. This is an incredibly hard thing to do, and most people, even the honest ones, can't do it because they fear offending someone or having to explain something they're not even sure about themselves.

For example, let's take the situation where you don't want to help someone in some way. You're busy, uninterested, tired, or whatever.

Rather than say you don't want to assist and risk having to explain why, you either lie about why you can't help or you inconvenience yourself by lying that 'yes, I'll do that', then begrudge the other for asking in the first place, and at the same time provide a poor, undedicated service to your friend. Tell the truth, even if you have to be careful with the words you use.

Infidelity

I had a single friend who was in a relationship with a married man, and she asked me if she was doing the right thing. Having established how fond she was of this chap, I asked this question: "If he has cheated on his wife, the one he promised to love until death did them part – how can you ever be certain that he won't do the same to you?" My friend went silent. In the event she stayed within the relationship, he got divorced, they had a child - and now they're apart.

People in adulterous relationships frequently justify themselves by blaming the innocent spouse/partner for not doing something which the adulterer wants, thus empowering their betrayal under the banner of 'serves them right'. Infidelity is, arguably, the ultimate betrayal. If you do fall out of love with your partner there are really only two, principled things you should do.

The first is to work harder on the relationship to make it work. It is said that one lady said to her counsellor that she wanted to divorce her husband because she no longer loved him. The counsellor suggested she make sure. She should go home and serve this man like she DID love him. Cook for him, be there for him, and serve him. If, after three months she felt the same, she should leave. She followed his advice, and after the three months discovered that she did love this man, after all. The counsellor knew a secret – DO love, and emotional love will follow.

The second, principled option is to tell the other person how you feel, and cease the relationship *before* embarking on any other. No adultery, only fair honesty. No matter how emotionally painful such a break-up can be, the lack of a third party influence and the spectre of adultery makes things a whole lot better for all concerned.

Disrespect

You can demonstrate disrespect in many ways. For example, you can dismiss someone in their presence and make it clear they are unimportant to you. You can question or challenge their capabilities, character, or other traits and do so in a fashion that allows no response. In effect, you can belittle them when it is not deserved.

Just like the expression 'little white lies', ribbing and banter are expressions that are used to lessen the gravity of what is essentially disrespect (even bullying).

People take the mickey out of each other. When relationships are sound this is acceptable, even welcomed as a bonding activity.

Where this is appropriately done, the *behaviour* of an individual is the subject of ridicule, not the person. It is something funny that they *did* that is found to be funny, not what they *are*. Communication to the other person that the emphasis is on the 'thing' that happened rather than the 'who' did it is key. (Incidentally, from the personal perspective, if you recognise that other people are laughing at what you did and not at who you are, your relationships – both with them and with yourself – will improve.)

When a person is being ridiculed for what they *are*, I have the following advice. Their response should be as follows:

Say to the person leading the ridicule, **"Are you trying to raise your own poor self-esteem by trying to lower mine – because if you are, it won't work."** That's it – say no more and do not engage in further communication about it. Don't answer any more questions, don't 'bite' to any further comments. Just say that and move on. Bullies can't emotionally bully the confident and confidence is born of character. A person of good character has nothing to feel guilty, less, or embarrassed about.

But the absolute *favourite* kind of disrespect is that which is demonstrated towards people who **AREN'T EVEN THERE!**

In '*The Seven* Habits', Covey wrote about showing 'loyalty to the absent', an excellent phrase that profoundly illustrates its meaning. This phrase means never talking about someone behind their backs or in their absence unless it is done positively, e.g. to praise.

In my place of work there was one team member who talked about people frequently; in fact, I recall one occasion when he was in flow about another's character and competence when, suddenly and in the middle of what he was saying, he broke off and just walked away. As he did so I could see the subject of his backstabbing making his way along the corridor towards us, which explained his decision to leg it.

I made it my business thereafter to correct this behaviour – when he started talking negatively about others who weren't there, I would gamely shout, "Is XXX not here then?" Eventually this behaviour lessened as he slowly took the point.

In the foreword to the '25th Anniversary Edition' of *The 7 Habits of Highly Effective People*, Stephen Covey's son Sean wrote about an occasion when his father was among a group of people that were chatting. Some of those present were speaking negatively and critically about a particular President of the USA and in time they noticed that Covey was silent. They asked him why he was silent and why he wasn't espousing his agreement with the group and he replied, "I may have a chance to counsel this man one day, and I wouldn't want to be a hypocrite." (In time, he did indeed counsel that President.)

That is what respect is, and what disrespect is not. People of character do not speak behind others' backs. Instead, they have the confidence and even courage to carefully word any criticism that they have, and to be willing say those words to the person who needs to hear them most – ideally, telling them first. And unless absolutely necessary by virtue of responsibility or position, to nobody else.

The same principle applies to the things you hear about others who are not present. You should not judge an absentee on what is said negatively about them unless there is objective proof available, and even then it should be only referenced and not used. I admit I was once guilty of this. I was running courses and an individual about whom I had heard nothing but negative thoughts – even evidenced thoughts – wanted to come onto the course. I admitted him, but because of what I had heard did not expect him to turn up. In the event he did not make an appearance but I had at least been willing to try accepting him even if my thoughts had been corrupted by gossip.

Each first meeting is an opportunity to let the other party and the relationship start afresh. If their character is not flawed, our unwillingness to listen to the backstabbing is rewarded by pleasant new experience. If the character *is* flawed, we start by trying to repair it with a positive motive. Even if we fail, we did so *after* we tried and not because we assumed the worst and never tried at all.

Ego

In the Daily Telegraph (15th June 2014) columnist Octavius Blank wrote:

"The scuba engineers were deep under the ocean fixing a problem with their oil rig. A warning signal told them to come back up by they ignored it, three times. The control room over-rode the automatic system and told them to come up immediately, but they carried on working. The chief engineer, whom they knew

and respected, told them their lives were at risk and they must surface NOW. They ignored him and continued. Moments later there was an explosion and all the divers died."

Have you ever heard the word 'Hubris'? The word Hubris comes from the ancient Greek and, "*in religious terms, means extreme pride or self-confidence that leads to offence spoken or done towards the God(s), usually harshly punished after. This religious meaning is sometimes transferred to denote overall highly unacceptable, arrogant and insulting behaviour that confronts ethical norms in a way that reminds one of the act described in Ancient Tragedies.*

Hubris is usually perceived as a characteristic of an individual rather than a group, although the group the offender belongs to may suffer consequences from the wrongful act. Hubris often indicates a loss of contact with reality and an overestimation of one's own competence, accomplishments or capabilities, especially when the person exhibiting it is in a position of power." (Source: Wikipedia.)

We all have an ego. Without a sense of pride, we would probably never seek to better ourselves, for self-esteem is an acknowledged driver of personal success and professional results. That said, when we think ourselves better than we actually are, or worse still consider ourselves to be better than others (without foundation for that belief), then we have allowed our ego to hide us from the truth and from principles. We may have better qualifications and be blessed with a talent, but while that distinguishes us from others it does not make us better. Believing you are better than someone else means you are acting under the delusion that you were the same to begin with, and that is never true. You are not better than someone else. They have different skills, talents, experiences and knowledge that you can use, not dismiss.

When you start to think you are better than others, that untruth can and will cause future pain. As Hyrum W Smith wrote in the book '*Pain is Inevitable, Misery is Optional*';

"*Of all the causes of pain (self-deception) is perhaps the hardest to root out, simply because in self-deception we twist truth and distort reality to make immoral or unethical objectives seem acceptable or justified*".

Self-deception is ego's greatest co-conspirator.

In the example of the scuba divers, their peer group hubris pressurised them into accepting the hubris of whichever one of them it was convinced them, either by word or by example, that he or she knew better than principles. They deceived themselves into believing that the worst could not possibly happen to them – they were experts.

Hubris is a by-product of an uncontrolled ego and, as suggested in the latter part of the definition, is often the motive behind arrogantly stupid behaviour that brings down people, and the organisations that they work for. Politicians believing that they are untouchable because although they swear to serve the people, the people end up being perceived, by those politicians, to be the servants. Celebrities, who treat their fans – their *customers* – with contempt. Police officers thinking that *they* are the law, and that 'the' law is not the law they swear to uphold, but their interpretation of it.

It is over reliance on their ego being the 'truth' that causes celebrities to lose their sense of character. They remain competent, but their relationships suffer because people know that competence cannot hide poor character. No matter how famous a celebrity gets, for example, there is no justification for some of the demands that some of them make in their work.

Those who accede to such demands (often of questionable character themselves!) detest the celebrities they pretend to adore. Those celebrities who shine briefly and then fade away are often those whose character is flawed. Celebrities *of* character are frequently venerated long after they pass on.

To remain venerated after death, however, does not require celebrity – ask yourself who *you* remember; a great teacher (often a first thought-of example); a parent or sibling; or a leader at one's workplace. None may be a 'star' celebrated or respected by the masses but in their circle, and often outside of it, they are remembered not only for who they were but for what they meant to those left behind.

Would *you* like to be remembered as a person with such levels of character as was possessed by those that *you* remember?

Ultimately, all of the above examples of bad character show how such traits hold us back. When we demonstrate bad character traits we stunt our potential through self-interest and through a failure to reflect reality in our behaviour. This includes any failure to recognise that other people's realities are as valid to them as ours are to us, and then acting on that misunderstanding.

When we act selfishly we believe we will achieve satisfaction only when *we* have enough, but that can never happen because inflated egos simultaneously tell us that there *isn't* enough. When we act generously we are rewarded immediately with sense of well-being, but not one borne of selfishness. Being good makes you feel good, even if feeling good isn't why you did it. In fact, even if you 'did something good' *precisely* to make yourself feel good – so what? You did good.

Revisiting the Second Resolution, how does the counterfeit of character - pride - hold us back? How does it restrain us?

Pride and Pretension

Pride is defined as *'a feeling of self-worth or esteem; excessive self-esteem; a sense of one's own importance; a feeling of elation due to success; to be proud of; to take credit for.'* (Webster's Dictionary)

Some of these definitions are not self-serving. Why shouldn't you feel elation at a personal success? Isn't self-esteem valuable? Why not be proud of something done, or to take credit for something for which you were responsible?

The key is that like nearly everything in life, moderation is good, excess is bad. Pride, in the context of the **Three Resolutions** and in particular the Second Resolution, is *excessive* pride. It is the over emphasis on self – excessive self-importance, or the big 'I AM'. It is taking personal credit for a team effort, or for someone else's work. It is hubris.

Why should we hold back on pride?

First of all, those with whom we live and work need to rely on us to be honest hard-working, congruent and reliable. We also need to rely on them to do the same.

Overly proud people tend not to play the team game; their self-interest threatens the relationships within *and* outside the team because their interests come first. In order to satisfy that interest, they can be expected to, or will act injudiciously, recklessly, even illegally to get their preferred result. They will, or they will be expected to, walk over other people to get ahead. If they get good results it is as much an enviable by-product of their action as it is the objective. They do what is needed, and no more. If they are overly-productive it continues only as long as they see they will get their ends met – once that end is no longer achievable, their efforts diminish and they move on to the next self-serving project.

In truth, people who will give us what we want need to be convinced of our integrity and character, not deceived into thinking something is present when it is not. Don't fool yourself – they know. They may occasionally provide you with your 'progression needs' but it's not because they are fooled. It is because they are as duplicitous as you and see that their own needs will be served if they give you what you (pretend to) deserve. Or they want to get rid of you.

(British readers will know of a TV comedy called 'The Brittas Empire'. The plot revolved around the keen manager of a leisure centre, Gordon Brittas. The predicate concept was that Mr Brittas was a complete idiot, if well-meaning. Due to his good intentions and efforts he could only be disposed of one way – by promotion. Exasperated employers would write him up in references with the intention of getting rid of him. This may be an example of a dearth of competence being the motive for upward disposal, but the concept remains – one way the unscrupulous can get rid of a threat is to send it elsewhere.)

The point is – once discovered, the prideful get found out. In their book 'The Peter Principle', authors Laurence J Peter and Raymond Hull defined their Principle thus: *'In a hierarchy every employee tends to rise to his level of incompetence'.* By this they meant that a person progresses along a promotional ladder until they arrive in a job they can't do, because although their competence (or perceived competence) *got* them there, their lack of competence now *kept* them there. And because they are incompetent things start to go wrong for the enterprise; and because they were promoted there, the unwillingness of the promoters to dispense with their services so as not to look foolish, allied to the protections of employment legislation, means they can't be disposed of.

This argument was applied specifically to in*competence*, but can also lie squarely under the heading of character. Those who lack character deceive to get ahead, professing or pretending to have good character. But when it is found that they do not, it is too late. The only way to get rid of them is to pass them on to some other poor sucker.

Given the 21st Century 'Me' mentality of success (the one which makes the talentless or mediocre demand uncritical acceptance of their singing on The X Factor, for example), and the lessons that schools, perhaps unwisely, teach that we can all have everything if we just work hard while our children are subliminally and simultaneously hearing the sub-text that we are all better than everyone else, how can 'pride and pretension' get in our way - surely they are essential to success?

No. Appropriate, unselfish self-esteem is essential to achievement, but pride as defined earlier gets in our way for the reasons we have discussed.

There is an easy way to show how some prideful character traits do hold us back, and that is for me to identify to you some of those which have come to my mind through experience, study and anecdotes. Some have already been touched upon in the previous paragraphs, others are just as relevant.

Being right. Have you heard people who state an opinion, have it proved to them that they are wrong or have their supporting authority questioned or even disproved - but keep on arguing their point despite the proof that they have seen? Such people have a need to be acknowledged, and their unwillingness to be proved wrong is the result of that need. It is as if accepting that they could be wrong means, at least in their mind, that they are lesser people. It does not occur to them that they can be wrong in one area while being wholly correct, expert and authoritative in another.

They have fed upon a societal norm that if one is wrong in one fact, one's opinion in other respects is therefore suspect – even though common sense tells us that this is not necessarily so. Common sense tells us that when I *am* wrong, it may be because I have been misinformed or I have misunderstood the context or the issue. Of course, if I am not aware that such possibilities exist, I cannot accept that they may be true. So I may simply be unable to objectively examine my own learning, values and beliefs. Consequently, when you attack these beliefs and I consider *you* to be uninformed, I defend them further.

Such character traits as those described above can all come under the heading of 'pride', even though pride is not necessarily the motivation. What *is* clear is that such individuals are unwilling to be taught because of the risk that to learn, one may occasionally first have to be wrong. Unfortunately, we align our social acceptability to a belief that to be accepted, we have to be right.

Social acceptance. Think back to Ruth Berenda's experiments. People who wish to appear right, also wish to be part of a group. When prideful people are proved wrong by a group, you will hear them rationalise why they thought 'differently' in the first place. They will justify the original error with, "Ah, but I..." and find a small contextual change to justify any change of opinion back to the group-think without feeling that they have been defeated. They will seek to connect with the group while still thinking they were right all along.

Social acceptance is not only evident in 'mind changes' such as those described above. We all want to connect, and most of what we do to connect with others is undemanding and does not cause us mental, physical, social or spiritual damage. If we join Manchester United fans in adoration of this year's team we may dress the same and sing the same songs. There is no harm in such behaviour.

But the world is full of people who *do* take up damaging behaviour in an effort to obtain acceptance in a social group. We use terms for those people like 'addicts', 'criminals', 'hooligans' and so on. They take drugs to fit in with their drug-taking friends, justifying it as normal because it *is* normal in that group, yet as they do so they knowingly try to defy natural laws because there is no apparent immediate consequence. Eventually, 'daring' becomes 'routine'.

Need to be fashionable. And this change from 'daring' to 'routine' is visible in fashion. I hear that children occasionally demand that they should stop wearing school uniform as it denies individuality. If the rules are relaxed, they usually respond by dressing according to their chosen groups' fashion diktats – your chosen social group dresses 'just so', and so should you. From one uniform to another! So the challenge to 'The Man' just becomes a slavish adherence to someone else's rules. *(Ever notice how anarchists all dress alike? The irony!)* At the same time, failure to dress in one group's preferred manner results in the main group ostracising those people who dress differently, and dressing differently causes unnecessary friction between groups.

Two-facedness. We are surrounded by them, aren't we? I have already written about a particular colleague who, more than anyone else I know, talked about people behind their backs. And worryingly, although we see it in others we cannot help but join in, either actively talking along, or at least listening in with a little relish about other people who are not there. Then, to their faces, we are all sweetness and light, friendly to a fault. We can't help ourselves because we, too, wish to connect.

How many faces do you have? Truly? Try *not* getting sucked into contributing to such talk. Accept that you have to remain because of a desire to be part of the group, but instead of joining in, suggest alternative subjects for discussion, or defend the absent. That is what having character requires.

Circle of Influence misalignment (i.e. being authoritative when not an authority). Do you have an opinion on everything, or is it just other people? Your circle of influence is an area of your life over which you have control, things about which you have knowledge, experience and, well, influence. Outside of that circle lie all the things which may be of interest to you but are things over which you have no authority, influence or control. Focusing on that inner circle is great; it means making things happen, coming through on goals, gaining respect for your knowledge and experience.

But what happens if that focus is abused, when, just because you are a genuine authority on something, you assume or are improperly awarded a sense of 'all-knowingness' that your position does not deserve. Consider those television panel programmes where politicians vie with comedians on matters of interest – what possible knowledge or insight could a comedian have over economic policy? They are *concerned*, of course they are, but should their opinions be awarded special merit simply because they are celebrated funny men and women? When someone expresses an opinion, question the validity by asking what experience/training/study they have in that field. You will either be better informed because they explain why they are expert – or you will discover that their opinion is ideological rather than objective.

Seeking success on the wrong wall. When you get to where you want to be in life or work – is it the place you thought it was? The world is full of unhappy 'successful' people, who've climbed the ladder of success only to be brought down to earth because other people find out how they got there. If it is the right wall, climbed in the right way, other people applaud, not deride. Ask people like Lincoln, Gandhi, and Mandela.

People who work in a hierarchy will be all too familiar with the individual who walks over others in the search for promotion. In doing so they destroy relationships with the very people upon whom they will rely when that promotion comes. Is this effective? Is it not an example of pretence when you offer to assist only out of self-interest, where your motives are focused wholly on your own results? The Peter Principle will catch these people out, eventually.

Seeking acceptance through our children. Some people feel as though they lost opportunities when young, and with these we see them desperately trying to mould their children to be what they were unable to become, themselves. If the child enjoys the same activities this has no negative consequence, but how many children have unhappily lived their parents' dreams and ambitions, only to never achieve their own?

How many parents seek social status through their children's achievements, taking some psychological credit for the work their offspring have done? Take parental pride, yes: inappropriate credit, no. Your children's success may be nurtured by you, but it is their success, not yours. They will be grateful for what you did, and how you helped them achieve; but they were the ones who achieved it. Don't pretend that their success is yours.

Avoidance of training because we consider ourselves beyond teachable. We all consider ourselves to be good at what we do, some to the point that they consider themselves unimpeachable, unable to do wrong. Others know they are not infallible but would die rather than admit it. Those with true character are those who know what they know; who accept and work towards discovery of what they don't know but know they need to know; or who just accept where their failings are, and work with other people to offset that lack of skill or knowledge. Indeed, that is what teams are *for* – to allow people to focus on what they are good at, serving the greater objective by doing what they do best while allowing others the same courtesy.

I was present as part of a group on one occasion when a speaker was delivering input on a subject we all 'knew'. One of us was quite insulted that we should be so addressed. For my part, I enjoyed being reminded of what I knew, updated on what had changed, and being altogether better equipped to deal with the subject when it arose in debate.

Being offended

Are you easily offended? I ascribe a lot of philosophical common sense to Charles R Hobbs, author of TimePower. In his book called '*The Healing Power of Forgiving*', Charles Hobbs defined the three component parts of 'offence' held by those harbouring a grievance. The Components are:

1.   The exaggerated taking of a personal offence.
2.   Blaming the offender for how YOU feel.
3.   The creation of a 'Grievance Story'.

Taking each in turn:-

1.   **The exaggerated taking of a personal offence.** Hobbs is not talking about being offended *per se*. We can be offended, that is human nature and all too common. Something is said or done which we find insulting, immoral, or which angers us in some way. That happens. What he talks of in his book is the *exaggerated* taking of offence, when we (more often than not) see something through the wrong paradigm because of a misunderstanding, and then we really go off on one.

I say the wrong paradigm. A paradigm is a pattern and for our purposes means the lens through which we see the world which, by virtue of its precise design, warps what we see. (I.e. a convex lens would provide a different view to a concave lens.) In this circumstance, and with a nod to earlier examples about my driving, if what we see is something we wouldn't do, we assume that the person doing it is deliberately acting in that way with the intention of offending us. If we are prejudiced, they're doing it because that's what they do. If we are tired, we just can't be bothered with all that nonsense. We judge others by what they do, and ourselves by what we mean.

Having 'seen' the offence through our (potentially) warped paradigm, we take offence. Or, to be more accurate, we *choose* to take offence. What's more, we choose to be really angry about it, which stirs up the emotion and conditions us to see it as even more offensive than it initially may have been.

2.   **Blaming the offender for how YOU feel.** Of course, it's not *our* fault they've offended us, so we reactively (and definitely *not* proactively) decide that it must be their fault we feel so angry. We don't like feeling angry, so their *making* us angry makes us even *angrier*. Of course, we could just decide not to be angry and take a moment to find out if what we saw as offensive really happened, was so intended, or was a misunderstanding. But that would make *us* responsible for the solution, not *them*, and it was *their* fault, after all. (Seeing the sarcasm, yet?)

3. **The creation of a 'Grievance Story'.** Having been offended by what may or may not have actually happened, and being further angered by their failure to make amends (without them knowing that they even have to), we start to tell *everybody* what **THEY** did, and each time we re-tell it we add a bit more 'fact' and get even *angrier*. Eventually, what **THEY DID** becomes a legend in our hearts and minds, and we are lost.

Next time someone offends you, try this little process.

1. Find out from them what they meant when they said or did that offended you. It might not be what you thought.
2. If it was what you thought, clearly but reasonably say that you found it offensive. It might, just might bring about the apology you seek and affirm the relationship you had a couple of minutes earlier.
3. Accept any apology without condition. Stop there if that is all that is needed.
4. If no apology is given, remove yourself from the relationship and take personal responsibility for not being angry anymore. It's gone, they're gone, it's over. Move on.

And here's the best piece of advice I can give.

If you weren't there when it happened and it was not directed at you, don't get angry in the first place because there's nothing you can do about it – yet. If it is something which is really, truly, badly wrong – don't get angry, start a movement that changes things. Bring it into your area of influence but in a proactive, constructive and (noble) purposeful way. That is what a person of good character does.

Emotional Control

The discipline to control our emotions is as great an example of character as any of the above. When something happens to us that angers us, it is *we* who have chosen – deliberately or by default – to be angry. Just as in most of the aforementioned examples, the point between what happens to us and what we do about it is where we decide or allow the rates to come into sight, or to remain hidden.

We can still be angry, but we can control what we do about that anger. We can stifle it, we can respond in a measured fashion or we can submit to our poorest of nature and go nuts. Good character is exemplified by those who respond appropriately, and not necessarily by stifling their emotions. Stifling is arguably a passive-aggressive 'I'll get back to this later' kind of reaction: an explosive response is the most aggressive; but a measured explanation of the situation as it affects you, expressed to the person providing the stimulus, is the mark of a person of great character.

If you bump your head on a low ceiling, however, you can swear all you like. The roof won't feel offended and will carry on hitting people regardless of your reaction.

Pride and Pretension are false defences against an inconvenient truth – the truth that we do not know everything and we cannot hide behind invented lives, incomplete study or incongruent character. Nor can invalid or exaggerated experience conceal reality for long.

Pride and pretension are false defences because you cannot defend the indefensible – once you are found out to be 'pretending' to be something that you are not, your lack of integrity becomes an open wound. It becomes a festering sore that cannot be easily repaired, if it can be repaired at all. Since the cost of broken integrity can be so potentially massive, why not stop pretending?

Assume a life of modesty and humility rather than one of false pride, and in time you will become an individual that is respected, even admired.

Moral and ethical behaviour.

Morals are temporal – what may be immoral today can later be considered acceptable. Please don't consider this prejudiced but for the purposes of illustration, good examples are the acceptance of homosexuality, extra-marital sex and teenage pregnancies – all once thought of as 'evil', now all societally accepted to different degrees and for different reasons. Your values will dictate what you think on each of these issues, and I respect your beliefs as I ask you to respect my own.

(The purpose of the above paragraph was only to show how 'morals' change. The examples used were used because they create heated, emotional debate – which means they are good examples to illustrate how things change.)

What ARE ethics? The dictionary describes ethics as 'the study of moral standards and how they affect conduct'. In other words, if morals can change, then ethics can change, too. Which is a shame - because we all pride ourselves on knowing what ethical behaviour is while the definition allows us to change the ethics and morals to suit the behaviour! When this happens, we see how the crisis in banking arose because of the bankers' self-interested behaviour – they changed their ethics to suit their morals, which were questionable. Other writers and speakers demonstrate how the culture changes as the behaviour becomes accepted, making ethics and morals much easier to change for the worse.

Legal ethics are another interesting example. Legal ethics allow for this comment to be acceptable: "I know emotionally and intellectually that my client did it and I know he is guilty, but I have not asked him if he did and I am therefore obliged by my ethics to defend him and, where he insists he didn't do it, **get him off**." Someone in the distant past, possibly for good 'moral' reasons, decided that 'truth' was relative and that a client (who is the source of a lawyer's income) is entitled to expect professional standards, or rather ethics, to change accordingly.

This may be because morals are not self-evident truths, or Principles. Remember, Principles are truths that stand up whether we believe them or not, wherever we are, whenever we have been, and exist independent of whether or not we observe them. The minute you change something (morality, ethics) you deny their existence as truth. But while you observe principle, and choose them as the basis for your ethical behaviour, then you are always dealing with reality.

Take Truth. No sensible reader would deny that Truth is a Principle, – believe in it or not, it is there, it always has been and it always will. We can lie all we like but we know the truth is not what we are saying.

If ethical behaviour is not based on truth, it is inherently unethical. There is no compromise. Once you lie, deceive or deliberately not ask so as to avoid the discovery of the truth - you are unethical, even if your profession's ethics allow for you to think otherwise.

Proof? Consider all those businesses that have been caught out acting in an unethical fashion. Note – when they acted in the way they did they could justify that behaviour within their inner circle. When caught out, their apologies reflected the fact that they *knew* that they had not acted ethically – which means they *knew* or should have known what truly ethical behaviour was, all along.

The Invention of Lying.

In 2014, while out walking my dog and listening to audio programmes which serve me intellectually (not just music, but books…) I was listening to Dr Laura Schlessinger PhD, author of *"How Could You Do That?!: The Abdication of Character, Courage, and Conscience",* an excellent book on those three subjects. She spoke of people who make stupid decisions and use the excuse, "Well, I'm only human". She responds (and I paraphrase the concept rather than her words) that being human means we are above the animals whose instinctive, reactive and unthinking responses to stimuli should not be reflected by a superior being, whose intellect can take us to the stars, cure cancer, eliminate smallpox and produce mechanical devices that can fly us through the air and into space. In her examples she writes about people whose moral behaviour is questionable – for all the reasons described in this chapter – who try to excuse what their conscience tells them to be true, to explain away the mess that their character proved to be, or to address their moral cowardice. Truly great morals are principles which we know to be true no matter how much we want to think otherwise when it suits us to do so.

Character requires us to obey our conscience and to act with courage. When we excuse our behaviour because it suits us to do so and protects us from admitting our flaws, we are lying. When we justify our conscience-defying actions we are rationalising. We are telling 'rational-lies'.

People will concoct a justification for something based on what they know in their hearts is a false premise, but because someone else does it – for example a celebrity or politician – it's okay for them to act in the same way.

In organisations like the Police and Health Service, seeing our peers acting inappropriately and getting away with it in the moment 'rational-lies'es our doing the same. But then someone gets caught, and we all prepare for the fall out. We then even justify ourselves as being different in some way from the person who's been caught! "Ah, it's different in my case because….." Rational lies!

Any lie we tell has consequences when it's discovered, of course. But when we lie, regardless of whether anyone else finds out, **we** know. And we suffer a little inside and our character suffers. And those around us who discover or even merely suspect that we have transgressed *also* know, and they treat us accordingly. Do this often enough and the trust is gone, and that has knock on effects for the relationship, future opportunities and your own mental wellbeing.

Don't lie. Even white ones. Hold your tongue – it is better to say nothing than lie. Let your thoughts remain your own and remember that a failure to act on those thoughts in the emotion of the moment, when you only know part of the reality, supports development of your character. This is particularly reinforced when that failure to lie or express an uninformed opinion proves, in the end, to have been the best course of action because the 'reality' turned out to be false.

In the final analysis lying, whether to ourselves, to others, or just about reality, is the ultimate expression of pride or pretence. Too much pride to admit that you're wrong, to learn from that knowledge, and to reinforce relationships. So much pretence that you eventually come to rely on others to not test you, because you know you will fail.

If we are to comply with the Second Resolution, we must resolve to never tell lies either verbally or through our behaviour.

Discover your own sense of good character, and then start to live in accordance with your discovery, by doing this exercise before you continue onto Competence.

Character Exercise

1.   Where do I act without conscience?

This may be a 'pleasure-orientated' answer. If it is, you're probably on the right track to discovering a vice/addiction.

2. What am I getting when I do that?

There will be a payoff for doing this 'thing' – it may be physical, mental or financial. Without conscience it is unlikely to be spiritually rewarding – quite the opposite.

3. How do I feel when I do that?

Emotionally – how do you feel? Probably quite good, but when does the guilt set in – before, during or after?

4. How do I feel *after* I do that?

If guilty, then it's a vice and you already know that you want to control it. (I nearly wrote 'stop it' but I know how hard that can be. Baby steps.)

5. What are my values?

Hopefully you've already done this exercise. If not, please do it now. Please.

6. What do they mean to *me*?

Remember – it's how you define them that counts, and your defining them clearly makes them easier to clarify if another's understanding of the term used is different from your own.

7. When do I act in accordance with my values?

Is it in a particular role or set of roles? If so, why in those roles and (perhaps) not others?

8. What do I get when I do that?

What's the positive payoff here?

9. How do I feel when I do that?

Good, innit? So do it more, then!

10. How do I feel *after* I do that?

If the good feeling is fleeting, maybe it isn't quite the right value for you OR you need to slightly redefine it. If it instils a warm glow, then it is absolutely right for you. Swim in it.

11. Do I have a Mission Statement?

If not, see Chapter Six.

12. Are there any situations *outside* my control (e.g. at work) when I find conflict between my responsibilities and my personal values?

Write these down, if they exist.

13. Can I resolve these differences?

For now, are you mentally or physically capable of resolving the differences? Keep going until you know your answer.

14. If I cannot, can I address my situation to avoid those conflicts?

You must consider either avoiding those situations in future, or you can consider moving away from that role. But a good alternative is to address the situation so that your values AREN'T in conflict.

15. If not – am I willing to walk away or to change my values?

DO NOT change your values to avoid the conflict –that's self- defeating.

16.   If I can, how?

What are you going to DO about this situation?

Now we move on to Competence, the second part of the Second Resolution and something we know that we need to possess if we are to succeed in anything meaningful. There is no question that you will see that there are a lot of cross-overs to character; there simply are a lot of parallels between Character and Competence, particularly in terms of examples.

Competence

Books on leadership rarely address Competence in any field other than the managerial context. In general, while these books instruct us in the competencies and methodologies of leadership they rarely discuss competence as a concept in and of itself. They teach you to 'do' leadership (or, more commonly, how to manage leadership in an organisation) but the rationale behind competence, and the building blocks to it, aren't so readily dealt with. Other training manuals are understandably focused on the 'how-to' of the task under instruction.

This means that there are a lot of books covering 'either side' of competence, i.e. how to identify what competencies are required, and what the specific competencies are, but I have not readily been able to identify any book that is *about* competence. Modern management science has also led to the creation of magnificent tables of competencies in every sector – the expected competencies of a private investigator run to hundreds, if not thousands of pages; a police officer thousands more. In other words, the competencies have been heavily drilled into to the point of describing how one should breathe in and then breathe out, but the *principle* of Competence is ignored.

Competence is not covered in leadership books except to the extent that they list and describe competencies in proactive thinking, forward planning, deliberate execution, and the acceptance and execution of relationship 'skills'. The books are about generic 'being and living' and as such could not and therefore did not spend much time on competence. Rationally, trying to address competence is difficult because competence in one area does not mean competence in another, and therefore trying to identify and express competencies in any way probably means excluding competencies that an author can't think of because it may be in a field unknown to them. But here are some suggestions about competence that can *lead* to achievement of competency in any area.

What is Competence?

Competence is defined in Webster's Dictionary as:

"the quality of being capable, sufficiency; capacity."

The Oxford English Dictionary defines it thus:

"being properly qualified or skilled; adequately capable."

Competence, therefore, is rather disappointingly defined in a dictionary as the lowest possible expectation that a person has of another when they expect something to be done. That said, one person usually has an expectation of competency based on *their* preconceptions and expectations rather than the objective realities, while another person may have a different set of expectations in exactly the same circumstances..

Despite the dictionary definition's lack of ambition, most of us have an expectation of a competency standard of *perfect*, or at least excellence, when it comes to what we expect from those who provide services. Conversely, we only need to be 'good enough'. "Is a puzzlement." *(The King, 'The King and I', Rodgers and Hammerstein.)*

Going deeper into the subject, and widening the context a little, competence in any area of work or play requires an ability to execute work and tasks to a level whereby the enterprise can progress and succeed. Anything less than competence threatens the endeavour, which means that while the 'dictionary definition' of competence is the entrance fee to employment, even moderate success requires application of the 'new', higher-level definition.

No matter how nice you are, how ethical, good-natured or attractive you may be, it is ultimately your competence that answers the employer/client/customer/community/family question, "Can you do what I need done and at the standard required?" And as suggested above, that standard is now perfection.

So while first impressions based on the character traits described in the preceding section may get you 'in', it will be competence *allied* to character that keeps you there. Good character traits will be helpful when making genuine, well-intentioned errors of judgement and are valuable for that reason (although not *only* for that reason), but they will not counter incompetence, or 'under-competence', for ever.

Conversely, reliance upon competence alone can be equally damaging. I know some very competent colleagues – but I wouldn't trust them with my secrets, my wife, or my money. One such colleague was good at his job, but everyone around him knew he was also a bit of loose cannon, ethically. Eventually he was dismissed over allegations of fraud in that he would consistently claim overtime while conducting his own building business. And when he went down he took some otherwise good colleagues with him because they saw only the 'fun' friend, not the 'unethical' friend. Such is the power of popularity that is not based on the principle of character.

For the purposes of the Second Resolution, Competence can be defined for the purposes of The Second Resolution as **"the ability to get things done in accordance with the technology, methodology, laws and ethics of the role being undertaken".** This definition takes into account your professional, personal and community roles. While competency usually relates to the former of those three areas of living, there is no reason to suggest that the seeking of greater competency in the other two areas should be ignored.

Someone who is competent is acknowledged, by that description, to know what they are doing, why they are doing it, and how it is done to a level of excellence. More often than not they have come to that status by having learned their trade, having been formally trained and having gained experience since that training ended.

There is another element to competence, however. Desire.

Competence as defined in The **Three Resolutions** is found at the nexus of knowledge (why to do), skill (what and how to do), and desire (want to do), which by pure coincidence are the three elements of Habit as defined by Stephen Covey.

Many people, myself included, have the first two skills as a direct consequence of the training and experience I mentioned. Many people, myself included, occasionally have trouble with the desire. Competence, however, requires all three. This is because a lack in *any one* of the three areas has a direct effect on the other two. If I don't know what needs to be done, I can't do it. If I know what needs to be done but I don't know how, I can't do it. But even if I know what needs to be done, and how and why it needs to be done, but I don't *want* to do it, it either won't get done or it won't be done properly – certainly not at the highest standard. Not 'The Three Resolutions' competently.

So while this approach patently applies to work, doesn't it also apply to 'life'? If I know I need a good relationship with another, but I don't know how to make it happen, then it won't. If I know I must, and know how, but don't want to – will any subsequent relationship actually work? If I know I must exercise, and I know how, but I don't want to – will I run or will I find an excuse? If I *do* run, how well will I run? In essence, we should seek competence in everything we do. If we do not want to be competent at something we should decide, here and now, not to do it at all.

Learning to be Competent

It is possible to provide advice on how to become competent in every endeavour we undertake. This is a sound developmental process that can be applied by anyone seeking competence in any facet of life, personal or professional.

1. *Training.* Find out who is teaching a method and get that training. Undergo the certification process, where applicable. Learn more than enough to pass – learn it so you can do it without having to think so much. Learn procedures so that they become second nature, but also be willing to question their validity when unusual circumstances arise. (And don't be ashamed to possess an Idiot's Guide – because only idiots ignore the benefit of having an available checklist.)
2. *Experience.* Find out who is doing something and join them in doing it. Watch, do, learn and improve by doing it more and learning more. Seek out opportunities to engage your training. Consider the old saying that it takes 10,000 hours to master anything and start today. Notice with interest the subtleties of what your mentor is doing; copy them as a way of integrating their thought processes with your own. Once you master their methods you can develop your own, and even improve upon them. I knew one master professional who, unlike everyone around him, kept a simple

blue covered, lined notebook in which he recorded details of meetings, decisions, rationales for those decisions, who he told to do what, and so on. I adopted that action and developed as a professional in my own right.

3. *Read, write and teach.* If you have to give a presentation on any subject properly, you will prepare and ensure that you know what it is you have to communicate. This may not apply to a whole career but it is a valuable method for learning important nuances and distinctions. In addition, having to know what you are talking about requires a deeper understanding, if only to avoid embarrassment! That said, don't be closed to alternative viewpoints that come from your 'class', as their input may be valuable and further develop your own competencies. And write about what you learn. I cannot quantify the massive amount that I have learned while writing this book. If you want to teach what you know (as a means of improving that knowledge) then learn how to make informative presentations, even if you do so only by seeking out a Toastmasters or Association of Speakers Club (ASC) style speakers club and gaining confidence in public speaking. My own experience was that once you make your first presentation at a Speakers Club you can't wait to have another go. In time, you develop so much confidence that speaking in public presents no fear, which in turn manifests better communication of ideas to your 'students' because of that confidence.

4. *Anticipate future needs.* I observed in my own profession that some enlightened people saw that new procedures and practices in relation to Information Technology and Computer Investigation meant that new training and qualifications were needed, and volunteered for that training and for the expected application. Notwithstanding the fact that they then became more valuable to the organisation, I also discovered that after many of these people *left,* their skill levels became *very* attractive to future employers and other professionals who could and would seek out these skills on a contractual basis. Future need became future profit. When new systems, protocols and procedures are mooted it is only a matter of time before they became so 'enshrined' that those who have taken the time to learn the protocols and the associated skills become an asset. Being current within your profession enables you to identify what needs may be marching over the horizon towards your organisation, and to seek out training accordingly.

And in each case, take that action persistently and never actually stop.

Once you have developed a competence it is imperative that you to seek out the opportunities to exercise it, as any machine loses efficiency when unused. Take every opportunity to exercise your craft because doing so keeps you sharp, and in truth further develops that 'sharpness' until it is YOU who defines the new 'cutting edge' thinking in your field. (Sorry.)

The Counter to Competence - Pretension

Pretension is defined in Webster's Dictionary as the 'claiming of great importance'. To a large extent this has been covered in the Character section but now we look at it from a competence perspective. Have you ever met someone who, to use a common expression, 'talks a good job'? Let's call him Fred. Fred is somebody who claims to have done this and to have organised that and to have achieved something else – and in truth Fred has either done none of these things or, more often than not, was on the periphery when somebody else, an individual or a team, did what Fred claims was entirely down to him? He pretended to be something he wasn't and was therefore pretentious. This example is apparently a common experience in many hierarchies and I have seen it exhibited in the Police Service where a job applicant said they had run an important investigation and achieved spectacular results only for a member of the interview panel to say, "I thought I did that job, and you weren't on it?"

We demonstrate pretension when we claim to be something we are not. The opposite of this is excessive modesty, when we deny being something that we *are*! We go all coy and despite the fact that we are deserving of praise we falsely defer responsibility to others, or simply suggest we were lucky. Somewhere in between is a positive truth, where we accept duly earned praise, give credit to others when appropriate, and place responsibility for success upon whom it is truly deserved, whether it be our team or even another party. Excessive modesty, like pretension, is a pretence we should avoid.

Pretension as a Restraining Force

Using the terms of the Second Resolution, how does the counterfeit of competence - pretension - hold us back? How does it restrain us?

How do we engage with and fight against 'pretension' as a restraining force when the arts (pop and TV business) reward 'pretending' – evidence the showy fashions, extreme behaviours, excessive 'campness' and outrageous celebration of the kind of 'celebrity' that is backed by neither talent nor skill - reality TV, in other words? How do we overcome a world that visibly rewards pretension with grossly inappropriate financial rewards and adoration – while seemingly forgetting that the vast majority of ordinary people have different, equally meaningful definitions of success and have a consistent, ingrained and congruent character? One where there is no pretence?

Put simply, we fight back by ensuring that we acknowledge the truth of our competence, and work to maintain and even improve it. We do not profess to know things we do not; we accept that we can be wrong and clearly state and show that we are willing to be proved wrong; and we can learn in order to discover the right way to do things. None of this involves 'surrender' or 'admission' of something which makes us 'less'; in truth, most people understand that an acknowledgment that we can be wrong enables them to question whether they are wrong, too – and as a result both can learn something useful, as well. Growth requires personal acknowledgement that growth is possible. Pretension prevents growth because pretension demands that we profess that no learning is required.

Growth therefore also requires character!

It seems to me appropriate that you should conduct the first part of a Competence Check at this point, before reading on.

Competence Exercise – Part 1.

1.   What are my roles?

Consider the roles you play – family, work social and teacher, for example. List them here.

2. Which roles do I excel at?

Which do you execute with excellence? Consider whether they are coincidentally those that you enjoy.

3. What strengths am I demonstrating when I do that?

Sorry – can't help you here, this one's down to you.

4. In which roles am I under-performing?

Again, coincidentally, are they the ones you don't like doing?

5. What knowledge gaps exist between the two, if any?

6. What skill gaps exist between the two, if any?

7. What attitude gaps exist between the two, if any?

If you don't enjoy some, is it a skills/knowledge/attitude gap? Would knowing or being able to do more improve your attitude to these role-related tasks?

Practical Application of The Second Resolution

So how do we demonstrate Character and Competence in our efforts to abide by the **Three Resolutions** in the many areas of our own lives?

Personal Life

It is a foundational principle that we, in our personal lives, *must MUST **MUST*** live with integrity. It is an absolute and unarguable requirement that those who achieve the greatest success in obtaining the respect of others are those who live in accordance with their stated values, provided that those values are in alignment with principles. (Again, we all know what that means because we know what 'unprincipled' means.)

Charles Hobbs argued that the essential element of high self-esteem is the desire and ability to live wholly in accordance with your own set of values. Hyrum W. Smith also argued that a personal sense of peace required the same compliance. This compliance is not ego-driven, because ego requires that you seek adoration from others and create sense of conceit within yourself, otherwise known as the creation of the big I AM. Those with the 'I AM' ego pretend they don't need external affirmation and respect, but in truth their bold claims are specifically designed to engender 'oohs' and 'aahs' from those around them.

No, self-esteem is a reflection of the respect one has for oneself, is the core ingredient of integrity, and is wholly intrinsic.

You can, of course, have values like greed, gluttony and sloth, and you can live in keeping with those values. But eventually your conscience will let you know you are out of step with principles, with reality. It will tell you that such values are not tenable in the long run – that they will fail you, in the end.

Your conscience knows that honesty, respect, nutrition, exercise, etc. are the principles which, if valued, will afford you the self-esteem that follows their observance. So consider the values you have and the level at which you live in parallel with those values, and then see if there is a gap that needs narrowing, or even closing. Once you have done this – once you have *truly* done this – you will start to feel 'right'. And once 'you' are right at a personal level you can start to apply yourself to feeling right at work and in your relationships.

Work

If you are like me, you *chose* the field within which you work: you did not 'accidentally' apply for, prepare, get interviewed and tested for, and then get given your job. In fact, these days, you have to jump through hoops to get into any professional job, walk over fiery ash to get semi-professional work, and bend over backwards to get even minimum wage work. Those who live on benefits by choice – there are some – arguably have some justification when they ask, "Why should I put myself through all that?" – but not much.

In his book *Life Matters*, A. Roger Merrill and his wife Rebecca Merrill wrote about the nobility of work, demonstrating through careful analysis and analogy how parents used to raise their children in the context of 'their' work.

While you may agree that the world has moved on a bit since 'those days' (they weren't that long ago), mothers showed their daughters how to keep a home, and men showed their sons how to ply the fathers' trade. But people no longer meekly or even willingly follow their fathers' trades and gender expectations no longer apply. The new approach is that seeking to live a life in which you serve others in the ways that *you* choose (professionally and socially) has a lot going for it.

Consider this – those who succeed most in their careers are often those who *love* what they do to the extent that they involve themselves in a search for what they need to know in order to be most competent when they perform. They do not merely accept training – they actively seek it out, and where formal instruction is unavailable they seek out mentors from whom individual assistance can be obtained. Notwithstanding the fact that they become super competent as a result of this approach, they simultaneously demonstrate high levels of character – eagerness to learn, the confidence to ask, the willingness to be wrong in an effort to identify what is right. These are *character* traits that support future *competence*, and in applying the 3Rs you will discover that the two work wholly together, and they are not effectively independent.

In the USA, medical treatment is a paid for service; it is not free at the point of service. An aspiring doctor was being interviewed about entry to an esteemed teaching hospital, and during the pre-enrolment interview was being questioned on ethics. He was asked, "If you had a choice between a dishonest but incredibly competent surgeon, and a highly ethical but less skilled surgeon, which would you choose?"

His response was quite astute and considered. He said, "If it was absolutely necessary I have the surgery, I'd choose the former: but if it was a question of *whether or not* I needed the surgery, I would choose the latter."

In other words, the lack of trust for the highly competent was a potential bar to use of his or her service. Lack of skill can be allowed for if trust is present, in some circumstances: but lack of trust can stop the highly-competent-but-unethical in their tracks.

Do you lean more towards one than the other? Do you focus more towards competence, or character? Or do you consider your balance to be about right? And if the balance is 'about right', is it 'excellent in both respects'? Or is it, "I do the best I can and I'm scrupulously trustworthy? Or is it "I have a truly excellent standard of performance and I only tell little white lies"?

I believe it is possible to have a 'high balance', where both your competence and your character can be at their best. That is the only truly acceptable balance and it is well worth working to achieve.

No, it isn't easy.

Achieving that level of balanced performance is not simple: for example, when you are tired or pressured it is easy to be short with people or to cut corners in an effort to get some small task done and out of the way. The 'secret' – the objective in applying the Second Resolution – is to be both competent and trustworthy as much as possible, and this requires personal integrity and personal honesty. It requires application of First Resolution discipline in an effort to avoid integrity-contravening temper tantrums and physical tiredness, and it requires the application of the Second Resolution to avoid pretending to be something you are not, and making sure that you perform exactly the way you should.

How does the Second Resolution assist in application of Character and Competence at work? Perhaps the answer to the following questions will guide you.

Do you turn up at work and just do enough, or are you someone who goes the extra mile and puts in that little bit more effort than other *regardless of pay or other tangible recognition?* Are you someone who insists you will do more when you are paid more, or someone who believes the more you do (first) the better the opportunities that will come to you? Do you honestly lie somewhere between those extremes?

If you are passionate about and committed to your work, I suspect that much of what you will read here will not apply. That said, even passionate workers can be tempted away from the 'perfect' path if something more attractive comes along. I have observed that even the most dedicated workers will accept an invitation to a working-time 'office breakfast' if their peers – equally dedicated – suggest it. Even the most dedicated toilers will fall into a passing conversation if the subject interests them. And I would argue that a passionate worker will also be attracted to corner cutting if, by doing so, they perceive that their results will be brought about all the sooner. I described, earlier, how in policing this used to be called 'noble cause corruption', where shortcutting the ethical evidential requirements was felt to be a good way of getting villains put away. Of course, nowadays this is no longer acceptable. What is amusing is that when it *was* accepted, even the villains played along.

Taking into consideration the processional impact of the **Three Resolutions** as they counter the Restraining Forces, can allowing ourselves to be susceptible to Appetites and Passions at work have negative consequences? I shall identify a few, and invite the reader to identify more, if they can.

First of all, cutting corners in order to get results quicker often contaminates that result. For example, a failure to comply with a system requirement can stall, or even stop a project. Not complying with a financial accounting process can result in costly fraud enquiries or time-consuming audits. Not sticking to a procurement procedure could mean the wrong kit being obtained, threatening future effectiveness. And to labour the police example, improperly obtained evidence can be thrown out and an otherwise justified prosecution stopped in its tracks.

These things can happen because of a need to 'get things done' and bureaucracy often seems to get in the way of doing that, but bureaucracy also protects us from costly errors and criminal acts. I need say little about how ignoring Health and Safety in the interests of (cost saving) efficiency has often been seen to have a tragically high human cost.

Next, failing to be disciplined and allowing appetites and passions to intrude into work can result in our competencies suffering, and therefore our future performance. I know that when I changed from a 'generalist' role into a 'specialist' role it wasn't long before I realised that had I been asked to return to the old job I would need re-training. While I may not have been at fault in that circumstance, a self-imposed neglect of competencies in the interests of self or for ultimate achievement can result in a loss of ability in essential skills. Then, when those skills are needed again, they have been lost or are executed incompetently at worst, or at least ineffectively. Discipline can include going the extra mile to maintain skills that, while not needed today, may be needed again in the future. Incidentally, the organisation for which you work should play its part in making sure that 'specialists' are kept as up to date as 'generalists'. If your employer doesn't do so today, enlighten your internal training providers about the specialist/generalist 'gap' as part of your effort to contribute – and stay current, yourself.

Other obstacles affecting our self-discipline and self-denial at work are the Culture within which that work takes place, and the effect of our ego – are we too good for the workplace, a particular task, or the people with whom we work? If we accept that this influences us, we can still ask 'how can self-discipline and self-denial address all of the issues I have hitherto identified?' Perhaps the following advice will help you find out.

Recognise when you are tempted by deflection or distraction. Once you realise that what you are doing is not what you ought to be doing, you use your self-discipline to return to the correct activity. This may require some self-denial on your part – focusing on work instead of work-time socialising. This way, results become consistent, and consistency increases the rate at which work can be completed. Once completed, then time can be taken away from the task. This process takes Character.

Always comply with standing procedures unless and until you or somebody else identifies an improved process. Such procedures have themselves been borne out of the experiences and knowledge of other people. They are perfectly valid until a change in the underlying circumstances, the availability of modernised resources, or knowledge improvement borne about in any other way. Compliance predicts the desired results – A action leads to B result or prevents it (if prevention is the objective). If new knowledge changes that system for the better, then and only then can any changes be proposed. This relates to Competence.

Accept, even actively pursue competency training. This includes *re*-training in a field where you may already believe you are competent. You may recall how I attended a conference where one of the lecturers provided input on a subject that participants were familiar with (or should have been). A colleague bemoaned the fact that this subject had been raised, implying that we were being treated like children by being re-taught the subject matter. I learned something new, albeit only a slightly newer perspective on the subject that would serve me in the future. This acceptance requires Character *and* Competence.

Be open to alternative views and be self-disciplined when trying to change systems. Self-denial requires that we be willing to accept that alternative views exist and that what we believe to be true may not be so. Self-denial helps us to take a momentary pause between being made aware of something we disagree with, using that pause to overcome the egotistical need to be 'right', leading us on to the discovery that what we thought was 'wrong' was, in fact, true. It allows us to re-assess situations *before* we act on incorrect input. Self-discipline is needed to consistently apply that pause. This takes Character.

People have often seen what is wrong with a system/process/organisation, etc. I have occasionally realised this the moment I have walked in! Of course, that initial assessment is based on personal and potentially uninformed perceptions, values and beliefs. And despite that, people will insist on telling everyone what they think. The others will resist, and as a by-product the critic will get a reputation as a trouble-maker, and an ill-mannered and ill-informed one at that.

Application of self-denial and self-discipline tells me to wait and assess a process, system or situation long enough to be able to not only identify what is wrong with it – the easy part – but also what may be done to correct that error and provide better results. It also helps me identify how to communicate this knowledge in a way that does not challenge individuals' beliefs but in fact takes them into account when making the suggestions for change.

Home, Family and Friends, Community

In the same way that competence and character apply at work, how many of us have given thought to the fact that they apply in the home?

I know from personal experience that some of the most competent and likeable workmates have poor home lives because while they are competent and trustworthy at a professional level, they seem unable to do the same at home, where their 'work' competencies curry no favour! The best pilot in the world cannot 'fly' her family; the best chef on the planet cannot cook his family. The competencies are different, even if (in the general work sense) they can be complementary. People skills work in either situation but here's the rub – using 'HR techniques' on family is not advisable, even if it works in the office or factory. A failure to be able to cook is forgivable; telling me that I am a poor cook when I have slaved over dinner is not.

Would I go as far as to say character is more important in the home? Thinking about it, I would not. I believe Character is of utmost importance and therefore important *everywhere*. But it would be reasonable to suggest that the consequences and effects of good - or bad - character are arguably greater in the home than they are in one's profession.

It is said that who we are speaks louder than what we say, and this is never truer than in the home, where our family knows us better than those with whom we work. Our workmates see us for 8 or so hours 5 days a week, while our families see us the rest of the time – and, particularly after a bad day at work, at our *worst* times.

Your family, friends and community deserve your best character and competence. You are the one responsible for making the effort to understand *them*, for example, not the other way around. As Bruce Lee put it, they are not there to meet your expectations and you are not here to meet theirs. Relationships – even the word implies a two-way street addressing someone's relationship to you and your relationship to them. Character-wise, your being your best, congruent self is the ultimate relationship responsibility. If you have 'one face' you can be trusted to act the same way all of the time.

Our children model us. Until they start to follow their peers, parents are their role models. What kind of (competence/character) parent or spouse are you? Are you teaching your children the 'right' things? By that, are you ever put into the position where you have to tell them, "Do as I say, not as I do"? If so, you have already breached the trust that your children need to have in you. Character requires us to live in accordance with what we believe, and we must act in accordance with those beliefs. The 'do as I say not as I do' attitude betrays that, and children see you act in that fashion – and then do it straight back at you!

Relationships involve competencies, but how we execute those competencies lies closer to our character when in the home environment because they are more emotionally founded than intellectually sourced. In the home, how our children see us act, and how they see us treat others, is far more important and real to them than what we *say*.

In terms of competence you can do no better that be prepared to listen without judging and without giving advice, a competency. In school we learn to read, write and count. Where were our listening lessons?

Consider what competencies, skills and talents you can bring to your relationships – all of them.

You can now complete the second part of the exercise you started earlier.

Character Exercise – Part 2.

1.   Am I willing to address the gaps I identified earlier?

If so, good. If not, why not – if you're true to yourself and simply don't want to, then now is the time to consider whether you want to continue in this role, even if you are frightened of discarding it.

2.   How am I going to address those gaps?

This is simply a strategy question. You've already done a couple of those, so do them again!

3.   Are there any roles I DO NOT currently carry out, that I would like?

Let reasonable ambition kick in, here. What would you genuinely like to do?

4.   What skills might I need to carry out those roles?

Think about interpersonal, as well as technical and skills. How should you be with people, and how can you achieve those characteristics?

5.   What experience and knowledge would I need for those roles?

Think about service opportunities where you can provide free labour while learning, from others, those skills or experiences you currently lack.

6.   What am I going to do so that I can be given (or so I can take) those roles?

Sometimes the easiest thing to 'do' is the hardest thing to consider – putting yourself forward and risking rejection. In truth, many organisations, communities (etc.) lack volunteers and will frequently snap up 'free' labour.

7.   When am I going to do it?

When would 'now' be a good time?

8.   Who can I go to for help?

Consider the slightly unethical approach of going straight to the top. Many people do so to achieve their own ends when the correct route isn't giving them what they want (which is often self-focussed), but if your interest is to benefit others this may get your foot into a door where you cans serve.

The Importance and Relevance of the Second Resolution to Trustworthiness

In your own experience of relationships, are there people who you like, whose company you enjoy and who you find amusing – but who you wouldn't trust to sharpen your pencil? Are there friends who you love, but who you wouldn't trust with your spouse? Are there people at work who are fun to be around but who you'd rather not work for, or even with, because they might do something that you will have to explain and, in doing so, you'll have to consider misrepresenting the truth?

I once attended a business forum in London at the invitation of a good friend, and the guest of honour and reason for attending was Stephen Covey, in his last London visit before he passed away in 2012. The guests were leaders from London's business and policing community and, to be frank, the lowest ranking police officer there was – me. In my estimation there were commanders and senior, *senior* officers present from the Metropolitan Police and other local forces. in fact, I stood in the urinal next to the then Commissioner. Bladders – the great leveller.

I was listening to a lot of talk about leadership but this one question bothered me because of my own experience with 'leaders' whose competence or character – sometimes both – could be questioned. Dr Covey or the hoThen came the inevitable opportunity - "Any questions?" In the ensuing silence I asked that question, "How important is the relationship between character and competence?"

Covey knew exactly which slide to go to, and responded that true leadership (personal OR organisational) requires that there be a balance between the two – it is NEVER a case of either/or. A leader must be competent and have (good) character. An incompetent will make mistakes that affect the results of any organisational (or personal) effort; but honest incompetence is merely a training issue and usually repairable. But a person of bad or no character will destroy the reputation of that endeavour. This may seem unfair – why should one bad apple affect the reputation of all others in any organisation? But look around, and unfair as I agree it to be, politicians, police officers, bankers – all are suffering because of the incompetence or dishonest self-interest (or noble cause corruption) of the few. And their respective professions suffer, too.

Sidebar: Coincidentally, the Commissioner next to whom I passed water was soon forced to resign having accepted favours from a third party. Corruption was never suggested, but the poor decision to accept an expensive recuperative stay at a convalescent home when other in-house options existed raised questions about his decision-making and ethics.

You may not believe that exercising good character and high levels of competence can have the reverse effect – you may feel that your little effort will never be noticed. But if it is noticed by your family, your team or your community it will have an effect for the good. And I assure you – it IS noticed. And you know it. It may not result in applause, medals and celebrity. But people *know*.

You may not be able to fight City Hall, but trustworthiness, honesty and the truth are weapons that cannot be overcome by deceit or corruption. Consider the situation of an expert witness in a trial. The opposing side will try to undermine the representation of that person's competence and character by attacking their intent and their integrity (their character), and then their capabilities and results (their competence).

THAT is how important it is to be a person of competence *and* character, to effectively execute the Second Resolution. If you have these, and if they are unimpeachable, you can fight off any attack on one or all of those characteristics. And in knowing that you have them, and by acting on that knowledge and in keeping with the power behind that knowledge, your self-esteem can never crack.

How the First Resolution serves the Second Resolution

Earlier, I explained in detail, and with an illustration, how the **Three Resolutions** inter-relate. For now, let's consider how the First Resolution can help us in our efforts to demonstrate competence and character.

Competence is obviously the result of a disciplined approach to learning new skills or to adapting old skills to new situations. We have to focus our attention on taking on board new learning, new concepts and new physical skills. An apprentice carpenter who has never worked wood before will start afresh; someone with a school-level certificate will have less to learn but will still have a lot of information to understand, while perhaps having some preconceptions which may – or may not – serve that learning effort. In most cases, whatever the pre-apprentice level of knowledge, some level of self-discipline will be expected by the person imparting that training. They will expect the student or apprentice to apply themselves and show some level of effort. The teacher may be accountable for the results but the student is the one who has to do the work if they are to benefit from the qualification that follows. Depending on the competence being sought there may also be a level of self-denial required of the trainer. A physical education instructor must present themselves as a fit individual if they are to have any credibility, so they must eat and exercise in ways that they may not wish to in the moment. All students at higher levels of learning should sacrifice their social lives (to a degree) if they are to achieve higher grades. In any case, how they spend their time is a good example of where the First Resolution can be rigorously and advantageously applied in an effort to support their application of the Second Resolution.

Character is the less obvious consequence of application of the First Resolution. Living in accordance with your values shows character, but how do you train to do that?

In my view, there is only one direct correlation between the First Resolution and the development and maintenance of a good character, and that is the self-discipline and self-denial that one needs to apply when, having identified, defined and committed to your value statements, you have to live them – and in that moment you don't want to.

This is when application of the First Resolution is MOST important. As suggested in the chapter on Appetites and Passions, it is easy to apply the First Resolution when what you want is served by it. But when what you NEED is served by the First Resolution, but you don't WANT to apply the physical or mental effort to get that need filled, then character is both underpinned and demonstrated by application of the First Resolution. Or put another way, the *absence* of First Resolution compliance *prevents* success with the Second Resolution.

You will recall the concept of the learning continuum where we start with unconscious incompetence and move forward to unconscious competence. Just as it applied to self-discipline and self-denial it applies equally to both character and competence. It goes without description *how* it applies to competence – that's a given – but how does it apply to character?

It applies because we can get better at being good people. We start out by merely having a desire to do the right thing but ignorance of what the right thing *is* can get in our way, especially when some of the people around us actively decry it as soft, not realistic, even undesirable. We can only start by knowing what principles apply (honesty being a more obvious example) and decide to act in congruence with that knowledge. As we develop we increase our own understanding of principles and we can apply that knowledge to our own sense of personal integrity, bringing the 'circles of behaviour and values' into closer alignment. Over time, we can better behave in accordance with our values because we now better understand the consequences of failing to do so – we become more mature and are less likely to pander to distractions. The key to doing so lay in application of the First Resolution. Once we became more disciplined and did the things we knew we needed to do while simultaneously stopping doing those things that we realised did not serve us, we discovered a better way –we became more consciously competent about what was 'right'. And in a bit more time we stopped having to think about it.

To get what you really want, you have to use self-discipline and self-denial to feed your character and your competence, to consequently make you a better person, the 'better person' that you have elected to be. There is a direct link between the First Resolution and the Second Resolution. The first serves the second, and it may also be suggested that the second also serves the first – people of character tend to be self-disciplined and deny themselves instant gratification in preference for the longer term objective.

In conclusion, Socrates said, "The greatest way to live with honour in this world *is to be what we pretend to be*." What a profound statement! Instead of pretending to be good, honest, compassionate, caring, productive, competent, healthy and so on *ad infinitum*, why don't we just *be* those things?

Chapter Five – The Third Resolution - Noble Purpose and Service to Others

"To overcome the restraining forces of unbridled aspiration and ambition, I resolve to dedicate my talents and resources to noble purposes and to provide service to others." S R Covey

Meaning. Purpose. Legacy.

We all need something to make us feel as though we have progressed or grown as an individual, and that we will be remembered for something. This need may not be obvious when we are young, but as we mature it develops. I recall a young person whose life was tragically cut short at 19 – she developed a sense of meaning when she was diagnosed with cancer at 16 – so perhaps a sense of meaning and legacy develops when we suddenly recognise we are mortal. Then, we start to seek personal growth.

Regrettably, many mistakenly interpret progression or growth as achievable only through professional promotion for its own sake; in the search for power, or in the seeking of success in the form of celebrity. Or we seek to show our progress and success through the possession of stuff. As money and influence are societally considered to be the modern measure of who has or does not have status, the accumulation of either does appear to many, on that sociological level, to be the sole objective of the achiever. Oddly, that view appears to be the same both for the selfish achiever, and for those who perceive wealth to be 'bad' on an ideological basis – those who judge the wealthy purely on the basis that wealth is, by its very nature, undeserved. Or so the press would have us believe.

The press appears to be of the view that anyone who has something others do not should, at some time and for some reason, be considered immoral, unethical, overpaid, corrupt, and so on. Sometimes they are right, of course. At the time of writing the bankers have come in for a great deal of criticism, as has anyone who wants and gets a pay rise above 1% in times of austerity.

But what of the wealthy and influential about which we, the media's clients, hear little or nothing?

The world is full of wealthy and powerful people who use those gifts in a way that should be celebrated, and these people are applying the Third Resolution. In recognition of what they have been given they strive to help others, yet the fact that they have money often renders them invisible and unrecognised for their charitable work. Partly, one suspects, because we recognise in ourselves an unwillingness to do such charitable work ourselves.

I once heard a friend deride Anthony Robbins for being a millionaire. For the few who don't know, Anthony Robbins is a respected coach or 'personal development guru' who has written books and audio programmes which are acknowledged by many to be the best available. He also holds events at which thousands of people are given three to five day seminars by him personally, on the subject. These events are akin to rock concerts, such is their power and atmosphere, except that rock concerts last two hours while Robbins' events last 4 days, 12-16 hours each day.

My friend had attended one of his well-attended events, yet all she could see was one millionaire 'making money from people' at the event. For my part, I pointed out that, as a multi-millionaire, he didn't have to do anything yet he travelled the world entertaining, educating and empowering people at what was a bargain price considering the usual corporate rates for one day programmes of that nature, and he also fed the homeless with his famed Basket Brigade at Christmas, with and through internationally-located volunteers who sourced and delivered food to the homeless.

Such is an example of a warped opinion based on scarcity thinking (that is, "you have more therefore I have less therefore you don't deserve it") falsely and ungenerously imprinted upon a person who yes, has wealth (Robbins worked for it, lost it twice, then had to earn it again), but also gives a great deal in order to maintain it. It should never be forgotten that people can only sell what people want, otherwise they invest (and therefore potentially lose) their own time and money for nothing. As many do.

Isn't Ambition a Good Thing?

Review the opening statement and notice that the Restraining Force is not 'just' aspiration and ambition: it is **unbridled** aspiration and ambition – the Restraining Force is unbridled; it is aspiration and ambition for their own sake and for the benefit only of the selfish individual. Seeking influence and wealth in the effort to serve others is not 'unbridled'. If one takes the view that unbridled means out of control (to use a riding analogy), then the alternative – controlled ambition and aspiration – implies (but does not confirm) a more ethical purpose behind those characteristics. Measured ambition can be used for good and evil, after all.

No one could possibly criticise ambition and aspiration *per se*. It would be ridiculous to suggest we should not seek betterment, promotion, growth and even financial security or success, as these are the drivers to the betterment of all, including society itself. Aspiration and ambition are two of the drivers of the Second Resolution – how can we better ourselves in terms of character and competence if we have no ambition to do so? If nobody sought these things where would our service industries be? Who would be responsible for supervising workers? Who would decide what we were going to work *for*? What would *our* objectives be if someone didn't start to show initiative and look for something that we wanted? Who would decide who cleans the cave and who hunts?

Seeking to progress for the benefit of all is to be applauded; seeking to progress solely for one's own sake is to be derided. That is the lesson of the Third Resolution, to rein in unbridled ambition and aspiration by seeking a noble motivation, and/or to use any power or influence obtained for the benefit or in the service of others.

How do you feel when you are asked for help? Most people feel a modicum of pride, because their opinion or assistance is being sought by someone who respects and recognises your ability to provide it. Provided it isn't an interruption to your day, or the request is not being made by someone who really should already know what they should be doing, you are inclined to assist. This is a noble act, even if not at a Homeric level. And your response is usually at your highest level, where you give as much as you can. However, if your first response and sole motivation is "What can I get out of this?", what level of assistance do you seek to provide? Just enough, if any – just enough to get *your* need met. The dedication isn't there. You do only what is necessary, and the relationship between you and your 'customer' suffers.

A well-known radio station I've heard quoted in this respect is WII FM. This station is "What's In It For Me?" and it has far too many listeners. There is nothing ostensibly wrong with this station – it's just that if it's your only station you miss the benefit of the alternative services. However, when considering and engaging in a truly co-operative exercise where one provides genuine service in return for fair benefit, our relationships improve and so does our life.

I had a saying that I frequently use when training others. It goes **"Nothing we do – nothing – is done unless it is done for someone, with someone or through someone."**

No matter how often I have tested this assumption I have yet to discover anything that isn't covered by it. Every example I have ever thought of is either deeply or tangentially covered by that tenet, but I have yet to discover something that is not. Test it yourself:

We drive cars designed and built by others, on roads designed and built by others, to go to work to earn money from others for the service we provide to others and with others, so we can go home and give to our families, service providers, bar staff, grocers, artistes and others who work to provide those services for our benefit, and their own. Life is truly interdependent.

Things you think you do 'on your own' required input from others – the clothes you wear, the books you read, the paths you walk *on your own* all required the involvement of others even if they weren't present when you played your part. Everything you possess or use is the result of a service provided by others, as you provide your services to them.

Quite often, but not always, the things we do include all three elements – me, we and them. Or to make it twee, me, we and thee.

When this works, it is because a demonstration of mutual respect is perceived by those involved as a starting point, not an objective. All parties must want to the other parties to succeed if they are all to get what they want without abusing what the others want, or need. When we abuse others' trust or needs we ultimately destroy ourselves in the process.

In summary, while there is nothing wrong with having considered the WII-FM question and finding our answer, the greatest successes occur when the needs of the others involved in the enterprise have been given sufficient, or as much attention as we gave our own.

Think of a rich person you have heard of who is known to walk over others to get what he or she wants. Do you respect them? Does anyone respect them but the selfish peers who rely on them for advancement? In fact, how much to people of character actually dislike such people, or at least their behaviour? And in that light, are these people truly liked at all? Or are they just tolerated?

If you seek self-improvement for your sole benefit, you may get what you want but discover that it is not what you expected. It is said that there are more depressed wealthy people than there are depressed 'poor' people. Is the reason for this because they have no sense of meaning outside their own amusement?

Imagine having all you wanted, and that you spent all your time doing what took your fancy at any moment. You would be surrounded by people you liked, all of whom expressed their like for you. Where would you find meaning? Buying things for friends? If so, could you then truly trust that their friendship was based on who you are and not what you have? How would you *know*? Don't misunderstand me. True friends will always be true and you'll know who they are because they demonstrate many of the characteristics of self-discipline, self-denial, character and competence already covered in earlier chapters. They only have one face.

But what if your friend is like this: someone who is constantly working towards the next promotion by creating opportunities to demonstrate and evidence their competencies while not actually *developing* those competencies once they have the position that their efforts brought them.

I know of one of my own past supervisors who seemed focused on advancement but never asked me about the work I was doing despite that work being their remit. (Oh, except when a complaint arose which threatened their peaceful existence and promotion prospects. Then I was 'Dave'.)

Another sign: do you know someone who 'works hard' at advancement when being paid to do so but does absolutely no volunteer work whatsoever unless it is clearly connected to that promotion drive. And once that promotion is achieved, the volunteer work such as it was, eases off? In the end, as an employer I would be asking myself whether such people were working for me – or was I working for them.

Changing the perspective – have you ever met someone put into a role they had previously avoided like the plague, only for them to suddenly become a zealot for that cause? True, they may have had a genuine change of viewpoint but they will find it hard to convince most that their sudden enthusiasm is not created out of self-interest.

Sidebar: *The dodgy ones usually release a wordy statement where they 'say' they are excited (etc.) to have been given this important opportunity a.k.a poisoned chalice..... blah blah.....)*

That is why we must avoid unbridled ambition and aspiration – firstly because it creates distrust; secondly because we need others to live their lives congruently and with the objective of service in order for us to live our own lives to the highest level of effectiveness; and thirdly, because our own lives become meaningful when what we do affects others in a positive way. It is mutual benefit, exemplified.

Unbridled ambition is surprisingly obvious when it is present.

The Effects of Unbridled Aspiration and Ambition

First effect – upward progress and increased income. Lovely. We all want those things. Well, actually, some of us are content with what we have, so our ambition is sated by having already 'arrived'.

But *unbridled* aspiration and ambition does tend to be demonstrated by the desire to go up and get rich. And to never get there because those whose motive is exactly that always want a bit more.

Second effect – burnout, destroyed relationships, disrespect from others, loneliness and disdain.

When your drive is solely self-interest you will, inevitably, come a cropper when what you seek is denied you. It may not be denied you because of your own lack of planning, or anything else within your circle of influence. It may instead be something outside your control such as a financial collapse, a political change, a natural disaster or someone else realising what you're up to. Once your unbridled ambition is thwarted all you have left is you, and by this stage what you have become is so focused on the (now denied) next step that you suddenly discover that you have no purpose, and now everyone else will be to blame. You will start to treat everyone badly, and they will distance themselves from you.

Those around you who watched such a fast rise to glory and 'know' that it was done out of self-interest will 'know' that every decision made, every policy introduced, every initiative, em, initiated, will be questionable because it is done subjectively and selfishly, and not for the good of anyone else. Such an achiever will not be trusted. Ever.

Am I wrong? Look around you at the successful self-servers. How many true friends do they have? How many marriages have they had? If their marriages are successful is it because they married a 'twin'? In which case, I would suggest that it is self-interest keeps them there, rarely love. Are they happy, or successful? How many are both? And of those, how many are givers, 'people people', and servers? I would gamble most truly happy, successful people give as much as they get.

Looking again at the progressive nature of the **Three Resolutions**, for those with unbridled aspiration and ambition, their self-discipline is rarely in question. They aggressively do what needs to be done. Their self-denial is less well exercised for the same reason, in that they will not deny themselves something which they see will get them what they have decided they 'want' – their need *is* their want, short-term as it may be. The only thing they will deny themselves is anything that will slow them down. Their competences will be 'proven' evidentially – it'll be on paper, in certificates, and it will be shown when they 'talk a good job'. But there will occasionally be little or no experience attached, little or no wisdom, and almost invariably no consistent application of true principles. For me, their character will be flawed and it will be evident to anyone around them. So, given that the second layer of their 3R sphere is missing or defective, how long will it be before their sphere collapses?

Again, I emphasise that these are the results of *unbridled* and *unprincipled, self-serving* aspiration and ambition; not controlled, principled, generous efforts to serve and make things better for oneself and for others.

The Third Resolution

If unbridled aspiration and ambition are restraining forces, then the way to progress and overcome those forces lies in application of Resolution Three – noble purposes and service to others.

i mentioned earlier that when someone calls upon you in the right way for advice or expert assistance, then if you are a person of good character you feel blessed, affirmed and respected. Your ego certainly gets a justified and fair boost. As you provide the service that has been sought you feel a sense of pride and contribution, not to mention appreciation for what you can do. Once delivered, you, the provider, are thanked for what you have done, and a sense of personal satisfaction follows. It would be unusual for this not to be the case.

So to the obvious question, then – if providing sought after service is so rewarding **why do you wait to be asked?**

There are essentially three ways that can result in our carrying out service to others. One is to wait and be asked, a second is for the unavoidable opportunity to arise 'in your face' and the third is to seek out the opportunity to contribute.

When we wait to be asked, we recognise that an opportunity exists, or soon will come to exist. While recognising, if you will, that there is potential for such an opportunity, we nevertheless rely on others to know what we are capable of, or to know what we know. We wait for an anticipated event happen to us. We know it will come, we know what it might look like, but we do not seek it out.

Waiting to be asked is not the 'best' route to noble service because it places too much reliance on someone or something outside our control. Waiting for an anticipated opportunity to arise requires a little more proactivity on our part if our service is to be timely – we need to spot that opportunity and be ready to take it. But at the same time this approach is still reactive, relying on something to occur before we can get involved.

The unavoidable opportunity may never happen because we do not know what it may be, so waiting for it is self-defeating even if we know that we have the initiative, resources and capabilities needed to cope with that challenge once it arises. The saying 'a ship in the harbour is safe, but a ship is not intended to stay in a harbour' comes to mind, in that having a broad skill set is useless if they are never used, and if we don't seek out opportunity we may never use them. Like any tool, they will rust through lack of use. Of course, you can keep them clean and oiled (Second Resolution) but that still isn't what they are *for*.

The third way – actively seeking out the opportunity – is by far the best, proactive approach because we can identify, prepare, control, and often even take charge of that opportunity. The approach is; "I have skills, how can I use them in a way that suits me and serves others?"

I have experienced this, to my benefit. Like many people, I was a bit of a shy back-seat sitter. When I entered a seminar or meeting room I went straight to the back to sit down, as if the building or room was built on a slope – which is a point I make in training sessions when I see it happen, and it happens *every time*.

In 1995 I attended a regional meeting of the Institute that I had joined some 5 years earlier. I had not long read the book "The Magic of Thinking Big" by David Schwartz. The book had been written in, I believe, the 1960s and this was evident by some of the examples of high income being $12,000 per year. The advice was timeless, however, and one specific example piece of advice I had read consisted of just 4 words, two of which were hyphenated.

The phrase was simply **'Be a Front-Seater'**. Schwartz wrote about how people who sat at the front in seminars and meetings 'got noticed' and had greater opportunities to contribute, partly because that willingness to be seen was evidence of self-confidence, always an admirable trait (provided it was not converted to Ego).

Any coach will suggest that there are two ways of looking at front row sitters. The first perspective is that 'successful and confident contributors sit in that front seat'. People who have confidence *first* are front-seaters. That is true, but it is half the story.

The second approach is 'people who *want* to be successful, confident contributors sit in the front seat.'

In other words, whether you are confident or not, sit in that front seat because *self-confidence will follow.*

At this regional event an opportunity arose to become the secretary and I volunteered, was seconded and appointed in 5 seconds flat. I initially wondered if I had just accepted a poisoned chalice but because of that new willingness to put myself forward I was later elected to the Institute's Board of Governors, which led to me serving as Principal, which led me to be confident enough to write a book and get it published. I went on to represent my colleagues at governmental level, to apply for and get better jobs in work, and so on. I often credit that one piece of literary wisdom *and my acting upon it* as the source of what success I have.

I had to know what I was capable of, of course. None of this personal progression happened in a vacuum. I knew I was reasonably intelligent, enthusiastic, studious and hard working. Without those traits I would have failed at the first meeting. Over time I learned a lot from some very good people, too. And I mean a LOT.

Knowing what you are able and willing to contribute is a key to identifying your noble purpose, and your identification of that purpose is a precursor to your providing a service to others. If you have decided upon the purpose of your life (personal, work, whole or part) then you can clearly identify what service you can give. You can find out what it is you need to know and what equipment or other resources you need to gather. And when you know *what* you are able and willing to give, you can seek out where you can provide it.

Self-awareness leads to Mission leads to Service.

Sidebar: *You may take the view that the opposite is true, that Service leads to Mission, and I would agree with you in the sense that accidental discovery and application of what we enjoy doing can, indeed, lead to us finding out what we ultimately wish to contribute, just as service to a loved one can re-create that love. The only caveat to this is that if the service we provide does not lead to discovery of a purpose but instead leads us to consider the service as drudgery or uninteresting, then it undermines our willingness to serve and prevents us from identifying and acting upon our noble purpose. It also requires something to happen to us before we act. If that 'something' doesn't happen, we lose out.*

For me to be able to do that in my own life, I had to overcome the very common distaste for public speaking. My own Mission included the desire to spread the word about self-leadership and I anticipated that I would have to train people in classes and seminars, so I joined a speakers' club and got to the stage where public speaking was sought out by me, rather than avoided. Later, I became a facilitator of this kind of material at a local comprehensive school. I had found a noble purpose and invested my time, my ego and my money in achieving it.

This approach works.

Conscience and the Third Resolution

It could rightly be said that the following paragraphs could equally well be placed under the Second Resolution, but they are placed here as a reminder that *character supports a noble purpose*. Indeed, it could also be said that a noble purpose can create and support character. While the two can be exclusive, they create synergistic, interdependent excellence when both are simultaneously demonstrated at their highest level.

A noble purpose requires a conscious application of conscience. Any murmuring from that inner voice which always tells us the truth, any rumbling of disquiet from our personal Jiminy Cricket that suggests that the purpose is not as noble as first thought, is the signal to walk away. This, I feel, was the signal ignored by so many politicians, police officers and the like who strayed from an otherwise decent, honourable and noble path into the self-serving 'end justifies the means' route to personal disaster and public distaste.

Being a good person means being honest, telling the truth, and working at the highest level of productivity and integrity. All of the time. Being a good person does NOT require the input of a PR consultant.

Charles Hobbs stated that the epitome of integrity (or in his terminology 'congruence') was to do the right thing in the right way at the right time whether you wanted to or not. E M Gray described successful people in a similar way, saying that successful people did the things unsuccessful people didn't want to do – they didn't want to do them either, but their distaste for the task was subordinated to the greater good. In other words, they did what they disliked because, in the end, it created the results they were looking for. But I suspect it also meant, as in the First Resolution, NOT doing the things which they wanted to do, because doing those things would get in the way.

People start working for noble purposes for different reasons. I suspect that when asked in interviews that eternal question "Why do you want this job/career/opportunity?" replies usually skirt around serving the public/company, doing something to contribute to the betterment of society/the company, and so on. The truth is that some people mean what they say: others want a career with great promotion prospects and financial returns (selfish) and others just want to do the job because it needs to be done and they value the opportunity to do it. In many cases there would be an element of all three motives in our seeking this work, and there is nothing wrong with admitting that. In my own case, serving the public was the last thing on my mind when I sought to join the police force – I wanted excitement in the form of car chases, fisticuffs and villain-catching. But in the interview I said things about community, serving, etc. (Cut me some slack – I was 24, and I wasn't as learned and ethical then as I am now.)

But here's my take on things when it comes to taking on a noble purpose as opposed to a 'job'.

When we are young, most of us just want to be a Hero or Heroine - someone worthy or deserving of respect, a positive authority figure who does something spectacularly good. It may be less of a motivation for some, but even the most quiet, introverted individual would like to be a hero just a little bit, or for a little while. Psychologists might say this is an emotional need for significance. Once we get into our role or job we chose different routes to achieving that objective, but there it is. The best within us drives the best of us towards a desire to be a Hero or Heroine.

Unfortunately, sometimes we forget that being one of the heroes means compliance with some sort of a Code of Conduct. In a moment of excitement, anger, stress, overwork or other influence, our standards slip and we fall short. Occasionally people fall so far short as to be criminally liable for their actions. And that is a shame. When good guys fall victim to a failure to act in accordance with a principled Code, we all lose something.

In 2014 the Home Office in the UK published a new Code of Conduct for police officers. I make no apologies for reproducing it here as I feel it represents a Code for 'heroes'. Read it carefully. Is there anything so wrong in its content? Isn't compliance with this code exactly what you should expect of a police officer? Or of yourself, context permitting?

Honesty and integrity

I will be honest and act with integrity and will not compromise or abuse my position.

Authority, respect and courtesy

I will act with self-control and tolerance, treating members of the public and colleagues with respect and courtesy.

I will not abuse my powers or authority and I will respect the rights of all individuals.

Equality and diversity

I will act with fairness and impartiality and will not discriminate unlawfully or unfairly.

Use of force

I will only use force as part of my roles and responsibilities, and only to the extent that it is necessary, proportionate and reasonable in all the circumstances.

Orders and instructions

I will only give and carry out lawful orders and instructions.

I will follow all reasonable instructions and abide by force policies.

Work and responsibilities

I will be diligent in the exercise of my duties and responsibilities.

Confidentiality

I will treat information with respect and access or disclose it only in the proper course of my work..

Fitness for duty

I will ensure when at work or on duty that I am fit to carry out my responsibilities.

Conduct

I will behave in a manner which does credit to my force and strengthens public confidence in policing.

I will report any action taken against me for a criminal offence, any conditions imposed on me by a court, and the receipt of any penalty notice.

Challenging and reporting improper behaviour

I have a positive obligation to report, challenge or take action against the conduct of colleagues which I believe have fallen below the Standards of Professional Behaviour set out in this Code.

Seriously, compliance with this is of course a legal requirement for police officers under the conduct regulations, but if you and I act in accordance with what our expectations would be of a good guy/hero, would we ever fall foul? These codes are, after all, the way professionals (doctors and lawyers) are expected to behave.

Look at the elements of this Code. It talks of duty, fitness, and compliance with the law of the land. It does not ask anyone to do anything which is wrong, only what they know in their conscience is right and proper.

When all is said and done, when I talk of a conscience-driven noble purpose I am setting you a challenge to aim for the highest professional and personal life standards achievable. If you want to be a hero, you've got to be a hero all the time, or you aren't a hero at all. Being a hero means compliance with your chosen, conscience-driven, values supported personal code of conduct. It means doing the Right Thing so that you can keep on holding the 'human right' to be called "The Right Stuff."

Any readers feeling uncomfortable about what they are reading should now know what action they need to consider if what they are currently doing is something they already know is ignoble, something that is not in keeping with their standards and integrity. Or when they realise that they are serving an otherwise noble purpose for immoral or unethical reasons, or in that sort of fashion. (Noble cause corruption, in other words.)

Stop.

Whatever you are doing that is immoral, unethical, illegal, undesirable, unconscionable, lazy or whatever, stop doing it now.

I'm not saying you should come clean and publicly acknowledge your wrongdoing – that may undermine your intention to move forward on a better road because of the negative consequences of such an overt admission, but just stop doing whatever it is/was that you were doing that you knew to be wrong.

Stop it Now.

Start living your whole life in accordance with the objective behind your designed or accepted code. Decide upon and commit to living in accordance with the standards you expect to comply with when you choose your purpose, and your part in executing and achieving it. And stop making excuses when you fail, as you occasionally will. Just accept the consequences fully, and move on.

We fail ourselves when we see another professional fail and accept the argument, "Well, if he/she does that, we can do it, too". Even as we say it we know we are lying to ourselves. Our conscience kicks in and shouts 'NO!' at the top of its voice. Listening to that voice ensures our noble purpose remains our focus, and ensures that we remain capable of serving it. That takes character.

Let your conscience dictate your own Code of Ethics and remind you to comply with your Personal Mission Statement, which we covered in Chapter Three.

By the way. If you DO fail – and you will, as have I – take the time to acknowledge that failure, and then forgive yourself. Stuff happen and take it from me, we all make mistakes, including even our accusers.

Talents, Skills, Knowledge and Experience

Occasionally people get asked 'what are you good at?' and, as any NLP practitioner would tell you, the eyes lift upwards in the direction of the individual's preferred 'memory-access' area in a strenuous effort to recall what their talents, skills, experience and knowledge are. They desperately seek the answer in the recesses of their mind and it is hard to find. Modesty may get in the way, but sometimes they forget what the answer is and have to give the question some deeper consideration. In truth, they're asked to consider that question so rarely that they can't immediately answer it.

This creates a problem; if they don't know what their talents (etc.) are they can't utilise them properly, so how do they know that what they are doing is the best use of their time, effort and resources?

You have spent many years in training, learning new skills and adapting them to suit new situations. You have exercised those skills in many diverse circumstances and as a consequence of simply 'existing' you have had to conquer the uncommon, the unexpected and the downright strange. Every time you have done that you have developed as an individual and, more often than not, as a team member, too. Thinking about that for a while, perhaps it's time for you to take stock and itemise what you have experienced, learned, discovered and executed.

Imagine you are writing a curriculum vitae/résumé with a view to getting the job that you've always wanted. You will put the extra effort into the task and you will try that little bit harder to make sure that your prospective employer is going to choose you because of the fantastic things that you've done. Take a while, now, to put something together. Aim for 100 events, certificates, courses and achievements.

Look at each and separately list what talents and skills you need to apply to obtain them. You'll be asked to consider these later in this chapter, and even if you don't use them later, you'll be impressed and even astonished by how great you are. (But remember – avoid hubris, be honest.) Spend time reminding yourself just what you have achieved, and what that means – the knowledge, experience, talents and potential that you have, put into words that you can use to remind you just what you have been capable of – and therefore that of which you are still capable. The objective? Finding out what you possess that you can use to serve others, and to discover (or rediscover) your own noble purpose.

By the way – you can be brutally honest because there is no point in being modest when you're only looking to impress yourself.

Applying the Third Resolution - Service

Naturally I would expect you to decide upon your own 'service project' but you may be like me in that you occasionally need a push to identify where you might apply your efforts, skills, talents and so on.

Starting 'close in', what service could you provide for yourself? Could you apply the First Resolution a little more consistently? Noble purpose can include just *being* noble. Nobility is a word that implies that you possess a sense of honour and a set of guiding principles with which you act in congruence at all times, a sense of greater personal integrity than the 'average Joe'. To me, being the best you can be produces an excellent role model. As role models are copied by others who choose to model you – including those who are still being conditioned (the young and immature) – the better *you* are, the better your 'followers' become. Being an example of excellence and a guiding light is often as great a service as any more open and salient act.

As an individual, you must also consider your 'noble purpose', which is a purpose that tends to transcend the immediate self and circle of family and friends. Identify it, strive towards its successful manifestation, daily wherever possible. More on that in due course.

Next, your family. Having decided to be a role model to all, they benefit in that way. Next, you actively encourage your family to be better, to be the best that they can be. This requires care and objectivity.

Expecting your family to be the best that they can be also requires recognition of one important fact – *your* best is not necessarily *their* best. They may choose a different path to your own in becoming what they want to be. The most important message that you can give your family is unconditional love first, then unconditional respect for their principled and ethical choices, even if they do not match your 'ideal' for them. I have 4 children. None have followed in their father's footsteps, and their careers currently represent their own interests. As a result, they are happy and so am I.

Let your children be what they want to be, not what you want them to be. If the two match, then good for you both. But a personal focus on encouraging your children to be what *you* wanted to be when you were their age is asking for trouble. Let them go and reap the 'love that returns', rather than push them towards what you want – but away from you.

How about your spouse/partner? They came into your life as complete human beings and you are not going to change them, at least not by conscious effort! Be what you are but let them be what they are, and dutifully help them in that objective. That is noble service.

Help around the home with the chores. You are providing an environment which supports you all, so all should maintain it. Small children should be gently taught (indoctrinated?) into maintaining their 'space' and the communal areas of the home so that all can live there in comfort. That includes careful treatment of facilities like entertainment and communications technology, tools and equipment and general cleanliness. This is service as much as running an international charity. Dag Hammarskjöld, former UN Secretary General, said, "It is more noble to give yourself completely to one individual than to labour diligently for the salvation of the masses."

Nobility and service begins at home. Even if that's as far as your noble purpose and service go, it remains no less noble and respectable than the provision of service to others.

Next, consider your friends. How can you serve them? Considering some of the earlier advice in this book, how about giving them loyalty, honesty, support in their endeavours without undue criticism, and a willingness to listen without judgement. Be there when you are needed and consider whether it might be better to be absent if you are not. An ever-present friend, as one philosopher put it, is a pest. Balance is essential in all things!

Professionally, do the best things at a level of excellence. Do the right thing in the right way at the right time for the right reasons, even when (especially when) it is hardest to do so. Assist your colleagues not only in their work, but in their personal and professional development as well.

To paraphrase Dr Charles Hobbs, "understand and perform congruently with the productive expectations of any organisation through which or for which you perform your services. Focus on your employers' vital priorities and motivate your colleagues to the same end." Make them better in their work and accept advice and assistance as they try to do the same for you.

You may not enjoy your work but it is (nearly) always a noble purpose. Notwithstanding that you (usually) choose the work you do and should be enjoying it at least most of the time, never forget that honest work is noble by definition. You have customers, even if they do not pay you directly. If you clean streets, make your streets the cleanest. People may not notice a clean street until it is pointed out to them but watch them bemoan the opposite. Take responsibility for the quality of your service – that is noble.

Be an example to others in your community. Your environment includes the public environment within which you spend much of your time. If that involves the occasional picking up of other peoples' litter, go to it. Make sure the authorities are made aware of the effects of other peoples' lower standards where appropriate, so that they can take the actions for which they have responsibility. Drive carefully and with consideration for others (which is valuable self-preservation advice, too).

Take part in community projects that interest you, and in social activities which develop you as an individual and which are in areas where you can contribute your own expertise, talents and skills where there is a need.

Service has been defined thus:

"Service is the virtue that distinguished the great of all times and which they will be remembered by.

It places a mark of nobility upon its disciples. It is the dividing line which separates the two great groups of the world --- those who help and those who hinder, those who life and those who lean, those who contribute and those who only consume.

How much better it is to give than to receive.

Service in any form is comely and beautiful.

To give encouragement, to impart sympathy, to show interest, to banish fear, to build self-confidence and awaken hope in the hearts of others, in short to love them and to show it, is to render the most precious service." (Bryant S Hinckley)

Consider the opening words of the second paragraph – "It places a mark of nobility upon its disciples." Disciple – a term derived from and comparable to the term 'discipline' because to be a disciple is to be disciplined in the philosophy being followed. Ignore any religious connotation of the word – focus instead upon its true meaning (remembering as you do so that the Bible was not written in English nor, I suspect, Latin). Discipline does not work in a vacuum. You must have something to be disciplined about. Being disciplined with a view to providing service is essential if it is to be *effective* service.

Nor does service need to be overly concerned with people outside your circle of concern. In fact, service to those most familiar to is often the hardest to provide yet the most rewarding. Providing anonymous or even acknowledged service to the masses, to specific charities or to smaller groups is valuable, noble and rewarding. Totally giving of yourself to one or two other people can be the most rewarding and noble service possible.

I recall reading a book by Blaine Lee called "The Power Principle" and there was within a story about a man with a wholly dependent (physically and mentally) brother, who could not speak or move unassisted. The writer told of how he would introduce girlfriends to his brother, and all would resist the introduction. In time, this man discovered his wife because of the way she gave of herself to this disadvantaged child – she fed him, talked to him, and made him laugh. (Even as I write that, the story brings a lump to my throat as much as it did when I first read it.)

The lesson here is that disciplined service to one, or to many, is a rewarding way of living in accordance with the Third Resolution. There are no restrictions on the numbers you serve. Just serve.

Success – _True_ Success – Results from Service

The key distinction between the success brought about by self-interest and that resulting from giving, is the legacy that service-orientated purpose brings about. Self-interested actions will be recognised only for as long as the person executing them sticks around. Routinely, once such people are gone they are usually forgotten except when something negative needs to be said about them.

One writer told the story of a man who ran a company with an iron hand and a selfish soul. After 40 years of progressing up the ladder by walking on others and ultimately heading the company with the management style of Attila the Hun, he retired. The following day he went back to the building in which he had spent so much time – and the security guard wouldn't let him in. Now, the guard had the authority provided to him by those in charge, who were in turn now free of the former chief's influence and power, and the guard was able to treat the ex-boss the way he had been treated – the way ALL the staff had been treated. The staff's combined hatred for this man legitimised and supported the treatment, indeed the contempt now shown towards him. He had lost the respect he thought he had earned, by discovering that all he had truly earned was fear and contempt.

Now compare that to someone like Gandhi, who is still venerated nearly 70 years after he died. Or Lincoln, or even Kennedy, who had his faults but was respected for the legacies he left. The common thread for all, and for others like them who left a legacy is this – they were all successful, and by that I include success in terms of fame and financial success, but they also left something behind that was beyond that temporal achievement. They left behind something positive that carried on after their untimely deaths. In our three examples they were even assassinated for what they believed in but you do not hear the assassins being venerated by anyone. These great statesmen made changes that benefited all, especially the powerless.

It isn't just statesmen and stateswomen who leave legacies. Scientists, entrepreneurs, businessmen and women, teachers, writers – all can leave behind positive legacies while still achieving the accepted trappings of success. The richest people in history are seldom remembered, but those who are fondly remembered were invariably philanthropists, giving away as much as they earned either directly, or in terms of external contribution.

They all combined their professional 'gain' and progress with an equally strong dedication to other projects, projects which served others either in terms of the provision of charitable services, or by teaching the disadvantaged how to be better. And while they did get respect, wealth and power for doing so (thus covering their WII-FM need), they did not do so primarily for that reason. They did it to serve a noble purpose outside of their own needs.

For many, that legacy might only be professional. They might serve in a profession or blue-collar field and decide that their efforts should be focused in that area. That is good, and many will be remembered for doing so.

But the ultimate legacy, many would say and few would argue against, is the legacy left with your family. Success within a family outweighs money and fame and can last for *generations* - so start there. Serve your family, give them what they *need* first, and then provide them with what they *want* when to do so serves their best interests. Love them unconditionally, treat them with respect, and define boundaries that help them develop their own good character so that they can, in turn, define their own boundaries having learned how to do it properly – from you.

Affirm them by recognising that they are different, but equal. I have a friend who sent his children to the same school. The first children were sports prodigies, but the third was more academically inclined. When the school told the father that they were 'disappointed' because the younger child wasn't so sporty, the father immediately took the boy away and to another school where this son's strengths could develop without the false societal comparisons with his brothers that were wholly irrelevant to the younger boy's success. I find that my friend's action was amazingly principled. Could you do that? *Would* you do that?

Family first.

Applying the Third Resolution - Purpose

Just as goals direct us towards achievement in specific areas, a noble purpose is something towards which the great achievers direct their efforts. For the famous and those with power, such a purpose can be quite magnificent — building giant bridges, setting up multi-billion dollar charitable foundations, starting new service industries or saving refugees from torture and slavery. For most of us, such achievement is beyond our reach. One might consider such missions as beyond our capabilities, and for me there is nothing wrong in believing that to be so because if that wasn't true we'd all be doing it. We'd all be doing something magnificent or we'd all be famous. For most of us our reach is, by circumstance, design or fate, much shorter. But that does not mean that it isn't there.

*Sidebar: And looking at it logically, if we were all superb achievers there'd be no-one TO serve, no employees and assistance to help us achieve. **There is nobility in all service, however small, and there is no shame in being the little cog that makes a larger machine work.***

In terms of the discovery of a noble purpose, we usually recognise that something 'floats our boat'. Some cause, activity or project *means* something to us, is important to us, is something we care massively about. Discovering what that is, is the first step in defining your purpose. At the end of this chapter I will invite you to discover that purpose, but for now imagine a life where you are spending your time doing what you love, with people who have a similar or complementary objective and are equally enthusiastic about that work, and in a way that you can clearly see does make a positive difference to other people.

How would you feel if you were doing that? How would you feel if you were doing that and getting *paid* to do it? How hard do you work? What standards are you demonstrating? How productive are you? Are you stressed – at all?

I would imagine and indeed guarantee that if all those things are happening in your life, then you are happy. BUT – taking the lessons on character into account – if you are doing these things wholly out of self-interest, is your purpose as noble, and if not, are you as dedicated to it as you make out? If the purpose is wholly designed to serve your self-interest, are you stressed?

Noble purpose certainly does serve ambition, but it does so only in the sense that the ambition that we serve is now a purpose that lies beyond our own interests – we seek to achieve but we do so to benefit not just ourselves, but others as well. Our families, our communities, our customers and clients, our world.

Think about these words when considering your own application of the Third Resolution. Is your own intended service something by which you will be, or could be remembered? This goes back to the 'what's in it for me' question. If a sense of peace, contentment and gratitude are the results of your intended service then even if you get paid for it, you are on the right track. Critics of many personal development writers and philosophers do so out of a sense of derision about the money they make from their work – but who is to say that they do not deserve to use their talents as a means to live well? Or that the value of their work is not representative of the customers' satisfaction with what they buy? And are their earnings any less deserved than those of a politician, entertainer or sportswoman? Are yours?

Seek out your noble purpose, and then work diligently towards its fulfilment. There is no reason why you should not do so, and every reason why you should.

Stress and the Third Resolution

The Chemistry of Stress

The brain is electro-chemical in construction and in the way it works. There are 4 well-known neuro-transmitters which control our thoughts, as it were, in that they affect the way we feel and behave to a large degree. They are:

1. Adrenaline – the fight drug. This gives us the instant energy to run from danger and is as old as us. It was designed to help us run from fast moving predators but now makes us run from large piles of paper (sorry, I'm being a bit critical of the compensation culture there….). Post-danger you get the shakes because, having used all the fuel, the body is exhausted.
2. Cortisol – this is the flight drug. It is an endurance chemical that allows us to carry on as long as we need to get out of trouble.

These are both necessary 'drugs' and they have to kick in when our brains have told us is something that is about to happen presents a danger to us. In other words, we're about to suffer something 'bad'.

3. Serotonin – the happy drug. We're all familiar with this.
4. Dopamine –This is what kicks in when we have a success and want to feel great about it. It is also the drug of addiction, which is why we like to seek more of it through the pursuit of little and large victories.

These latter drugs are the counters to the bad but necessary drugs of Adrenaline and Cortisol. If we can get more of these than we get of the former two narcotics (*sic*), we don't suffer from stress in the acknowledged, poor fashion.

The Third Resolution Response

Hans Selye, an expert in stress, wrote that there were two kinds of stress. They were *distress,* which is an understandably negative and debilitating form of pressure on the individual; and *eustress*, which is diametrically opposite in that it was pressure that benefited the individual. There's no need to further delve into distress – we all know it when we feel it.

Eustress consists of two parts. The prefix *eu-* derives from the Greek word meaning either "well" or "good." When attached to the word *stress*, it literally means "good stress".

Describing eustress would involve identifying pressures that make us feel good. It's the deadline we know we will meet, it's an important piece of work we do that we know will cause positive effect, and that we know we can produce to a high standard. It's playing the important game with the confidence that we will be victorious. It's having a message to spread and possessing the opportunity to do so. It's publishing a new work, and it's discovering a new way of doing things that makes for better results.

The common thread I'm sure you will notice is this – all of those activities involve the possession and manifestation of the one thing Selye himself described as the 'cure' for stress. He said that the real cause of a long, healthy and happy (un-distressed) life is the "making of contributions, of having meaningful projects that are personally exciting and (which) contribute to and bless the lives of others."

I suggest In those words you find the ultimate answer to the question WII-FM?

Service and noble purpose.

We serve ourselves most of all when we execute on the Third Resolution, when we execute on a firm foundation of the First and Second Resolutions by diligently and competently providing conscience driven, principled service. We know that we feel great when we act in that way, but part of that feeling must be in the knowledge that what we are doing is appreciated by, or at least benefits, other people. We like to be acknowledged for what we do, even when we do anonymous service and we are only acknowledged for it by our own ego.

When we serve, we do get a lift – our Serotonin and Dopamine levels are given an upwards shove and that, many scientists believe, is a healthy way to counter the 'anti-bodies' of unhappiness, Adrenaline and Cortisol.

Find meaning in what you do, and stress is diminished.

Please take the time to discover the meaning in your life by identifying your own purpose and opportunities for the provision of service to others.

Service/Purpose Exercise

1.   What am I capable of? What do I love to do?

The answers to your other exercises might be of assistance. What you've already identified as 'talents' might push you to finding the answers.

2. How can I serve with the talents, skills, knowledge and experience I possess?

In architecture form follows function – that is, the design must suit the purpose. You wouldn't dig a hole to gain height, would you? Do your talents, skills and other resources point in a specific, even a vague direction which, if followed, will take you where you want to be?

3. What charities, institutions, and associations (etc.) would I be interested in serving?

There are some. Look up charities and your preferred field in Google. They're there. If they aren't – start your own!

4. Why aren't I serving them already?

Truthfully. Is it fear? If so, just do it! If the answer is geographical find a way of getting closer to the charity, or even bringing the charity closer to you.

5. What would they expect or require of me?

If you don't know, here's a tip from an investigation consultant – ask. That'll be £250, thank you.

6. How much of my time am I willing to provide?

This can vary according to your own situation (including financial resources) but again, only you know what the answer is.

7. Who must I contact to start providing that service?

Back to Google.

8. When will I make that contact?

Ahem. When would 'now' be a good time, for the second time of asking?

9. How should I prepare for that contact?

Ask yourself not only what you need to know, but also what you anticipate they will need to know about you. That way you'll be ready when they ask the question 'WII-FM'? (See, it works both ways.)

10. Who else can I serve?

Now, did you include family in your previous answers? If not, please go back and think about what you did......

Serving Suggestions

Join a charity as a helper, and work up to organiser level

Provide specialist training related to your profession/hobby in local community colleges

Join your professional/vocational body and serve its interests

Write articles on your expertise

Start a website and do any or all of the above

Volunteer as a bus driver for a community service

Do the accounts for a local organisation

Do an elderly neighbour's shopping, or help them do it online

Do talks for local organisations

Give more to charity

Have a sort out and donate unwanted clothes/'stuff' to charity

Dig someone's garden

Do a better job at work – seek, research and help implement improvements in processes

Take more responsibility for housework

Join the PTA

Give your first class seat to a young mother

Provide support for a colleague without being asked

Buy lunch for a homeless person

Plan and execute a charity event

Serve your family without complaint

Hold your partner for two minutes and talk to him/her

Wash your partner's car without being asked

Exercise patience

START a charity

Keep your environment clean, tidy and organised

Listen without judgment

Set an example

Buy someone a copy of a book that will help. 😊

Take the lead on a table full of strangers

Live ethically

Apologise

Say Thank You

Be punctual

Give blood

Keep your promises

And many more – use your imagination

Chapter Six - The Importance of a Mission Statement in Executing the Three Resolutions

When you discover your mission, you will feel its demand. It will fill you with enthusiasm and a burning desire to get to work on it.
W. Clement Stone

The corporate world is full of mission statements. I fully anticipate that anyone subjected by their own organisations to the triumphant trumpeting that surrounded the publication of theirs probably responded with some resignation. After all, who has ever been consulted on the content?

I like mission statements but, like you, I sighed with dismay when I read my last employer's declaration of what the organisation stood for, having experienced the way individuals in that organisation – individuals who must have had input into that corporate mission – routinely failed to live up to the expectations they were imposing upon me. Of course, no-one had asked me my opinion.

Having said that, if you look at these declarations objectively, you have to confess that if the organisation and its staff (and its creators) *could* live up to those fine words, then it would undeniably be a great place to work and to serve.

Writers on leadership (Kouzes and Posner, Collins, Covey, etc.) have consistently made the case that the great, long standing and successful companies have mission statements. However, they go further and emphasise that those great, lasting companies not only *have* them but they conduct their business activities *in accordance with* them. It would be naïve to observe that the odd individual, or the odd decision, fails to demonstrate religious compliance with the corporate mission statement but, in the main, these great companies are successful because they believe in and comply with their missions and value statements. Top to bottom, inside and outside.

What I am going to propose is that you write one for yourself, one with which *you* know you can comply because it is *yours*.

What is a Personal Mission Statement?

The easiest way to illustrate the concept of a mission statement is to ask you to consider the Constitution of the United States. Whether you admire or dislike that nation is irrelevant, as is the specific content. If you prefer you can use the motto of France (Liberty, Equality, Fraternity), North Carolina State (To Be, Rather Than to Seem), or any other national, corporate, school or voluntary organisation's mission statement. The reason I am using the US example is because I understand it enough to use it as an example and, I suspect, so do you. And like any other mission statement, you will note that religious observance is frequently absent.

The US Constitution is a written document. It is the foundation for the way that nation creates its laws and governs its society, and upon which that society bases its conduct and culture. It is a fall-back document against which all US laws are tested. If a proposed law is not 'Constitution-compliant' it cannot be passed. (A least in principle – others may find loopholes in the argument.) As always following a mass shooting (and that line is regrettably always up to date), there is another argument in the US over gun control because the second amendment 'right to bear arms' is so strictly read and applied by many as a constitutional right, such that any effort to even monitor gun ownership is resisted. For many Americans any threat to the Constitution is a threat to America and to its citizens, which demonstrates how emotionally important it is to them. Servicemen and women fight for it, and they die for it.

Viewers of the US TV Drama 'The West Wing' will have noted how important it is to the characters and to the plotlines. There is a moving moment in the final episode. President Bartlett, a father of three daughters, had an assistant, an Afro-American named Charlie who Bartlett had engaged as his personal assistant. Over time, Bartlett came to see Charlie as the son he never had, and their relationship was such that on conclusion of his term of office Bartlett handed his careworn, personal copy of the Constitution to Charlie as the latter left for law school. Knowing what the Constitution means to a President, you can imagine how important and emotional a scene this was, at least to American viewers.

But most relevantly for our purposes, the US Constitution is a document or credo which the President swears to uphold when taking office, and it is a document to which new citizens swear allegiance.

It is also intended to be unchanging. There would be no point in having a mission or constitution which swayed in the wind of popularity, changed conventions, morality swings or religious variety. The idea is that there should be something unchanging, something upon which the people can rely in order to live without confusion about the future.

A Personal Mission Statement (PMS) is intended to follow that intention: namely being an unchanging central credo or code of conduct with which you comply, and against which you can measure that compliance. It is a document (or other source of reference) in which you clearly state your rules for living, and then live them.

"What about those amendments you mentioned?" I hear you ask.

Life happens. When the USA set out its Constitution it did so in 'its' present, specifically in the aftermath of a War of Independence where half of the continent remained unexplored and unpopulated, and where the population was relatively small. No electricity, few enemies, a settled society that was new to having its own destiny in its hands. The Constitutional Committee created, in that moment, what it felt was enough.

Then things changed, society developed, people learned new things and science made new discoveries. As a result, amendments were made because of new knowledge and newly enlightened attitudes. Occasionally there may have been an 'Ah, but!' moment when a phrase or paragraph in the original document needed clarification. Lawyers probably got involved. That is the way of existence, and so it will be when you create your own mission. (Except you won't need any lawyers.)

For an individual, changes come as relationships develop and the ultimate change for a single adult would come the day you fall in love, which leads to getting married and having children. That is a massive change that will undoubtedly permit an amendment – although you can make a PMS that anticipates such events. Not only would such a circumstance permit an amendment, it would create an opportunity for the creation of a partnership/family PMS. The same principles of creation and implementation would apply, but now as a partnership or group PMS.

I have already encouraged you to seek out, identify and define your personal values. My objective was to help you discover what is important to you so that you could behave in such a way as to get more of that. Happiness *is* achievement of what is important to you, or at least avoidance of what threatens that which is important to you. And in **Three Resolutions** terms, one of the things which threatens your living in accordance with your values – is you.

Living with integrity means living in keeping with your values because you have decided that your values represent your 'truth'. Fully understanding integrity is essential because if you are to be disciplined, you have to be disciplined about *something*. If you have nothing against which to measure your efforts, how will you know you have achieved integrity? Your values, already defined by you, are the foundation of your PMS.

The Personal Mission Statement is *your* opportunity to set or raise your own standards, the standards against which you will measure your integrity, and the standards which, when met, will create that contentment, happiness and success you seek.

Your mission statement is an extension, a legitimate extension of the value statements you made earlier. In fact, the simplest of Mission Statements is a list of values, set alongside their definitions and behaviours. But if values dictate how you are going to love your life, the PMS is somewhere you can define what you are going to do with your life while living in that way. It is a way of stating what you are going to do *with* your values.

"I will be healthy and fit (so that......)"

"I will manage my money carefully (so that.......)

"I will be a loving wife and mother (so that.....)"

Your values are a means to an end, but not necessarily the end in themselves.

That 'end' is the ultimate, most important aspect of the personal mission statement, and the most important parallel with the Constitution example.

When challenges arise in your commitment to any endeavour, including to the way in which you wish to live your life, you may wonder what to do. There will undoubtedly be moments when two or more competing actions are available to you, and you feel stuck between those options. The PMS and your values statements are where you find the answer.

For example: suppose you work in the financial sector and a respected colleague asks you to cook the books, to make false accounting entries, to lie for him or to merely exaggerate a product's effectiveness in order to sell it to an unsuspecting customer. You are financially challenged and the potential personal or professional rewards look interesting. What do you do?

PMS can be a guide whenever a difficult, or apparently difficult, decision is called for. Any confusion or crisis of conscience over what to do next can be resolved through recourse to your Mission Statement, because that document should, if properly drafted, prove to you that you have already made that decision. In fact, your PMS can be your written conscience, it's potentially that powerful.

For example, in the financial sector example above, you would (I hope) have already decided that your honesty and integrity were too important to you for you to compromise them in the interests of a fast, dishonest buck, or you would know what to refer to in order to remind you what you had decided.

I have used my own PMS that way. Occasionally I won't want to exercise. On countless occasions, a serendipitous reading of my own Mission Statement has sparked me into my Lycra and onto my bike.

Writing your PMS can be challenging, but anecdotally those who have taken the time and put the concentrated, conscience-directed effort into doing so have all recognised the benefit. I know I have.

The Benefits and Consequences of a Personal Mission Statement

A properly considered, carefully drafted and beautifully presented PMS looks wonderful in a frame, in the front of your personal planner or, for those like me with an acceptable level of digital ability, on the home screen of your smartphone. However, just as a ship is safe in the harbour but was not created just to sit there, a laboriously penned PMS has a purpose other than (a) being a completed 'to-do' and (b) looking pretty.

You don't write a PMS and leave it at that. This has been a failure that many have reportedly made. Just as so many mission statements in the corporate world have been created, widely marketed and then ignored, there is a possibility that you will fall into the trap of preparing a PMS only to then ignore it. The objective in making and possessing a PMS is that it should have an emotional impact on you, an impact so great that once it exists it drives you to committed compliance.

There are quite a few good reasons for creating a PMS.

First, as you consider the value statements and lifelong goals and legacies that will eventually represent its content, you should be taking the time and making the effort to look deep inside yourself to discover the 'true you' and what the 'true you' needs. The most impactive PMS is one that sobers you, even brings you to tears. I'll be frank and suggest that such an emotional connection is rare, but if the words you write make you cry because of their beauty and connection to your very soul, you have your perfect PMS. For most of us, we are there when we look at what we have written and just 'know' that this is 'it', that we have in front of us our ideal 'me' and describes what 'me' stands for and what 'me' is going to do. It is at once both sobering, in that we have set a challenge and now we know we must meet it, and exciting in that we suddenly see a clear way forward.

Secondly, it is something that creates a personal accountability, something against which you measure your actions and progress from the day you conclude its creation and commit to its content, and subject to any amendments of the kind I mentioned earlier, it should do so until the day you die.

Next, for those with the confidence to allow it, it can be made public so that not only will you want to comply with it, those around you will, supportively or maliciously (it doesn't really matter which!), make sure you live by it.

Some writers have different takes on this. If you have a goal – and compliance with your PMS is a goal – then you have two options. Keep it to yourself so that your failures remain personal, or spread the word so that the judgement of others is utilised as a tool for compliance. Some say that if it is a 'stop' goal (e.g. smoking) tell the world, but if it is an achievement goal, keep it to yourself because others may wish to hold you back. Those who support you will help by keeping you honest, and those who bear you malice will make it pointedly obvious when you falter. If you are willing, and you recognise the difference between and the benefits and disadvantages of both approaches, then make your PMS – and your desire to comply – public.

Once it exists the PMS, like the Constitution, is a marker for your behaviour. I've already detailed how a PMS contains the rules for your future, but now let's look at the practicalities, and for that I base the following on my own experience.

Like you I occasionally feel under-motivated, tired, stressed and otherwise uninterested in doing something that needs to be done. It can be anything; a work project, a telephone call, taking exercise, writing a book, mowing the lawn, absolutely anything. Now and then, when these things aren't truly important, letting them slide won't be a problem. But when they relate in any way to my self-discipline, professionalism, character, the service I provide to others or my ultimate goals, such malaise is a threat to my integrity. My conscience kicks in and, as I've described before, I start to slip and make excuses for my lack of progress. My conscience is shouted down or ignored.

Then I look up and see my PMS, which I have turned into my computer's wallpaper. (It's also in my planner; and in abbreviated form on a wristband and a dog-tag I had custom made. Oh, and on a badge in icon form. Yes, I am sad. Moving on.)

I read the commitments I have made and I take action. Countless times I have been feeling tired, yet I have got out of bed or off a chair and gone for a run. I've done that because of the commitment I made and because of the physical presence of that reminder. I've made those telephone calls, I've written articles, I've agreed to attending meetings, and I've even spent money. (If you knew me, that one would shock you.)

The power of the PMS is that it supports your conscience. I repeat that because it bears repetition: your conscience has been created by you to support you in making the decisions that need to be made that mean you continue to live in compliance with your values; your conscience is the voice of your integrity. In the same way as your nerves communicate pain when you cut yourself, your conscience only speaks to you when you have threatened to disrespect it by failing to act in keeping with the promises you have made yourself, whether consciously or unconsciously. The PMS represents your promises, and they are promises you made to yourself.

A PMS need not be overly wordy, although I feel I should qualify that statement. Going back to the values exercise in the last chapter, you recall that we chose a word, made it an action statement and then further defined it. A PMS can contain many words, but you can reverse the values process to make it more compact. You can have three words that mean an incredible amount to you because you know the meaning of the hundreds of words that lay behind them.

Even two words can have impact. One example of a young adult's PMS, in the book in the book 'The Seven Habits of Highly Effective Teens' by Sean Covey, simply read 'Nothing Less'. I cannot but guess what life philosophy lies behind that but you can sense the potential and profound impact on the creator's life. In my own experience in delivering such training to young people, I was bowled over by one young man whose PMS read, "Surprise Myself".

Emotionally, and logically, a PMS is something of exceptional value.

How to prepare your Personal Mission Statement in the Context of the Three Resolutions

As the 3Rs apply to your whole life (self, work and relationships, and contribution), it makes sense that a PMS can be created utilising the 3R 'headings' as a guide when drafting it. Remember, the generic 3R headings are

- *Discipline*
- *Character*
- *Service*

In terms of self-discipline you may want to write about your physical self – how you will live in terms of your health and fitness, your personal standards, and so on.

What physical fitness regimen will you apply?

What diet rules will you follow?

What habits will you keep, and what addictions will you deny yourself?

How might you manage your environment with those declarations in mind?

WHY?

When it comes to your work you may consider the specific roles and responsibilities you have and write down how you will perform in those areas.

First, what are those roles and responsibilities?

How will you carry them out? What rules will you set for your own level of performance?

How will you obtain and develop the competencies required to do that work?

What resources might you obtain and maintain – in terms of equipment, location and the people around you (team members, clients, suppliers)?

What character traits will you need, or apply? How will you know you are demonstrating them to yourself and/or to others?

WHY?

Finally, when it comes to contribution you may wish to specify those voluntary groups for whom you provide service, or areas within which you may consider doing that (if you are not already involved in such activity).

Who will you serve? What issues are so important to you that you want to bring them under your influence?

How will you serve? What will you actually DO?

How much time and effort will you contribute? What other resources, e.g. money, will you commit?

What will the end result look like?

WHY?

Interwoven within these three 'headings' you may find ways of expressing how you will relate to the people you live, work and volunteer with.

Who are the people with whom you have personal, professional and social relationships?

How will you treat them? What are your expectations of them?

WHY?

Not everything you write in answer to the above questions will make it onto your final written document – a mission statement with a declaration of how clean you'll keep your bedroom may seem a little twee, and certainly not something you might like to put up in public as a teen – or as an adult, come to think of it - but consideration of such questions might make you adapt your PMS in some way.

Just as a way of illustrating what I mean and demonstrating to you, the reader, that I am committed to what I have written in this book, this is my current PMS. I use it here to show how I've taken the **Three Resolutions** headings and made behavioural statements under each, statements that represent what is important to me.

It reads:

I solemnly recommit to the covenant I made with my mentor - that I will live with integrity, pursue excellence, and live my life in observance of the Three Resolutions.

I am committed to the exercise self-discipline and self-denial

- I regularly and sensibly enjoy exercising my body through running or cycling. I maintain an active, balanced lifestyle with careful eating priorities.
- I seek a healthy body and effective mental acuity. I enjoy exercising my mind, I read broadly to improve my knowledge and my intellect, and I am careful in how I use the media.
- I exercise a disciplined approach towards doing what must be done. I carry out my tasks in the appropriate way, at the appropriate time, and to the highest standard. If I fail in those aims, I am willing to work harder.

I work constantly on my competence and on my character.

- I am committed to living with unquestioned personal integrity, in accordance with my Unifying Principles. I am always honest.
- I project an excellent professional image: I take pride in my appearance, I demonstrate exceptional self-confidence, and I possess, pursue or maintain superior knowledge and competence in my work. I provide quick and effective demonstrably excellent standards, responses and results in any given role or task.
- I exercise personal courage and by doing so I continually enjoy new adventures, challenges and experiences.
- I demonstrate mastery in my driving.
- My actions are always ethical.

I use my talents and resources to serve noble purposes.

- I am an excellent husband, father, friend and colleague – helpful, supportive and, where necessary, forgiving. I am dedicated to the wellbeing of my family and I provide for or support them when they cannot provide for themselves.
- I freely contribute in ways that serve others, and volunteer to that end when time and commitments allow. I give due respect to other people and I make the effort to be loyal to the absent. I remain open-minded and willing to be wrong, and I apologise when necessary.
- I am creating a home environment in which I can take pride, and which serves me in performance of all my roles. I focus my financial resources on investment in that objective, in saving for the future, and in ensuring my own and my family's security, happiness and education.
- Through my behaviour, and by use of the written and spoken word, I spread the philosophy and methodology of Principle-Centred Leadership.

If I haven't been quite as clear in this chapter and in using this illustration as perhaps I could be, let me restate the aim.

Values underpin behaviour; our happiness is served through achievement of results that are representative of our values; our behaviours create those results; the **Three Resolutions** *reinforce those behaviours. There is a thread between commitment to the behaviours that serve the values that represent our true happiness – and success.*

Or, perhaps put more simply, Values dictate behaviours dictate results; therefore, applying the **Three Resolutions** to those behaviours (and perhaps also choosing self-discipline, good character, competence and service *as* values) will get us what we want.

The Reverse Process

As I intimated when turning the **Three Resolutions** sphere inside out with the suggestion that although the **Three Resolutions** should be progressively applied '1 to 3', an alternative perspective when planning your PMS could be to decide what service and purpose you seek to provide and achieve, and to then 'reverse engineer', i.e. move '3 to 1'. Rather than starting 'bottom up' as you do when *applying* the **Three Resolutions**, you should work 'top down' when developing *why* you seek to apply them.

Stating at the bottom might not even be the best approach unless you are really starting out on your personal development, and discovery of a purpose is still to come Planning a PMS 'bottom up' means deciding to be in great physical and mental shape, achieving high levels of self-control, and *then* deciding what competencies you have or intend to obtain.

For the average reader there are some competencies which they already have and are happy with – it's the bottom level where they have most challenges. More commonly for those who have discovered the need for self-improvement they may already be involved in the provision of some kind of service (e.g. a 'job'), but seek an improved personal approach towards that purpose; to widen it, rediscover it, or even to replace it and find new options.

For someone yet to start 'living' and who is in a position to start from scratch, designing a PMS bottom up might be an appropriate approach, whereas those who are pretty content with what they are doing but feel they need a new perspective could start 'top down' and rediscover the new competencies, depth of character and levels of personal discipline that will improve on what they already love to do.

Nevertheless, even for those with an almost completely blank slate, e.g. those starting out in life, or about to start a new life stage (graduates, school leavers, recently unemployed), the reverse approach might be better. The point is – you decide, then go ahead and do it.

A reverse approach, therefore, is planning and writing your Three Resolution-compliant Personal Mission Statement by looking first *not* at Resolution One, but at Resolution Three.

What service do you want to provide, and for whom? Who will benefit and how, including you and your own benefit? Thinking wider than just the service, how will you know when it has been properly provided? How will you know when your mission is on course, even completed? Why do you want to do that?

Having decided on the 'end' first, the next questions can be addressed.

What skills and talents do you possess or can seek out, in order that the mission/service/purpose can be achieved successfully and effectively? What character traits would a person who provides that service, or is capable of providing that service, need to possess and demonstrate? How and where will you obtain them?

Finally, the disciplines.

Having decided on the skills and character traits, what do you need to do, or not do, in order to support and nurture the competencies and character traits that you have identified are needed for your ultimate mission to succeed?

Writing your PMS this way can be both exciting and alarming. Exciting because you identify what you are *for* before you even consider how you're going to make it happen. And alarming because having completed the first task you might realise just what a challenge you've set for yourself. This calls for some deep emotional consideration – on the one hand you don't want to frighten yourself off from your desired outcome, but you don't want to set yourself up for failure. One way to avoid this is to make sure it is **your** mission and not someone else's mission wrapped up to look like yours – you have to discover your own.

The Personal Mission Statement is YOUR document (if you have decided to write it down) or motto, and so it *must* be a reflection of **your own words** and emotions. You can read other people's mission statements to get an idea of how you may want to create yours, but above all, *above everything,* the content and intent **MUST** be your own. You will never passionately pursue someone else's mission in the same way you pursue your own. And it is this passion, the commitment you make to your *own* mission, that you seek.

As I have alluded to you before, you won't lose weight until *you* want to; you will never perform well at work until *your* passion and dedication is aroused within you; you will not contribute in the same way to *other* peoples' causes as much as you will to one you have chosen yourself.

Create something *great!*

Chapter Seven – An Academic History of the Three Resolutions

The following chapter contains references to religion and may stop you reading further, but please read on for reasons that will soon become clear to you. Instead of putting the book down, take the view not that values are religious but that religions adopt values. Recognise that religious references are often merely metaphors for explaining common sense. Take the 'religion' out of your 'belief window' and just read this next section for what it is, a history behind the thinking behind the Three Resolutions.

Dr Stephen Covey (1932-2012) was born into a business family, and was expected to enter the family business when he grew up and started work after college. As luck would have it he discovered that his own calling was not going to be commercially-orientated; as a result of input from others he found that what he was meant to do was teach. And what he was destined to teach was not simply what he, himself had learned from others. Instead, he was to learn for himself what he was to later teach the wider world.

His own discoveries in teaching method and how to live a principled life, along with the studies he carried out in order to obtain his educational awards, led him to the discovery of a philosophy of personal and interpersonal leadership that has not been matched – often quoted or copied, perhaps, but not matched – in the 30 years since it was first published.

After many years of teaching he left mainstream education to start his own leadership training company, first as Stephen R Covey and Associates and later as the Covey Leadership Centre. In 1997 CLC merged with a company called Franklin-Quest that had been founded by his friend and co-learner Hyrum W. Smith, that merger creating the now well-known and respected FranklinCovey, a global   company with millions of satisfied learners in over 140 countries. He passed away in 2012 after complications arising from a recent cycling accident – he counselled living life in crescendo, as if the best is yet to come, and at 79 he was still on a mountain bike. He lived his credo.

In an effort to improve your comprehension of the kind of person Stephen was I looked out for some good quotes by famous people about him, his life, and what he meant to them. There were many, but in the end I concluded I should use my own.

"I credit him with who I am today, because reading his words improved my self-understanding, self-esteem and ultimately self-expression. I grew from being a

nervous, undirected man into a self-guided missile. I can talk as I write, proactively thinking about what I am going to say before or as I say it, rarely using 'gap' words (sort of, actually, like and "obviously" – my most hated new gap word). Being able to communicate clearly, and with the needs of the individual I am with being taken into consideration, has helped me achieve a lot. I became a 'life-long learner', seeking out education, gaining qualifications, becoming more and more professionally relevant. I have overcome or addressed challenges because of Stephen, including the emotional upheaval of being told I had cancer at the age of 45.

I've written books and had them lauded. I have become head of my professional body. I ran half-marathons. I developed along many other goal-led paths. I learned to teach, and I coached.

All because I found a man who told me what I needed to hear. And he kept doing so for 20 years. What a debt I owe."

That eulogy may seem a little self-indulgent but it accurately reflects those produced by many of his readers, and certainly of those who knew him most. But, moving on.

It is for his books that Dr Covey is most famous, and for me the developing history of those books is of great interest.

Dr Covey was a religious man, and his earliest books were written in that context.

His first 'real' publication was entitled 'The Spiritual Roots of Human Relations (1970)'. He described it as a book intended to address the roots of the problems people face in the world and was written, as is clear from the tone and content, for students of his church.

The book was published when he was a 'mere' 38 years old and looked at a number of 'roots' or bases for living, specifically vision (purpose), commitment to that vision, understanding and example, communication and, finally, self-discipline. The book's chapter headings reflected the intent described, but one of the chapters under the generic heading of 'Vision' was entitled **"The Three Temptations; Understanding and Overcoming."** This was the 'in-print' birth of Covey's **Three Resolutions**, which were themselves, as I understand it, the result of listening to an authority within that church. In this chapter Dr Covey wrote of three temptations, calling them

- Flesh vs. the Spirit, or Appetite.
- Appearance vs. Reality
- Aspiration vs. Consecration

In this original generation of the **Three Resolutions** concept, the first temptation was very much about threats to our physical wellbeing – excesses, sleep, gluttony, etc. It was intended to help readers overcome society's proclivity to encourage a lifestyle that seemed so good in the moment but which did not serve them in the longer term. One need only look around at the way so many young people are being taught by celebrity and some elements of society that 'things' and 'fun' are the way to live properly, only for the same young people to find out that such a lifestyle tends to crumble around them as they are forced to meet new challenges and responsibilities. "Eat drink and be merry" may sound like great advice, especially when young, but if we rewrite it for accuracy, the next phrase is "for tomorrow you will suffer the obesity and physical ailments you are setting yourself up for."

The second temptation was about how we prefer to be seen as *we* want to be seen, not necessarily as we truly *are*, and how we therefore portray a public persona that is not necessarily the accurate image of what and who we truly are. As has been put by Henry Fielding, "Fashion is the science of appearance, and it inspires one with the desire to seem rather than to be". Looked at 'in the round', this approach to being is a direct result and reflection of the social drive to be like everyone else, having 'fun' and possessing 'stuff', and essentially following the crowd we choose to emulate. When we emulate others, we lose sight of what we are and of what we know is right. If we fall victim to this temptation, we live our lives 'seeming rather than being'.

Covey used as his illustration the example of college students' cramming for examinations, doing enough to pass without really having to work hard at studying, a crime of which he was himself guilty. And he used Jesus Christ as the alternative example of a person being, before seeming.

The final temptation was living life selfishly, interested only in ourselves and approaching every interaction with others with a 'what's in it for me' motive. The consecration in this original work was the ideal that one should live to serve God's glory, not one's own. I'm not going to suggest that – religion is wholly a matter for the individual and I'm going to neither promote nor decry it. I do, however, encourage the seeking of a noble purpose, and the provision of service to others.

Covey's sources for 'his' Three Temptations were the temptations laid at the feet of Jesus Christ as he spent 40 days and nights in the wilderness. Satan tempted Christ with food, challenged him to prove his godliness, and later offered him great power, but Jesus' adherence to His own **Three Resolutions** pulled him through the ordeal. Despite the offers of food and water he honoured his body by fasting as intended; he proved his character by not answering Satan's calls to show off; and he preferred service to God and his future followers above the personal power offered. These were succinctly rephrased by scholars as temptations of the flesh, of pride and of selfishness. Looking at these 'temptations' and the Resolutions you have no doubt already come to see the obvious parallels. To save time, I repeat and explain - Satan tempted Christ with food (body, flesh, hunger), challenged him to prove his godliness (to demonstrate his competence at the expense of his character), and later offered him great personal power (appealing to his pride and ambition – neither of which Jesus possessed).

Covey also opined how we should develop a principled response to the first temptation – mastering our minds and bodies, preparing ourselves physically and mentally before addressing the second temptation, and then reinforcing our character and competence before addressing the third. For Covey, the concept of progressive development has always been a key to his approach to teaching.

These three temptations were not the only ideas promoted in this early work – they are specifically detailed here because of the objectives of THIS book. The book also made references to principles such as honesty, truth, integrity, discipline, and so on. Dr Covey defines Principles as undeniable truths; they are universally true (apply anywhere), timeless (have always applied), extrinsic (existing outside of our understanding whether we believe in them or not) and accepted. To decide if something is a Principle, he wrote, try arguing the opposite and see if it makes sense. My use of the words Principle and Principled have had that definition in mind.

Sidebar - *Let's briefly consider the idea that for many people, any writing connected to or associated with any religion is suspect.*

Psychologists and readers of psychology-based literature will be familiar with the idea that society accepts what it knows and is suspicious of the unfamiliar. It also speaks of how, when we do encounter the unknown, we try to rationalise or compartmentalise it into something we DO understand, and if it does not fit in with such understanding we routinely deride or even attack it.

Examples would include what is now the wholly accepted fact that the Earth revolves around the Sun, which itself circles within the Milky Way. Prior to Galileo, Ptolemy's contention that the Earth was the centre of the Universe was the accepted norm. Galileo was able to show the truth but was cast out from society and placed in house arrest.

Another example is arguably racism, which (one could argue) starts out as an understandable, even natural mistrust of the unknown when one race encounters another, but which becomes hatred when fed with the wrong 'facts'.

So consider the suggestion that people associate the word 'Principles' with 'Religion'. **_DON'T MAKE THAT MISTAKE IN READING COVEY'S BOOKS._** By the definition being used here, Principles are NOT religious concepts – religions accepted principles. This is an important distinction, and acceptance of this may make it easier for you to open your mind to what this book promotes.

I believe that Covey realised that people tend to confuse the two, and that his religious upbringing and his use of religious metaphor and experience could be a bar to greater understanding of the principles he was trying to communicate to others. I emphasise that this does not necessarily mean that your blind acceptance of what he wrote is sought – I ask only that you read this material and seek to obtain as objective an understanding as you can. What you do with that information once you have it, is entirely up to you.

So, as I suggested earlier that the religious context within which Dr Covey wrote his first books must not be allowed to put you off, I ask now that you put any such prejudice aside, real as it may seem to you in the moment. Consider that no matter how religious or secular you may be, you probably believe in or have faith in something that science still cannot prove – for example, love. So if you start out by mistrusting someone who does the same thing, but with different rules and objectives for doing so, then this is not a great precursor to understanding or learning something new. If you have concerns, please read on and THEN decide if what I have explained does or does not make sense. And whatever you do, please take religion out of the equation. If you wish to do that.

I once read that an 'academic' was shown a copy of The Seven Habits and this 'academic' read a few sentences and handed it back dismissing it as 'written by a Mormon' because it promoted Mormon values. Which is like saying that Truth *is a religious value because the Bible says you shouldn't lie. Try spending your life constantly lying and see how you get on.*

Once again for emphasis – Religions adopt values. Values (and Principles) are not religious.

In these earlier books, which were aimed at his peers, he used religious experiences and beliefs to provide examples or demonstrations, either directly or through metaphor, to show how they worked. This made sense – his audience needed to understand them, and one thing about Covey was his incredible ability to communicate ideas.

In recognition of the possibility that using scriptures to illustrate the principles he had followed may not be the best way to communicate them more widely, I believe Covey decided to rewrite his books in a way that made sense to people WITHOUT the 'baggage' of religion attached. In an effort to widen the prospective audience he did not have to alter his beliefs, he only saw that he had to make them effectively secular. He had to change his approach so that he avoided the danger of people concluding they were associated with religion, and then dismissing them with that incorrect paradigm in mind.

In 1989 he published the book called 'The 7 Habits of Highly Effective People', and this changed things. Over thirty million copies of this book have been sold, often to business men and women who are seeking something more than 'just' professional success. I'm not entirely sure how many 30-year-old books are still routinely on shop bookshelves, but this one is of note. In a nutshell, these readers are discovering that the lessons implicitly taught throughout the 1980s – greed is good, put yourself first, climb that success ladder and focus only on doing that – were then, and remain an incomplete and even inaccurate way of seeing things. These readers realised and continue to realise that something is/was missing in their lives – they had money and power but felt no sense of meaning or purpose. And when the money was gone…….

In 1992 he published a follow-up book called 'Principle-Centred Leadership', and it was here that he updated the concepts initially written about as the Three Temptations. In this new book the concept had been revised and described differently, but the message remained valid. The three 'temptations' were now called **Restraining Forces** and were identified more clearly as

- *Appetites and Passions.*
- *Pride and Pretension.*
- *Aspiration and Ambition.*

Now the (positive) solutions were clearly stated, instead of the (negative) challenges - and these were the **Three Resolutions**, which are:

"To overcome the restraining forces of appetites and passions, I resolve to exercise self-discipline and self-denial."

"To overcome the restraining forces of pride and pretension, I resolve to work on character and competence."

"To overcome the restraining forces of unbridled aspiration and ambition, I resolve to dedicate my talents and resources to noble purposes and to provide service to others."

In clearer language, Covey now identified not just the 'temptations/restraining forces' but now provided a set of clear phrases that identified their principled counters, their antidotes. In three simple sentences he helped the reader identify both the causes of their problems and the solutions. Instead of just naming the problems and writing about them in general terms he now effectively paraphrased them to the degree that a reader could see exactly what he or she needed to do to overcome those challenges.

And it is the new perspective that this book sought to explain, interpret and expand upon.

Chapter Eight – What Now?

To briefly summarise what you've read this far:

- You've had a look at your own current situation through completion of the exercises;
- You've been told about **The Three Resolutions** and how they serve each other. You've also been told how they are not simply the philosophy of one man, they are principles that others have acknowledged and explored and accepted to be true;
- You've been fully advised about the Restraining Forces, the forces which prevent our achieving meaningful personal advancement, success or achievement (whichever term you prefer to use);
- You have been given 'food for thought' on each of the **Three Resolutions**, and their potential impact has been explained;
- You have read suggestions on how you can apply what you've learned through reading the book;
- You have been encouraged to write your own Personal Mission Statement as a precursor to living it; and
- At each step you've been invited to look at what you've learned as it applies in your own life, with a view to implementing that new knowledge to make your life more like what you know it could be, and you want it to be.
- Finally, you've been told the history behind the **Three Resolutions**;

So – what now?

It's entirely up to you.

Writers in the field of personal development are emphatic on one specific point – just reading this material is not enough. Anthony Robbins emphasises that the responsibility for change is not his as an author or speaker, it's yours as the client. Jack Canfield says, *"The principles work – if you work the principles."* (My italics.)

The world doesn't change to suit us – change must start within us, change is 'inside-out'. The consensus is that it is not the writer or speaker or book or audio programme or preacher or ***anyone else*** who is responsible for making things happen after you've read or heard the material that you paid for – it is YOU, and only YOU who can do anything about it. You change first.

That said, and taking The Third Resolution into account, another pre-requisite for successful personal progress can be summed up by the words of Zig Ziglar, who says, "You can get anything you want provided you help other people get what they want." That quote reminds us that we don't live in a vacuum – we do everything we do with someone, for someone, or as a direct result of what someone else has said or done. Our lives are connected 100% to the lives of others unless we are alone on a desert island, and even then we rely on others to take action to rescue us. **The Three Resolutions** reflect that reality.

In the forward to his 15th Anniversary Edition of The 7 Habits, Covey said, "*I have found living the 7 Habits a constant struggle – primarily because the better you get, the very nature of the challenge changes, just like skiing, playing golf, tennis or any sport does.*" He observed that as we get more disciplined, better behaved and more helpful, we discover that there are even more levels of discipline, character and service to be found, and the number of opportunities to execute the **Three Resolutions** grows rather than shrinks. As a golfer gets better he discovers how much better he has yet to get. The differences may be subtler at the higher level but it is only our development to that point that makes that subtle difference visible to us.

As we execute our personal commitment to the **Three Resolutions** we discover that what we thought was 'enough' doesn't have to be – we can get better still. You may be at the beginning of this trip (I deliberately avoid the word journey) or you might be half way there and just a little mired in some obstacle or another, but the truth is that once this exodus begins it never actually stops unless and until you decide it should. Either way, the next step onward and upward is entirely down to you.

At the end of each segment or chapter I invited you to carry out an exercise. Many readers either put it off until 'later' or never do the exercises at all. There may be a good reason for this, but the only good reason that is (arguably) acceptable is that they 'got it' the first moment they read it and knew without further analysis what they had to do. They are lucky people, or I am a great writer. I'll rely on them being lucky, because like most of you I have to think about these things for a while before I am willing to make a Resolution. In truth, I waited longer than I should have done, as many do.

I encourage you to do those exercises if you haven't done them yet. If you have, let's move on.

The world is full of nearly people. In his book 'How to Be Brilliant', Michael Heppell tells the story of a man we'll call John, who went to school with a friend of his, a good friend, called Richard. As they passed through school Richard was always coming up with weird ideas about projects and always invited John to take part. John was cautious and would initially promise to help but would then find excuses to avoid participation. When they left school Richard would still invite John along, but John would still prevaricate. In the end, Richard Branson became an entrepreneurial billionaire and adventurer. Who is John?

I'm not for one minute suggesting that execution of your plan will make you a billionaire (even though it might). I AM suggesting that *inaction* will probably keep you where you are, though. And I am assuming that as you have purchased this book and have read this far into it, you don't like that place. But your situation may get even worse.

If you keep money in a drawer under your bed, interest rate rises and inflation mean that over time your money will buy less, so it actually lessens in value. If you put it in a bank, particularly a safe bank, it will grow, at least in keeping with inflation (okay, probably just under). If you speculate wisely you might make that money increase in value, potentially by some high degree. It is the same with this book. If you put it in a bank….

Sorry to be flippant. If you stay where you are, in that uncomfortable place you've decided isn't where you want to be, things will get worse. If you're fat and do nothing, you'll get fatter as you get older and it'll have serious health consequences. Are you planning on having a Stennah Stairlift, to driving around the local shops on an invalid carriage motor-scooter, and to having your bum wiped by a nurse as you dribble over the side of the bed? If you have no job and you do nothing, you'll probably freeze to death in your seventies because you have no pension to pay the fuel bills. If you are a person of poor character and do nothing, you will likely live a long lonely life before dying alone and unloved because people know what you truly are. If you don't contribute in some way, even in the meaningful but simple ways suggested, you will be forgotten. If you suffer from all these maladies, you die fat, alone and forgotten after spending a long time in healthcare/nursing home purgatory. That is what will happen if you do nothing about what you've read here. (Scared, yet?)

It may not come to that. You may be part way to being a semi-disciplined, healthy, employed person of good character with some community involvement that benefits others – but you want more or you wouldn't be here, would you?

But you won't get 'more' if you do nothing. 'More' requires effort, learning and contribution. It requires that you stop doing what doesn't serve you, start doing what does, start living with integrity with principles, ensure you're current in working practices valued by employers, and you purposefully provide some service that benefits others in some way. It requires compliance with the **Three Resolutions**.

I invite you, now, to review the answers to the exercises – YOUR answers, not mine, remember – and start writing down specifically what action you are going to take in respect of your responses.

Do It Now.

That's a favourite phrase I used in my time management book, one that I initially wrote specifically for colleagues. It's a self-discipline catchword that recognises that the best time to do anything challenging is now, in this moment, in the moment when your mind has accepted the truth of what has been suggested and hasn't yet looked for 'rational-lies' to justify procrastination. It means making the call you've been avoiding, spending the money on something you need but is expensive, going for the run when you're tired. Just as you feared doing the exercises because of the inherent possibility that your answers would mean you oblige yourself to act on them. If this book is working it would be inevitable that some of your answers would have been uncomfortable to write down, because writing them down made them even more real.

To avoid stasis and in recognition and acceptance that the answers may be uncomfortable reading, do the following exercise anyway.

 Make a list of things you ARE going to do about your situation, the things which will be commensurate with your Resolution to be disciplined, to be of good character, to exercise excellent levels of competence and to serve others in some way.

(Pause for effect)

Okay, you've reviewed the exercises and you've made your first list of things to do. I say 'first list' because if you are anything like me you missed some things out that you are not wholly committed to, yet. Leaving that aside and assuming you don't want to **Do It Now** even though I heartily suggest that you do so, start working on that list.

If it means researching some health-related websites and making contacts to start doing the work required to get healthier and fitter, **Do It Now.** If it means emptying the fridge and freezer of poor foods, **Do It Now.** If it means joining a running club or gym, **Do It Now.**

If it means registering with a recruitment agency, **Do It Now.** If it means signing up to a community college or university course, **Do It Now.** If it means writing letters of apology or making peace with someone you have offended, **Do It Now.** If it means committing to stop using bad language, **Do It Now.**

If you seek the opportunity to start providing a service to others, find out who you need to contact and **Do It Now.**

If you haven't started drafting your Personal Mission Statement, DO IT NOW!

Under all three headings, in all **Three Resolutions**, there are actions you are willing to take – and there are actions you will be reluctant to take. That's life in a nutshell. The difference between who you were before you read this book and who you are now willing to become is dependent upon whether you are willing to take the reluctant step forward. Anyone can do the easy stuff- it's the stuff we don't want to do that, when done, makes all the difference. Remember Gray's quote from The Common Denominator of Success – successful people are successful because they are "doing the things failures don't like to do" *(sic)*.

It takes a bit of courage to admit that there are changes to make, but through your completion of the exercises you have already demonstrated a little bit of courage - perhaps courage in privacy, but courage nonetheless.

Having stretched those 'courage muscles' I now call upon you to exercise just a little bit more. Make the phone call you're avoiding, speak to that person who can help you, spend a little cash in pursuit of the 'better' that you have identified. If it's a purely 'physical' action you need to take, like exercise and diet, just throw yourself into the next action required to create and then maintain momentum. For each success – even for making that fearsome telephone call – make an entry in that journal you started at the beginning (I hope). Each exertion that overcomes the inertia that was the crux of your existence, is another step forward to improvement.

Don't be tempted to rest on your laurels – that usually causes slippage and you have to re-create that momentum. It's like doing press-ups. Work at it until you get to 20 and stop – and in no time at all you're back at 10. You don't stay at 20 because you got there once. You need to maintain the pressure just to stay at 20, and then increase it a little bit every day to move towards 30.

Commit to action. For those it may suit I have drafted a Personal Contract document in the Appendices for you to complete, laminate and pin up in front of your computer (even to pin ON your computer as the wallpaper, like me). This your declaration of intent, your promise to yourself that you will act in accordance with the **Three Resolutions** so that you can get what you want in a principled way.

Nothing need stop you now.

But - are you scared of what people will think when you commit to all this? I was.

In 2001 I started wearing a number 7 on my tie, as a personal commitment to the Seven Habits. (I'm still weird like that.)

It was handy that my police collar number (still called a collar number even though it's been on police officer's shoulders since the early 1960s) was 679 and I had a few spare 7s. I wore this number 7 in plain sight as a personal reminder of my commitment to live in accordance with the 7 Habits' principles. One of the first things that happened was people would ask, "Why have you got that 7 on your tie?"

And I wouldn't tell them. It was years before I told one close colleague, and a few more before I was willing to declare my allegiance. I feared what other people would say and I was scared that I wouldn't be able to adequately or competently explain the principles and the philosophy. By 2006 I was in a new, more specialised and professional department with people who, on the face of it, I should have been even more frightened of in terms of how they might (and occasionally did) respond to my public declaration of trust in the Habits.

By then, though, I was properly committed and possessed a greater self-confidence. And in truth I had also matured and learned that what they thought of me and my beliefs was of absolutely no consequence to me or to those beliefs. What I believed in was real, undeniable (as are all principles) and set out in a communicable manner. If they asked, I told them. When I was appointed to teach colleagues about personal development I used the lessons I had been taught, many of which are in this book. I was publicly spreading the word and thus was expected to live in their accord.

I suppose I am now asking you to do the same. Embrace what you decide is right for you. If the **Three Resolutions** fit that description, embrace them. If you don't want to tell people yet, then don't. Wait until they comment on your improved health/fitness/competence/character/ helpfulness/life, and then tell them what you did.

It won't be easy. I had the most difficulty with the First Resolution and gained several pounds (okay, 51 of the buggers) because no matter how much I exercised I also ate like a pig. In the other areas, I like to think I held my own (but could always do better). Unfortunately, I was trying to do a lot of this in a vacuum without the necessary or desired support of others, which would have been nice to have. But in 2014, having properly committed to the **Three Resolutions** like never before, I made a LOT of progress in that specific area.

Perhaps that's the lesson. Tell people what you are trying to do and ask them for their support. Those who offer the opposite should be avoided. Those who support you should be embraced. But ultimately the buzzword here has to be communication. Tell them – "I am trying to get fitter/slimmer/more competent/a better character/more helpful and I'd like you to hold me to those objectives. Don't tempt me with fatty foods or high calorie drinks. Don't take the mick. Tell me where I can be better, not just where I am wrong." And so on, according to your own objectives.

I'm not exceptional by the definitions of sport, celebrity or power. That's the reason I haven't included stories about 'exceptional people'. We can all aspire to be as congruent as Gandhi, as fit as Usain Bolt, as rich as Bill Gates or as talented as Pavarotti. The truth is that most of us just want to be as good as we can be at what we do, and as integrated as possible. We just want to do our bit to make things better for others. And we feel, now and then, that life is not letting us do those things. All I want you to accept now is that I am responsible for my situation in those three areas, and you are responsible for yours.

Be healthy, slim and as fit and disciplined as you feel you can or need to be. Be the principle-centred, congruent person you know you can be and align yourself with your values. Then do the best you can at whatever it is you chose to do.

And serve others in a way that you know, in your heart, reflects the most noble of purposes. That, in this world, is itself exceptional. It's as exceptional as you need to be in order to be happy and to live a satisfying life.

In fact, given the table of Restraining Forces in Chapter One, here's a 'post execution' table based on the same criteria.

Appetites and Passions	Drink and eat wisely. Sleep restfully but not to excess. Identify what is the right thing and focus on doing that.
Ambition and Aspiration	Recognise that the provision of service will result in progression of a kind that is longer-lasting and more meaningful than false plaudits.
Pride	Demonstrate only congruent pride, that is pride limited to a sense of a job well done when the job has been done well.
Pretension	Put simply – walk your talk. Clearly state what you believe and always act in accordance with those statements. Be proud of your own, genuine accomplishments while also happily giving due credit to those who helped.
Comfort Zones	Step outside, stretch yourself so that what was uncomfortable becomes comfortable.
Social Mirror	Accept genuine criticism but ignore false praise. Don't live your life through unthinking, ill-considered adoption of others' standards and behaviours.
Procrastination	Do the thing that needs to be done, the way it needs to be done, when it needs to be done and at or above the standard necessary, whether you want to or not.
Routine	Create new, better routines but always be willing to alter them as situations require. Think on your feet, be adaptable. Accept changes imposed by others so that when they don't work your opinion is not tempered by distaste for the new way and is completely objective.
Internal Dialogue	Use affirmations such as 'Do It Now' or 'It is worth the effort, and now is the time.'

I'd be interested in how you go. Don't consider the end of this book as the end of your efforts, it is just the start. What I would like is for you to let me know what your situation was when you started exercising the **Three Resolutions**, and where you are having exercised them for a while. Let me know if you find that the trip is likely to get longer, as I suggest.

I'm contactable at threeresolutionsguy@aol.com.

Appendix A – Three Resolution Goal Setting

Overview

Jim Rohn described self-discipline as the bridge between goals and their achievement, and in this book I encourage adherence to that philosophy and suggested that self-discipline is not something that can exist in a vacuum – you must have something *about* which and *in pursuit of* which you can exercise self-discipline and self-denial. Without a goal there can be no discipline. Even if you don't have a clear idea what the purpose of your self-discipline actually *is*, I bet that if I asked you why you may be dieting or exercising you would provide a 'goal' response, even if you had to pause for a moment to think about it.

Goals. Targets, dreams, intentions. Whatever you choose to call them, 'goals' are the objectives we have that give our days, and eventually our lives, some meaning. As Zig Ziglar puts it, "You've gotta have goals" or you become a wandering generality instead of a meaningful specific. Instead of leading a purposeful life towards some achievement, you just go from day to day complaining that the world is giving you nothing.

In his seminar on goal setting, Zig told of a great archery exponent who he described as being able to hit a target bull with an arrow ten times out of ten at amazing distance, and to be able to shoot a 15 foot shark in 20 feet of water, or a 20 foot shark in 15 feet of water – "Either way, it was big and way down there!". Then Zig claimed that despite his own lack of experience in archery, he could quite easily out-shoot this expert – provided the expert wore a blindfold. Inevitably you may ask, "How can he hit a target he can't see?" To which Zig would parry,

"How can you hit a target you don't even HAVE?"

Charles Hobbs considered goals to be events which we wish to bring under control. In another insightful observation, he also described them as an 'intended conflict with the status quo'.

Goals are dreams that you wish to make happen, to come true. Assuming you already have some idea of the things you wish to bring into being, I need not labour that point. You know what goals are, so it makes sense that in a book of this kind there should be a section on goal setting. In *this* book, of course, such activity must be in the context of The **Three Resolutions**.

One important term you may like to consider is that of the **Wildly Important Goal**. Other writers have called them HUGGs – Huge, Unbelievably Great Goals – and BHAGs – Big, Hairy Audacious Goals.

A Wildly Important Goal (WIG) is a goal of such importance that not achieving it would have a severe, even fatal effect on all other activity of the entity concerned – including an individual. That definition may seem a bit extreme but in a world where an unachieved goal results in lowered self-esteem and worse, mental health issues, perhaps it is ot so wide of the mark.

I like that term - WIGs. A WIG has a greater chance of being achieved - the term Wildly Important Goal means that it is really wanted. In terms of your mission statement or values statements a WIG is one that wholly motivates you and which you would love and strive to achieve. It has an emotional grip on you – you want it, and you want it bad. When reading the rest of this chapter on goals, consider your WIGs as the ones to which these paragraphs most specifically apply.

Traditional Methodology

Anyone involved in a management role would be familiar with the goals' mnemonic 'SMART'. SMART, in its most common form, means goals that are Specific, Measurable, Achievable, Relevant and Timed. Or Agreed, or Realistic, or whatever a particular writer feels stamps his or her own identity on a particular version. I've even heard of SMARTER and SMARTEST goals, such is the evidence of the inventor's desire to be different, and to sound extra clever. all the same, such mnemonics are a good guide to forming goals and provided it works, I would encourage you to use whichever mnemonic appeals to you. For those few of you who don't know the traditional meaning of SMART, I will briefly cover it, here.

SMART means...

Specific. How specific was your goal? Was it 'lose weight' or 'by the 31st of December 2010 I will weigh 13st 7lbs'? Was it, 'own a sports car' or was it 'By my 40th birthday I will own a black Reliant Scimitar S5a with beige leather trim'? (In the end, I bought a Toyota MR2.)

Do you see the difference? Which is likely to focus your attention the most – a generality or a specific, timed and even visible objective? That's the first secret – being as specific as possible.

The human mind has a faculty called the Reticular Activating System (RAS). This system alerts the unconscious mind to things that are important. At the time when we were just cavemen it would shout 'TEETH' when something crept up behind us. Now, it identifies things of importance in less direct ways. For example, have you ever bought a new car and then noticed how many other people had the same model? I know that since my wife and daughter both bought Citroen Xsara Picassos there are MILLIONS of them on the roads, and I keep waving to complete strangers.

The purpose of specificity is to make the image of the goals' attainment so important to your subconscious that it spots the opportunities to make progress towards your goal for you, rather than wait for you to see them consciously. For example, if you did want a Reliant Scimitar S5a, the RAS would pick up the one passing you with the For Sale notice in the window – it certainly did for me. If you did want promotion, the RAS would pick up the adverts for accredited training courses in professional journals. If you did want to lose weight, the RAS would bring your attention to the fat bloke's image looking back at you from the shop window! (I know that one is true.)

Be specific where you can, and also be as specific as you can. (There is more on this, later.)

Measurable. Can you measure progress? Of course, some goals are apparently only measurable on completion, such as buying that sports car – you don't have it, then you do. But some goals are the result of progression towards an end, pertinent and even clichéd examples being weight loss where weekly progress can be monitored, and progress towards an athletic goal, e.g. weight-lifting or a marathon, where weight lifted or distance run can be measured as time passes.

In the corporate world, and saliently in the world of the 'public authority', the truth is that 'what gets measured gets done'. (See Appendix B, *post*.)Targets drive behaviour in that workers' behaviour is directed towards achievement of the end objective. I won't go into how this occasionally corrupts activities, that's for another time. But this concept, true as it is, can be used legitimately to achieve a lot. I used it to progress from running 'a little' to running 6 times a week and to doing some more serious mileage – and I am not an enthusiastic runner. But ticking off the daily running record provided a sense of achievement (serotonin/dopamine) on the days I ran, and a sense of relief on the days I didn't have to!

Achievable. As a 52-year-old, former fat guy I did not set a December 2015 goal to win the London Marathon in April 2016. That would have been a stupid goal. Had I been 25 and a competitive runner, then given time and proper preparation it may at least have been reasonable.

The idea is to look at your circumstances, decide what is slightly beyond 'reasonable', and identify a goal that stretches you. I have heard it suggested that you should consider setting three levels of such a goal – a minimum expectation, a target result, and an outstanding result.

The target is what you think of when you set the goal, the minimum is what you would settle for if the ultimate target became impossible to achieve for external reasons – and the outstanding goal is what you would go for if your circumstances actually improved as you worked towards your target. I would be mindful that having the minimum goal would require having an allied sense of self-discipline to ensure that it did not become the target through laziness or settlement for less. It is a back stop to support self-esteem, not a rationale designed to undermine it through becoming an excuse not to go for the target. It is ONLY there if the target becomes unreachable – for example, say your target was a half-marathon in 6 months, and your minimum target was a 9-mile run. You'd got up to 9 miles and broke an ankle; then your earlier selection of a 9-mile run as a minimum would be acceptable. If you bruised a toe, it would not.

Relevant. This is an important part of the formula. Setting a goal that does not reflect your personal value system, or that is not a requirement of your professional role (assuming that you chose your profession), means it is not a valued goal, and is arguably irrelevant. Ask Ben Franklin.

A goal that is not relevant or valued is doomed. If you have no heart or sense of involvement in the goal's creation or its success then you are unlikely to put in the required effort, and when you 'fail' because of that disinterest your self-esteem plummets, and like a line of dominoes it affects everything else you do (if you aren't careful). That said, when a goal *is* imposed on you and/or you select a goal that isn't immediately accepted on an emotional level, then the solution may be to either redefine the goal so that it *does* reflect your values, or subject it to analysis to see if there is something about it that might serve your values.

For example, if you are told to do a piece of work that really does not float your boat and is not helpful in achieving any of your more obvious professional ambitions, you could look at your value statement on 'demonstrate professionalism' and decide that regardless of your distaste for this task, you will nevertheless create the most professional result possible. I used this quite often in my days as a police detective. I hated major incidents because they interrupted my 'real' (vocational) work, but when I was directed to work on them then my values 'required' me to do the best job I could. (And quickly, to get them over with....)

It is therefore important that when you set a goal it reflects your mission and your values, or it is one which you can redefine so that it does. Again, for those whose professional role requires them to occasionally do work that does NOT reflect your mission or values, remember that you chose your profession – and it's not unreasonable for your employer to ask you to do some work, is it? I repeat – find the values-based connection to the unwanted task.

Timed. This simply means set a deadline for the goal's completion. For most accepted objectives that fit the broad 'goal' definition, this is straightforward. 'I have a black Toyota MR2 by the end of this October' is easy enough. Goals which are never-ending do exist, however. 'I will maintain a healthy and fit physiology' never has a deadline – or at least a deadline you want to set. Maintaining it until you die is the aim but setting such a 'dead' line may be unattractive.

Okay, that's SMART covered. You could add E for exciting and R for Realistic (which duplicates Achievable) if you want to be 'special' but that's a matter for you.

I believe SMART has its place, especially the S&M (eh?), but in the book First Things First, Stephen Covey identified what was, for me, a slightly different spin on things when he wrote of the Context Goal, where goals are planned in the context of your various roles and your personal values. The specific drafting of goals he suggested, should be done using the What, Why and How 'method'.

To illustrate how to set goals using this method, let me take you through a process.

For the moment, just write down some notes, some simple jottings as to what your goals might be, e.g.

- Lose weight.
- Seek promotion.
- Buy a sports car.

You have a general idea about where you intend to go, but no sense of the detail. This is the secret of effective goal setting – not the simple identification of the goal, but four other factors of EXTREME importance!

The factors are:

- Specificity   - What
- Motivation   - Why
- Method   - How
- Action!   - Now

Specificity – Revisiting the earlier examples, how specific was your goal? Was it 'lose weight' or 'by the 31st of December 2010 I will weigh 13st 7lbs'? Was it, 'own a sports car' or was it 'By my 40th birthday I will own a black Reliant Scimitar S5a with beige leather trim'?

Do you see the difference? Which is likely to focus your attention the most – a generality or a specific, timed and even visible objective? That's the first secret – being as specific as possible.

As indicated earlier, the purpose of specificity is to make the image of the goals' attainment so important to your subconscious that it spots the opportunities to make progress towards your goal for you, rather than wait for you to see them consciously.

Again – Be specific where you can and be as specific *as* you can. You may elect to include the 'Timed' deadline in the specific definition of your goal. It is the best place to do so.)

Motivation – why do you want to achieve this goal? What about it keeps you interested? What will it mean to you as you work towards it and when you achieve it? How will you feel? How will life be? What values will be met? Is it part of your ultimate vision?

Silly questions? I think not. Goals that get carried through are goals with meaning. It's the goals that fail that are a reflection, I would argue, of the fact that you never really wanted to achieve them in the first place. Or you didn't want to do the required work.

For example: how do you feel about goals that are set for you? I suspect they get a grudging 'I will do enough to be seen to be doing enough' response.

Why? Because someone set them for you, that's why. You have no investment in getting the objectives met. You don't see the benefit, to you, of doing the work that someone else feels is so important. That's not a bad thing, it's just natural. When you were in school some subjects grabbed you and some did not. As you developed your interests and hobbies, you became passionate about some things and were disinterested in others.

So when setting your goals, decide why it is you want to achieve them. Create a passionate desire to get what you want by imagining what it will be like when you have it.

Method – having decided what you passionately want and in specific detail, the next phase is planning HOW you are going to get it. There are a number of ways to do this, as we will discuss later. This, if you like, covers the 'Measured' element of the SMART template. They are the steps needed to come through on the objective, each of which can be 'ticked off' on completion as you make progress.

Action – get off your backside and MAKE THINGS HAPPEN. Don't expect things to fall into your lap. They might if you wait long enough, but time is wasted in the wait. Don't spend all your time 'getting ready'. Having made a list of things to do in the Method (how to) stage, the idea is to DO those things. I know I have fallen victim of 'perpetual planning' in the past, making long lists of things to do and then procrastinating like heck until, finally, they get done. And then I regret the missed opportunities that resulted from my not being ready because of that waiting. **Do It Now!** Whenever possible.

Re-examine those brief goals you mentioned earlier, and then rewrite them in a more specific fashion. You can use the now clichéd SMART mnemonic if you want, but I would just write something like, *"I want a black Mercedes SLK coupe, less than 10 years old, with beige leather seats and a Bose sound system, by my 40th birthday."* That is timed, specific, measurable and achievable without being too rigid on SMART.

Then do the motivation part.

"I want this because I love fast sports car made with class. I really do believe that I will look good driving it, and the feel of the chassis as I negotiate bends and roundabouts will be magnificent! It will look beautiful on my drive, and I can smell the leather even now. Owning it will make me want to be a better, advanced driver. Etc."

Then, the how.

"I will need the money to buy it." (Loan, overtime, change career, inherit it.)

"I will need enough money to insure and maintain it." (Loan, overtime, change career, inherit it.)

"I will research the options available on the internet." (Identify websites, check Glass's Guide for prices, and look up Owners Clubs for good deals. Visit auctions. Etc.)

"I will visit a dealership." (Telephone Mercedes dealership tomorrow and arrange a test drive to get the feel. Etc)

"I will arrange advanced driver training." (Research and then contact either RoSPA Advanced Drivers Association, the Institute of Advanced Motorists, or the High Performance Club.)

Etc.

The 'how' is often a matter of initiative and imagination. You can brainstorm by just start writing down the first things that come into your head with the intention of organising your thoughts later. You can consider a backwards plan, where you think of the last thing you need to do before the goal is achieved; then the last thing before that last thing, and so on until you get to the starting point and act upon it now.

Then act in some way on what you have written down. Make a call, an appointment, do some research, make a new friend, go for a run, whatever. Make a start on that goal you feel passionate about, and then use the momentum that first action creates, to keep going.

For all the goals you set and about which you still feel passionate enough to do this valuable work, do the What/Why/How exercise.

Three Resolutions Perspectives

Having read this advice on how to set goals, the time has come to decide on the goals that you will set in terms of the **Three Resolutions**. I have written two sections on this. The first is on setting **Three Resolutions** Goals; the second is on applying **Three Resolutions** to 'any' goals. Either approach will be valuable.

Part 1 – Setting Three Resolutions Goals

This section is about identifying goals in terms of the **Three Resolutions** – goals which create and require self-discipline, self-denial, character, competence and a sense of service – all in the context of your Mission Statement (noble purpose).

First Resolution Goals

The traditional goals set in respect of the First Resolution are those which relate to your physical wellbeing and, given the further impact of 'addictions' on that area of your lives, you should consider setting goals in their regard. The particular areas are

- Weight;
- Exercise; and
- Vices

So consider at this point what goals you might want to set in terms of the First Resolution. For me, it was a weight goal.

Using the What/Why/How template, I created this goal sheet.

Wildly Important Goal (SMART)	Relevance to PMS:
By the 1st of December 2014 I will weigh between 182 and 196 pounds.	**First Resolution** - health and fitness. **Second Resolution** – character – show I am capable of execution of First Resolution. **Third Resolution** – to be able to prove to others that the Three Resolutions work, and to write accordingly.

Lag Measure	Weight measurement on target dates (below)	

Lead Measures	1. Continue Slimfast Diet daily.
	2. Eat 'normally' only for celebrations.
	3. Target weight loss to achieve goal by deadline:
	   a. 8lbs a month
	     i. 1/9/14 – 210lbs
	     ii. 1/10/14 – 202lbs
	     iii. 1/11/14 – 193lbs.
	     iv. 1/12/14 – 182lbs
	4. Start formal running programme 1/8/14. Target distance/time estimates:
	   a. 1/9/14 – 20 minutes easy
	   b. 1/10/14 – 30 minutes easy
	   c. 1/11/14 – 45 minutes easy
	   d. 1/12/14 – 55 minutes easy
		√

Deadline:		

As you can see, my Wildly Important Goal was to go from an unstated 16st 9lbs (233 pounds) to somewhere between 13st and 14st (182-196lbs) by the end of November 2014 – my intended publication date for the first edition of this book. My reasons were as stated, and they all related to my **Three Resolutions** Personal Mission Statement.

I established how I would do it – I would use the Slimfast© diet, I established my only intended exception, and I identified interim targets against which I could measure progress. My exercise goal was included within this WIG because it served the weight loss efforts as much as it served my fitness efforts, and as you can see I also included interim targets for running, too. I had separate measuring tools in my personal planning system which related to the running programme, (see Appendix C) but this goal 'statement' was the Master Plan, so to speak.

I would now encourage you to do the same, using the same form if you want to (available as a download from www.threeresolutionsguy.com).

Do It Now.

(For vices your approach may be more about application of self-denial through self-discipline. Find a support group, or even just a website that provides a method for overcoming the vice from which you suffer, and which you want to avoid from now on.)

Second Resolution Goals

Goals set under the Second Resolution relate firstly to character, then to competence. Taken in that order:

Character

Character goals are harder to measure because achieving them is an ongoing process, which is why a deadline template may not easily apply. Each time you demonstrate character you have completed that goal for the moment but the next opportunity to demonstrate character is still on its way. There is, arguably, no scope for a completion date – fate will decide that.

Relationships. What goals do you have for your relationships – with friends, family and community peers? How will you treat people? How will you make and keep friends? How will you prepare yourself to maintain effective relationships – how will you communicate, and how frequently? Set some goals in this area, now.

Behaviours. How will you behave? What standards will you choose to adopt, and what circumstances may occur that will challenge those choices? How will you respond when those challenges arise? Anticipating obstacles to improved behaviour will increase the likelihood that you will respond in the way you have chosen, rather than in a reactive, and therefore negative way. At the same time, you should choose goals in terms of what behaviours you will no longer demonstrate, and measure any subsequent failures just as you measure successes and progress sin other areas. Learn from the mistakes as a method of reinforcing the good behaviours you seek to enforce on yourself, and that you want to show others.

A lot of the goals set in terms of character will relate to the character traits and behaviours you identified when writing your personal mission statement. They are – and I cannot emphasise this enough – *your* chosen traits and behaviours. Not mine, not imposed – *chosen*. Having chosen them, seek the opportunity to exercise your new standards. **Do it now.**

Competence

Competence has two 'sides' – the achievement of qualifications, which is (almost) finite in the sense that each qualification can be an end in itself; and the obtaining of higher levels of competence discovered through the application of effort and skills, and through self-discovery of new and improved ways of doing things.

Work. What competencies do you need that you don't already have? What competencies do you anticipate you will need in the future (remember the opportunity benefits of being trained *before* a need arises)? How will you gain these competencies? Who provides the training, and at what cost? Who will pay for it? Are you willing to obtain that qualification, in the sense that you need to anticipate both the advantages of having a skill, and the potential disadvantages in terms of additional responsibilities that (perhaps) you aren't looking to have? Do you need to move to a different department, office, even organisation? How about a new career, even? Do you want to earn more, or even work *less* and take the financial hit, in preference for more time on other projects, or with your family? If so, what new skills (Skype-use, IT capabilities, time management) might help you work from home?

Hobbies. What are your favourite pastimes, and how can you do more of them? Is there an association that you can join, through which you can learn new skills, or update and develop the ones you already possess?

Now, having considered the questions in those two paragraphs, set some goals in terms of character and competence. **Do It Now.**

In respect of competencies (certainly) and character (less so, but still relevant), the achievement of Second Resolution goals will still be reliant upon your adherence to the principles of the First Resolution – self-discipline (mainly) and self-denial. This is in keeping with the illustrated concept that each Resolution builds upon the first. For example, learning a new skill or competence, particularly one that is a level or two above your current capabilities, will certainly require the disciplines of study and application. It may also require that you discard prior beliefs and understanding in preference for the new thinking required for such a quantum gain in your professional and vocational skill levels.

But read on.

Third Resolution Goals

The Third Resolution requires us to consider our noble purpose (in the sense of our development of a Personal Mission Statement) and how we will serve others in a way that also serves us.

It remains my contention that establishment of your noble purpose through drafting and then execution of a Personal Mission Statement is key to your achievement.

You have already read the chapter on the subject of the Personal Mission Statement. It is for you to decide whether you will write your own, and if you haven't done so yet I heartily and enthusiastically encourage you to consider it a goal – not only a goal that you 'should' aim for: it is one that is easy to achieve, yet will have enormous impact on your ability and motivation to achieve all of the other goals you have considered so far. As all meaningful goals will derive from your personal values/unifying principles and from your Personal Mission Statement, and that PMS will motivate you to carry out the tasks needed to successfully achieve your goals, then you can surely see just how important it is that you set a goal to write your PMS – and that you then act on it quickly. It is achievable in the short term, and creating it will give you that sense of personal victory that is essential to making progress. So, if you haven't done it yet, go back to the chapter on the making of a PMS – and act on what you read. **Do It Now** – it is a *must*.

Having set goals in the two earlier Resolutions, you are about to enter a bit of a loop. You have probably already figured it out by yourself, having considered the goals you have set, but having higher levels of self-discipline and self-denial, having decided upon higher standards of (characterful) behaviours, and having identified ways to improve your levels of skill and ways to utilise your knowledge and talents, you must realise that you have accidentally identified opportunities to serve.

If you have greater skills, knowledge and talents in one specialist area it is nigh on inevitable that as you discovered them you also identified other people, other specialists and associations who recognise and support people like you. There are associations, professional Institutes, charities, representative bodies and so on, who need people like you – professionals, authorities, experts, enthusiasts – who have a capacity to make a positive difference for those of a similar persuasion.

First, consider one goal to be to identification of such a body, and then another to join it. Ignore the costs: the benefits will usually outweigh those. Make your choice carefully and don't simply choose the easiest one to join – I am familiar with such associations, who exist only because their members would not or could not join the 'better' ones because they weren't able or willing to comply with the higher expectations. Find the best one for your circumstances. Choose one, for example, that has the ear of the authorities that regulate that field – that provides you with greater opportunity to make positive change for yourself and for others.

Once you have joined such a group, learn how it works and be willing to be an active rather than passive participant. If you have been a member for some reasonable time, or after you become a veteran (so to speak), the next step – and the most compliant with the Third Resolution – is to seek office within that organisation. You don't necessarily want to be at the top, although I suggest that application of all **Three Resolutions** will eventually see you get there. For the shorter term, get in there, commit to serving the body and to making a difference. The rewards of a well-chosen service opportunity are *incredible*, I assure you.

Set a goal to identify 'your' professional body, then seek to join it. Find a local chapter and make sure you become a frequent flyer at their events – put yourself about in a modest sense, make sure they know who you are and that you are willing to contribute something. Then make the decision and take the action needed to do so.

If the organisation has different levels of qualification, e.g. membership, diplomate, Fellowship, then make sure you start to do the work to progress along that upward spiral – a Second Resolution goal with a Third Resolution benefit.

As you can again plainly see, your Third Resolution 'service' goals will still rely on Second Resolution character traits and competencies, which in turn rely on First Resolution disciplines. In TimePower, Charles Hobbs wrote about how long-term goals are served by achieving medium-term (intermediate) goals are served by ticking of immediate goals. He wrote how the goal 'Getting a Pilot's Licence' was served by the goal of 'taking flying lessons' which was served by the goal of 'finding a suitable flying school'. One immediate goal led to the successful completion of an intermediate goal which supported the achievement of the 'ultimate' goal.

Three Resolutions goals are similarly progressive. The execution of First Resolution goals, which develop self-discipline, enable self-denial and ultimately serve our ability to take on new knowledge and gain competence in new skills by fine-tuning the equipment through which we carry out our roles – specifically, the 'tool' that is our body, and the mind within that controls it. With a fit body and a clear, uncluttered and guilt-free mentality it is much, much easier to learn and apply the competencies needed in our working-life and private-life roles. It is also easier to resist impulses to slack off and waver from our chosen path if our bodies and minds are up to the task. First Resolution goals serve our efforts to give effect to Second Resolution goals. And since it is our competencies and character that dictate our ability and willingness to serve ourselves and others through execution of our personal mission statement, those Resolutions serve the Third Resolution. Just as each successive Resolution is founded upon the one that went before, goals set in respect of each Resolution are *also* founded upon successful drafting and achievement of the goals that went before.

Part 2 – Applying the Three Resolutions to Goals

An alternative to the 'Create Three Resolution Goals' is to come at goals from the opposite direction, by identifying goals and *then* applying the **Three Resolutions** to those goals. It is not altogether different to the What/Why/How, it just asks you to consider slightly different questions in a different order – specifically, What/How/Why.

Decide what your goal is going to be, but in general terms that lay somewhere between 'lose weight' and 'By X I will weigh exactly Y pounds'. Your 'what' is now in mind, even if it is not yet specific. You don't want to make it too specific, yet, because the answers to the following questions will dictate whether the goal remains a goal or is discarded.

Now ask the following questions, and in this order:

1. **Where and how will I apply self-discipline in my efforts to achieve this goal?**

A goal worth achieving means overcoming what 'is' in order to create something better. Occasionally a simple goal like 'buy a new computer' won't take a lot of self-discipline but if you have to earn the spare cash to make that purchase then self-discipline may be a factor in whether, or not you get that new equipment. For personal development goals discipline may be a bigger factor. The most common examples would be weight loss or physical fitness, neither of which will be achieved without self-discipline.

Ask yourself what you must do that you aren't doing now – whether that's because you haven't actually started or because you have just been reluctant to do whatever it is – and write down the answer. Do nothing further, just yet.

2. **Where and how will I need to apply self-denial in my efforts to achieve this goal?**

A lot of goals require missing out on something else. Goethe would say 'the best must never be at the mercy of the good', meaning even good things must be cast aside if something better is available. On a diet, the application of self-denial is patently obvious. If it is a desire to have something else, you may have to deny yourself something. Perhaps you want a big home or family. Will you have either of those while you spend money on partying or a fast car? Of course not.

If you discover that you are not willing to exercise the necessary self-discipline, and/or that you are unwilling to deny yourself those things you have identified in your answers to question two, then this goal (at least as drafted) is not for you. You won't achieve it. You're not willing enough to apply some of the How, and if you go ahead with this Resolution missing you are doomed to failure. Either abandon the goal or reconsider how you want to draft it. Only when you have a draft goal to which you are willing to apply self-discipline and self-denial in your efforts to achieve it, should you move on.

3. **What competencies do I have and will I need to obtain in my efforts to achieve this goal?**

This question does need careful consideration. Once you have identified the competencies you have, you may already be satisfied that this goal is achievable. But what about competencies you don't have? Are they learnable? Is a course of training available? Can you afford it? Do you think you have the intellect or physical dexterity to pass the training course? If the answer is 'no', it may be prudent to abandon this goal. If the answer is 'yes', then you must return to questions 1 and 2 to see if you are willing to be disciplined enough to learn!

4. **What character traits will I need to demonstrate in my efforts to achieve this goal?**

This is a good question. In my view, people reading this book have most of the character traits required to achieve any goal – it's just their willingness to act they have trouble with. That said, look to your Value Statements/Unifying Principles/Personal Mission Statement to remind yourself of who you are, and your capabilities.

Those four questions effectively covered your 'How'. Next, the 'Why'.

5. **Does this goal enable me to work towards my noble purpose/personal mission statement?**

Remember that the imposed goal is less likely to be achieved, so a goal that does not reflect your values should be either avoided, or they should be redefined in such a way as to be compliant with your mission/values.

6. **While I serve myself in achieving this goal, will I or can I serve others in doing so?**

Think broadly – what appears on the face of it to be a self-serving goal may just as easily be reinterpreted or refocused to be one that serves others. In his book 'The 28 Laws of Attraction', author Thomas Leonard altered my thinking in this regard. He wrote about how the understood term 'selfish' could be reconfigured to mean 'self-ful'. Self-ful meant wholly concerned with one's own interests (in other words, what we would understand selfish to mean!), while HIS version of 'selfish' meant that we put ourselves first ONLY to the extent that by doing so we became better able to serve others. If we maintained our mental, physical and emotional selves through self-focus, we could better serve others with the fit, healthy and considerate person that resulted from that 'selfishness'.

With that in mind, does your goal serve others, either directly or indirectly?

I would agree that the difference in approach may be subtle, but it is different. One makes Three Resolution goals, while the other applies **Three Resolutions** to goals made *before* the Resolutions came into the mix.

Either route is, I would say, effective. Either way reinforces the fact that The **Three Resolutions** are a route to personal achievement, and the '**The Three Resolutions**' make a great life philosophy.

3R Goal Sheet

Earlier, I showed you a form I used which allied a goal to the **Three Resolutions**/Personal Mission Statement. You may wish to use the same method in your own goal setting efforts.

As you can see, the 'What' is large, in your face and clearly in view. The **Three Resolutions** are then looked at as part of the 'Relevance to PMS' section; this is the Why. Why do I want this goal? Where will I show self-discipline? Do I have the competence and character to do it, and have I declared that intent in this goal plan? Who and how will I serve, and am I included as one who is served?

Goal Sheet

Goal (SMART)	Relevance to PMS:	
	Resolution 1:	
	Resolution 2:	
	Resolution 3:	
Lag Measure		
Lead Measures		√
Deadline:		

The Lag Measure is how I will know I have achieved the goal, and the lead measures are the steps and actions I will take in my efforts to get the goal 'done'. The Deadline is self-evident. A Word document copy can be downloaded from http://www.threeResolutionsguy.com.

Appendix B – Time Management applied to the Three Resolutions

What is time management and how can it help you in your efforts to apply the **Three Resolutions**? I know so many people who resist training in this science on spurious grounds such as 'It's an American thing (what, like Microsoft, Apple, most of the TV you watch and things you like?)", or "It's for yuppies with Filofaxes."

The argument about the latter prejudice is that those 'yuppies' were successful, even if they weren't necessarily nice, but neither argument stands up to much scrutiny. The one which makes me laugh the most is the argument that applying time management skills 'prevents spontaneity'. It implies that utilising improved time management methodology stops you being creative, or having fun, or just going with the moment. This thinking is 180 degrees away from the truth.

Time management allows for creativity and makes what is created possible to achieve. Time management serves spontaneity because it makes sure that those things which need to be done still get done. Spontaneity does not absolve you of responsibility, it just allows you to move such things to their appropriate moment in time. And as for fun, isn't it more fun to be able to enjoy yourself without having to feel the guilt of a job unfinished, a relationship soured or a client properly served?

The application of time management serves everybody but in the context of this book I need to focus on how that science, art or skill serves your intentions and efforts in respect of The **Three Resolutions**.

First Steps

In the Foreword I encouraged you to start a journal in which you carried out the exercises that were to come, to record your own thoughts and developments on the **Three Resolutions**, and anything else that came to mind as you read this book. By the end of this Appendix I will ask you to consider investment a bit more of your time – and possibly your money – in starting to apply time management in a way that serves your efforts to 'be better', but to do that I suppose I need to explain my thinking.

The first thing you need to get over is the term 'time management'. Having just used it for the last few paragraphs that may seem a bit of a paradox, but here's why. Einstein provided an explanation as to how the term 'time management' came about, and Charles R. Hobbs of *TimePower* fame expanded upon that. He opined:

Time has no existence other than by the events by which it can be measured, and the order of those events in sequence, one after another. One event happens, then the next. A minute goes by, then another, then 60 make up an hour that passes before the next one. If 'things' didn't happen we wouldn't need to measure 'time' and therefore 'time' would not need to exist.

Management is the act of control. It's about making things happen, ensuring resources are available, that people do the things that need doing, and that payments be made where appropriate.

Therefore, by extension, time management is the act of controlling events. Of course, the contradiction remained that the one thing we want to manage – time – can't be managed because we can't put it where we want to, we can't save it for later, and we can't invest it to get more in the form of 'time interest'. What we have, we have. When it's passed, it isn't coming back.

The arguably better term for our purposes might be self-management, where we manage ourselves in the context of the time available to us. We make other people do what we need done while we do something else at the same time, maximising its use but still not managing 'it'. Extending that idea further, we don't manage time or ourselves, we manage ourselves in the context of time *and* the context of the people with whom, for whom, and because of whom we spend that time. Other people cause us to act, we cause others to act, and what we do requires the actions of others for it to be of value to any of the parties involved.

Having decided that we are now talking about 'life management' (in the context of time and people) rather than 'time management' alone, the next obvious step is self-*leadership*.

What was called time management is or should be re-termed self-leadership. Before you manage yourself as a 'thing' to be resourced, directed and controlled you must decide what it is you are leading yourself *for*. You must discover *why* you are doing what you are doing. Strategy comes before execution. But to return to the purpose of this Appendix, once you HAVE (through your Mission Statement exercise) decided what your strategy is going to be, you must decide how it is to be executed. You must manage *you*.

The Core Management Method

For anyone who works for someone else, there is one thing we are aware of and that is the fact that the organisation has targets. And we are equally aware that we need to measure if/when we achieve those targets or woe betide us for failure. Poor targets are those which are only measured at the end – pass or fail. We only know we're on track when we discover that we never were because we failed. Good targets, on the other hand, show us that as we head towards them we are on or off-rack. These targets are often termed intermediate goals. They are not the end goals, but we know that if we don't achieve these part-way objectives we still have time to adjust our actions to achieve the ultimate success. And these intermediate goals have shorter term goals on their back to bite us, to paraphrase Swift's treatise on fleas. (**The Siphonaptera,** *based on Swift's works*.).

And from this situation comes a phrase many have heard and have learned to distrust. The management motto is, "What gets measured, gets done."

I know that in my police role we found that what got measured got done. Someone decided that how fast we answered a 999 (911) call must be measured, so we measured it down to the millisecond and patted ourselves on the back when we achieved a 99% success rate in terms of the target set. What we didn't measure was what got done after we'd answered the phone so fast. On one occasion the poor service following the successful achievement of the pick-up target resulted in a fatality. A good example of what got measured got done – but we measured the wrong thing.

That's the important difference – I am going to suggest that you DO measure your activities, but that you *first* decide, clearly and sensibly, what you are going to measure. You are going to measure *your* right things and definitely NOT someone else's.

Measuring the First Resolution

In the exercises you carried out in respect of the First Resolution you most likely stated your fitness, weight and behaviour targets. You identified what it was you needed to achieve. It may have been a specific weight loss. You may have decided to start training to get fitter, faster or stronger. It may have just been a desire to do something every day that until now you had resisted for some reason. This is where your first measurement plans can focus.

You read earlier how I did this with my diet goal plan. I created lag measures (long term goals) and lead measures (daily running on a programme, weight loss targets each month). That way I knew whether I was on target and if not, just how wide of the bull I was headed. I invite you to do the same, or something similar that suits your own plans.

For many it may be a weight loss target, so on the next page there's an example form you may consider using.

This sheet would be the tool you use to measure what you do on a daily basis in accordance with your intentions. As you completed it you would measure what action you were taking, and at the end of each time-frame (I would suggest weekly as it allows faster redirection in the event of deflection) you **know** whether you need to change tack.

Parents among you may be aware of the fabled Star Chart used to stop children wetting their beds. Many such parents will also explain just how successful it was – even the child accepted the value of a daily measure, visibly and clearly telling them how they were doing towards their ultimate goal. It seems so simple, yet many would resist using this simple method – because it is so simple.

You decided how and to what you wanted the First Resolution. Now create a measuring tool to achieve what you've set out to do.

(Another management motto – 'if it's simple it couldn't possibly work and management must complicate it'. Discuss.)

EXERCISE / DIET SHEET

Week starting: _____

Meal Record

Start Weight	Breakfast	Lunch	Dinner	Extras
Saturday				
Sunday				
Monday				
Tuesday				
Wednesday				
Thursday				
Friday				

Exercise	Mon	Tues	Wed	Thurs	Fri	Sat	Sun
Run	Dist/Time	Dist/Time	Dist/Time	Dist/Time	Dist/Time	Dist/Time	Dist/Time
Stretching							
Other Activities							

Measuring the Second Resolution

Measuring your progress in this area is done through basically the same method, but there are some adjustments you may have to make because many of the measurements you make are going to be on intangibles. For example, how you treat other people, how well you drive (subjective, more often than not!), how good a job you did. These are often the measurements of the character traits you want to develop. Not so easy, but possible. Other Resolutions are easier to record, but harder to do so objectively. Like speaking the truth without qualification. *Really* hard.

Competence measurements may be slightly easier. Educational qualifications are pass or fail, but daily study can be planned, scheduled and measured, as can each staged assessment.

Anything can be measured and recorded. I once had the honour to work with someone I considered to be the best investigator, manager and 'people person' I know. His method for measuring his competence was to keep a book in which he recorded every decision and action he ever made, and to carry that book around with him all the time. He was also a man of character, sticking to his guns in a promotion when he argued that a senior management requirement that everyone above a certain rank — and I mean *everyone* — attend a meeting at 8am every day regardless of their potential for having any input. Standard management theory that. This, of course, meant that they had to get into work earlier to make sure that they prepared for the meeting. The person demanding the meeting be held was childless, wholly professionally focused and had no time for people who had different commitments. My friend told the promotion board that it was a waste of time for those who did not need to be there and had nothing to contribute. He did not get promoted, yet everyone who knew what he did knew that he was undoubtedly the best person for the job and would have improved things for everyone had he got it — including the organisation.

His book was depository and album of decisions made and lessons learned. It guided his progress professionally, as it did those who worked for him and with him. I suggest that you consider trying the same technique. Record what you do as you go along, including what you learned from what you did, good and bad.

Measuring The Third Resolution

You decided what your noble purpose is, and how you would serve others, including family, clients and the greater community. How do you measure your Resolution?

In truth, having measured your activities in the first two Resolutions there isn't so much to measure here as there is to simply record, for your own benefit and for the benefit of the others that you serve. And you should not only be recording your actions, but you should also *plan* your future actions. Time Management (self-leadership) serves you in that its application allows you to prepare for those things you anticipate you will want to do and those actions you will have to take in service and in your personal life.

Where will you plan and measure these plans and results?

I'll save you time and tell you that I do it in a personal planning system. I counsel you to do the same. The To-Do list could be a start but a To-Do list doesn't lend itself to the maintenance of records, to detailed planning and scheduling or to proper prioritisation of tasks. Here's my full take on things.

The Practice of Self-Leadership

Putting First Things First

If you have read this far I'd bargain that, by now, you have established your Roles and your Goals. You know what you do and you have goals that aren't being achieved because of your wavering compliance with the advice in these pages – that's not a criticism because you wouldn't have read it if the situation were otherwise.

If you haven't identified your roles and goals, please take the time to do it. Do that for the simple reason that having made those respective lists and having defined them to your satisfaction, you have decided what, in your own mind, are the most important areas of focus in your professional and private lives and therefore what you want to be disciplined, competent and ethical about. Having done the work you will have to agree that the reason these lists exist in their current form is because **you** decided that they were important. I didn't, and nor did anyone else. You did. No more excuses, reader. You have identified what you want to put first, or what you accepted should come first in your own life. You have, like it or not, officially taken responsibility!

The problem is that 'life' has a nasty habit of getting in the way. Other people, politics and politicians, supervisors and other circumstances have a propensity to place obstacles between what you want and what you can have. Things happen that interrupt you and make you change your focus.

The question is: do the interruptions have to cause you to take your eye off the ball for good? Or even at all?

Diligent time management students will know that the answer is, of course, 'No!' Of course, events can interrupt; of course they can make you redirect your focus; but with the exception of life changing events they do not mean that you MUST change your focus on what you want.

Occasionally, in the moment, it may feel like that has happened. You don't get promoted on time, or you just started a new job and immediately got dragged away from it for another task that will take up a lot of your time. A close family member dies and it feels like the end of the world, or (maybe) worse still a colleague is injured, killed or diagnosed with a terminal illness. All of these events can cause you to lose perspective for a while, but none of them need stop you achieving what must be achieved – what you decided is important to you. Those are the First Things. And they must come First.

How do we make sure, then, that we prioritise those 'things' in our daily activities? How do we become disciplined, and people of good character who do what needs to be done, when it needs to be done and in the way it needs to be done, whether we want to do it or not?

Prioritisation is the process of allocating relative importance to a number of events or tasks in order of a properly considered priority, so that they can be acted upon in the appropriate order and/or at the appropriate time. In time and life management, it has been accepted that there are two primary measures for identifying and allocating our priorities. These measures are Urgency and Importance.

Urgency is time critical, and means that we need to carry out an assessment about how long we have available to get something done (a deadline), or when something must be acted upon (e.g. an appointment). Importance means that it is critical to the achievement of the ultimate objective; that there is a performance/profit/success consequence in its achievement, or failure in the absence of that achievement.

Here's the thing: in identifying your roles and goals you decided what was important. In doing so, you made these your truest priorities. Anything else is NOT a priority in terms of your life, even if they are a working life priority. Other things may be a priority to somebody else but that does not make them yours by default. You may choose to make them priorities based on the other party's place in the hierarchy; for example, their being a client, a boss, a friend or a department. But outside of your own responsibilities and accountabilities in your roles, they are not ordinarily priorities.

Deciding what is important and what is urgent influences the order in which we do these things. But how?

Convention has it that the best way to make this decision is to decide where the task fits into the time management matrix,.

Convention has it that the best way to make a prioritisation decision is to decide where the task fits into the time management matrix. Charles Hobbs and Stephen Covey explained this concept in their books TimePower® and The Seven Habits® respectively and it is now used as an industry/science standard. The matrix looks like this:

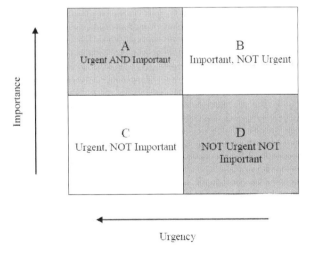

Quadrant A is where things (events, tasks) are Urgent AND Important. That means they relate to the Mission (yours or the job's), and they have to be done within a certain time frame. Simply put, there is a deadline surrounding something that is essential to our professional or personal objectives. For example, it might be attendance at an appointment relating to important work.

Quadrant B is where things are Important, but we have as long as we want to get them done. We are not pressed for time and can do them when we want to, or while we are doing something else as well. For example, exercising, planning our work, studying for exams.

Quadrant C contains things that are Urgent, but do not relate to our purpose. Things that happen here may be the submission of reports 'now', or changing a flat tyre. They have to be done 'now', but if they weren't done nobody would notice. Sometimes, they feel important because they reflect the priorities of someone we trust/like/value, but in truth – they are often their priorities and not our own.

Quadrant D contains things that are neither important nor urgent. In other words, things we shouldn't be doing anyway! This is where you watch Eastenders or the X Factor. It is wasted time by any stretch of the imagination.

(Just re-read that part – it is vitally important that you understand it. Ask yourself which Quadrant some of your own tasks may have been in, and where they should have been, if different. Get your head around the idea.)

The objective is to spend as much time as possible in the Important Zone. Time spent anywhere else is time wasted. (I hear you say, "But what about having fun?" True recreation is important. Watching Eastenders is not, unless you truly enjoy it. You place your own importance – or not – on what you do for 'fun'.)

We don't *get* what we think is important if we spend our time *doing* what we know to be unimportant. Goethe said, "What matters most must never be left at the mercy of what matters least"

Take a moment or two, now, to look at those things about which you want to be more disciplined (or that you are going to identify NOW because you failed to do so when you were encouraged to do so the first time. Don't you get it yet? This stuff is important AND urgent!) Number them in order of importance, just 1-2-3 for now. Which is the most important for you, which is next, and so on.

Do it Now!

Taking on board all that has been described up until this point, which is the theory behind the mindset of effective time management, the point arrives when we need to ask, "So what? How can I use this information?" A fair question.

Time management is the management of time in the context of our responsibilities, accountabilities and personal purpose towards and with other people. We do not live, and therefore cannot manage our time, in a vacuum. Everything we do involves some kind of relationship with other people. Therefore, everything we do must be prioritised in that context, too.

So when I plan something, I need to take their needs (etc.) into consideration, and that includes their priorities. And in our 'whole life' perspective, that means our supervisor/ team/ organisation/ family/ community/ us as well.

When we are at work, it is normal and reasonable for other people further up the hierarchy to expect that their priorities come before our own. That includes the people we serve. But that expectation is often based on routine – in other words, putting them before us is the default position, the starting point when it comes to deciding who does what, when. This is usually quite correct and it certainly isn't being suggested that this is wrong. In the vast majority of circumstances, it is the norm. It's what people are paid for.

Occasionally, however, that default position is NOT the right position to be in.

For example, you may be torn between two tasks – one which serves you in the long term and one which does not. The latter, though, is tempting because of its convenience, pleasure quotient or potential intrinsic value (money). In other words, something which tests your willingness to comply with the First Resolution.

Or you may have something you need to do in work that is a higher priority than what the boss needs, possibly because what you want to do is in Quadrant 1 – important and urgent – while what he wants is in Quadrant 2 (or possibly 3!). For example, you may have a time critical job to do, while the boss needs a report 'now'. With some jobs, no matter how 'important', that task must be assessed against (for example) a statutory requirement that something be done by a certain time, and your interrupting it to do your boss's bidding may threaten that deadline. Any distraction will have a negative effect on the job at hand. The choice is whether to comply with the Second Resolution – or not.

The answer is that you look at the whole situation and let your conscience decide. But that conscience-based decision is based NOT on the 'nice' thing to do but on the most effective thing – the one that complies with your Resolutions.

Always, always, ask yourself what the most effective thing to do is, in terms of your Resolutions and the Mission Statement that the Resolutions are designed and intended to serve. It is much easier to justify a decision if you can show yourself that you made the right one based on your values/mission and the Resolutions, than it is to justify the wrong thing by quoting other 'priorities' you know were just an excuse to procrastinate on your ultimate aim to live correctly.

I would suggest going through this process when prioritising:

Ask - What do I expect of myself? At work this is arguably the most important question, based on what you are expected to do by your employer and the clients you both serve. Sometimes the answer is not the one you may want to hear, but the answer you get is the truth. It's what you signed up to do. Remember, you volunteered to do your job, you weren't press-ganged. There may be elements about your work that you detest but, assuming you chose the job for a good reason, the rewards outweigh the disadvantages.

Ask - What are the consequences of doing (this)? What are the consequences of doing (that), instead? Once you have decided what the correct, mission-compliant action is, you can still decide what to do with that information. You can identify a different priority, yet still have options about when and how you act upon that analysis. Remember that having a priority does not mean it has to be done first; only that it must be done. When you do it is often influenced by other factors such as availability of resources – people, transport, and so on. So when you ask this second question you take the consequences of your alternatives into account and move further towards your ultimate decision.

Ask - What are the job's priorities? Occasionally, work priorities come into play that stop you doing the personal or professional 'fun' activity that serves your mission. There will be times when it is obvious; the job will have to come first and the Second Resolution can be applied. Other times the job will have to play second fiddle to a personal event – the balance between character and competence will allow you to make the right decision, and your self-discipline will ensure you take the action you decided was correct. The point is that knee-jerk priorities serve no-one: conscious thought about activity serves everyone.

The taking of your own and your work priorities into account does not require either be put first, only that they both be fully considered and properly assessed.

Ask - What resources do I need, and which are available? Knowing which resources are needed and available can influence your prioritisation decisions. If everything you need is available, act on the priority. If you know that people or equipment or information are not available to do the job, either make them available or put their collection first. The collection becomes the priority. Otherwise you simply cannot put the 'job to be done' at the top of your priorities - unless you want to do it badly.

Ask - What does this mean to me? Yes, you are allowed to take yourself into account. There may be perfectly legitimate reasons why you can't do what is asked of you, either 'then' or 'ever'.

Ask - If I do (that), can I do the other thing better/faster/first? Here you will find the answer to a question that may be asked later as to why you did one thing and not the other. If you put someone else's priority behind another, they will ask why you did so. It's what bosses do. If you have the answer ready because you genuinely considered it in your prioritisation questions, the 'right back at you' timing will clearly demonstrate that it is the truth.

An Alternative Perspective

In criminal investigation training, one of the decision making processes promoted in respect of Major Incidents is this: to ask what MUST I do now?: what SHOULD I do now?: and what COULD I do now? The idea is that answering these simple questions directs you towards taking positive action on the answers in direct proportion to the question. In other words, having decided on what MUST be done, there is no question that the shoulds and coulds take precedence, is there?

Well, yes – in an ideal world. Because all too often the MUST cannot be done immediately because of availability or otherwise of other people, equipment, the time of day, any one or more of several factors outside our control. However, this unavailability only means we have to move on to the next priority (sometimes a must, occasionally a should) to see if that can be actioned instead.

The coulds, incidentally, are the tasks that you might be able to 'shove' into any available space left when all the other priorities are planned.

This system was used by the founder of US Steel Andrew Carnegie nearly a hundred years ago. He would list his priorities for the day, every day. He would then attack the most important job until it was done (or progressed as far as circumstances allowed) and then move on to the next thing on his list. Anything left over at the end of a day was either a priority upon which no action had been possible, or it wasn't a priority at all. Left-over tasks went on to tomorrow's list.

He ascribed his enormous success (and life balance) on this simple system of prioritisation. (And he paid Ivy Lee $25,000 for the idea!)

Managing Workload

Take personal responsibility for doing a good job.

Years ago, I was working as a police officer and a non-urgent call came into the Operations Room, whose job it was to allocate incidents to available staff. Unfortunately, what they tended to do was to allocate jobs to any staff, regardless of their availability and current workload. Proximity, workload, capability – all these factors were secondary to getting it off their screen into their 'allocated' pile. If someone genuinely responded, "I'm busy (albeit more politely and less bluntly) the Ops Room controller would say' "Add it to your list", meaning that you now had more work while someone else, who may have just done their last allocated job, had nothing to do. The controllers were reducing their responsibility for managing their work, by dumping everything anywhere so they could say' "I've done my bit."

Read my lips: "I don't do lists". In the context in which I said it, what I meant was that I don't just add things to my list to take responsibility from the individual whose list it should be on. My motive was not to avoid work – it was to control work. My intention, clearly stated to the operator, was that I would let them know when I was available and if the job still needed allocation, I would do it. But I was not prepared to make a never-ending to-do list and create unnecessary stress. I explained all that that once to the Ops Room operator and never got asked to make a list again. But I also created a reputation for doing good jobs on what I did manage to do – which was still (quite often) everything on their list. I still had to come through on my promise to ensure I told the operators when I was free – if I had been found, just once, to be avoiding rather than controlling workload, my reputation – and that work management method – would have been lost.

Lists should be appropriately managed in that I should manage my list and you should manage yours. If I am appropriately allocated work, it goes on my list. If you are responsible for allocating work it stays on your list until you allocate it appropriately, not just dump it and tick it off as gone Furthermore, if you delegate a task to me (appropriately) then I should also be given the authority to make prioritisation decisions, too.

Inappropriate allocation of work is one of the main reasons that mistakes are made. If I am given a task that I am not competent to carry out, it is not my fault – it is the fault of the person who allocated it to the wrong person. If you are allocated a job you are not competent to handle, make it known to the person giving you the job and (time permitting) seek training, guidance, assistance or re-allocation.

Productivity

The best time to do something is always Now. As Tony Robbins puts it when discussing procrastination, the question is "When would NOW be a good time?" NOW gets things done. NOW gets things out of the way. NOW results in progress being made. So NOW is one of the keys to success.

But wait! Sometimes you can't do something NOW.

Occasionally a project or activity will take three hours and you only have one hour spare. Or you have a planned appointment and an event needs a level of attention that will take you away, possibly for days. This happens. ('This' is an anagram, you know, and that anagram happens a lot in many jobs.) But that doesn't absolve you from responsibility for getting that project done, does it?

The answer is to at least try to do everything as soon as practically possible, and to not let excuses get in the way.

Let me illustrate by example. To the best of my knowledge (which is limited by experience in this case), very few people will be seconded to deal with a crisis AND still be expected to get all their routine tasks done at the same time. To most of the people I worked with it was either/or – "I am dealing with the crisis so I cannot do the other things". So the other things wait for action, because they can't just go away – and then people claim that they suffer stress when those waiting, important 'things' suddenly become urgent.

As a 'time manager', however, my thinking developed differently. My belief is that there is time to deal with both, provided I am careful, I plan properly, and I take advantage of opportunities as they arise. Many's the time I have been on a major incident and dealt with my own routine tasks – appointments, for example. If I had an appointment and I was on a major incident, then because I knew I had that appointment I could plan for it. I could carry out major incident actions either side of that appointment 'window'. I could get that planned job out of the way and out of my head, and still do what else was required of me. My colleagues tended to cancel their appointments (if they remembered) and thereby created a future work-load and its associated stress. My attitude, put simply, is and was to Do It Now.

Here's the Key. If the task you are considering will take 2 to 5 minutes or less, always and without exception, Do It Now unless it is physically impossible through lack of equipment or information. That is the advice of the great success and management writers.

The alternative is to procrastinate, widely defined as putting things off because you fear doing them now. You either fear the effort itself, the nature of the action to be taken, or the potential consequence of taking that action. By using the word 'fear' I am including all the levels of fear such as concern, disinterest and disquiet, through to absolute panic. For example, do you remember when you were a child and you wanted something – you chose to ask the parent from whom you expected a better, patient response rather the one you 'knew' would say No. You would usually approach Mum rather than Dad, am I right? (My 22 year old son still does that!)

That was an example of the 'fear' of being told No. A minor fear, but an example of what I am talking about. By procrastinating, you avoid what you don't want or what you expect will happen if you take the action under consideration.

My answer is the same – Do It Now. Face the fear, do what has to be done and get it over with. Jack Canfield includes amongst his Success Principles the principle 'Act as If', where you 'pretend' you are the opposite of what you are now, or 'as if' you have what you lack. In this context, I suggest you 'Act as If' you have confidence in your ability to get what needs to be done, done. Overcome whatever fear it is that is stopping you. Lack of confidence? Act confident. Lack of knowledge? Act as if you know what to do. Fear of the person involved? Act as if they are not as important as you (they aren't). And so on.

Another excuse resulting in procrastination is 'inconvenience'. What that means is that you consider that you have something more important to do, and the new action doesn't quite fit in with your need to do that other thing. Occasionally this is true. Often it is a lie, and you know it. I often like to hear people use this argument for not doing something and I remind them about Rationalising, you will recall, where you argue something using often spurious or exaggerated argument to make something 'right' – like the smoker who argues for his habit, or the drinker who says he is not an alcoholic because 'I can stop any time I want', apparently the first sign of alcoholism! They make sense only to the speaker, who makes the facts fit the argument, rather than the other way around.

When putting things off, therefore, ask yourself why you are putting it off, and if the answer is truly 'fear' or one of its levels – Do It Now. Including the exercises and planning I have recommended throughout this book!

Another question to ask when deciding whether or not to do something, therefore, is 'What will happen if I delay/abandon this activity?' If the answer is 'nothing', and the consequence of inaction has no effect on the ultimate result – perhaps you should not be doing it anyway. If there is a consequence, then knowing what that consequence is can help decide what action to take, and when. It is a conscious assessment of the situation rather than a (typically management driven) 'that's the way we do things' judgment call.

I recall a dispute I had with a colleague when he was in CID and I was in uniform. A young lad had been assaulted the night before, and we knew who'd done it. On the first day of the enquiry, two offenders were arrested. Quite correctly the DC insisted that we get some evidential statements before interview, but as the day moved along we could only take one or two, despite trying to find other witnesses. I suggested we get on with the interviews, because if they admitted the offence we'd have the result (and I'd finish on time), but the DC insisted on visiting all the missed witnesses again – burning up the detention clock (the time allowed for a person to be held in custody before release was required) but enhancing the overtime opportunity. At one point my own sergeant asked why two of us were doing all this investigating when one could do it, and the answer the DC gave was "That's the way we always do it". The sergeant said, "Not with my staff" and sent the DC off on his own! At this point the Detective Inspector panicked and we did things my way – we did the interviews, got the confession and took our time getting better statements from witnesses afterwards!

As in many cases, the result was more important than blind (or malicious) compliance with the process, but sometimes people get bogged up in that process. Occasionally, distinct parts of the process can be considered and left (procrastinated) until later, while still getting the results.

It is necessary, indeed essential, that conscious effort be put into analysing situations rather than just 'doing it the way we've always done it'. That is how processes develop, speed up, and allow for creativity – using the massive computer between our ears to ask simple questions. And that conscious analysis can and should involve those others involved in the matter under consideration: it should not be your assessment alone, because the involvement of others makes sure that the things you either don't know about or that are outside your experience or knowledge, are also considered.

So it is okay to procrastinate occasionally – so long as the rationale has been fully identified and planned for.

Life

All the advice I have provided in this Appendix is as applicable to being at home as it is to being at work. Arguably more so.

At home, I procrastinate more often. Why is that? I suspect that for me (and possibly for you, too) the fact is that in work we are disciplined, we have processes and procedures that are laid down and monitored. We have the resources we need in terms of equipment and people. And ultimately, we are also accountable for failure to do what is expected or required of us.

At home, we have as long as we want; we are accountable only to ourselves and our families, we have only whatever equipment we own or can borrow, and our families do not like to be considered as resources! And in the last analysis, that self-accountability can be self-defeating because if 'we' are only answerable to ourselves then 'we' can excuse 'us' if we want to. And we often want to – and do so. This kind of thinking is contrary to that needed in our commitment to the First Resolution.

Overcoming procrastination is simple, in theory. Remember, Jim Rohn said that discipline is the bridge between goals and their achievement. You know that is true, don't you? Sometimes the truth hurts, and it hurts because it is a truth that we cannot argue against not matter how hard we try and how much we want the converse to be true.

We want to 'know' that waiting for something will get it done; that success will come to us and we won't have to chase it; that the garden will dig itself, or someone else will cut the 3-foot-long grass. (In my case, my neighbours once had a late night party and DID cut my 3-foot grass. For shame.) But we know what the truth is – nothing gets done until we take action towards its completion. Work or personal life – the rule is the same. And we know it. It is discipline. And I covered that in chapter 1.

Take my advice, and whenever possible, Do It Now!

Overcoming Procrastination

Sometimes it isn't easy, I know. So occasionally it pays to have a strategy for overcoming its ugly drag. Here, then, are a few suggestions.

Just Start. Occasionally, when you sit there looking at the task that must be done, the best way to get it finished is to just start. Once started, momentum takes over. One bite at the task leads to the next, and in no time it is done.

Set a time limit. If the above idea didn't completely solve the problem, set a limit of 5 minutes to work on the matter. At the end of 5 minutes your integrity is safe and you can, if you wish, stop. Do that 5 times in a day, and you've probably done the job – not all at once (which was unwelcome) but at the very least, in time.

Start in the middle. Sometimes the problem isn't the job to be done, but the order in which it must be done. You don't get to do the best bit until later because protocol dictates that you should start 'at the beginning'. If possible, decide instead to do the bit you like doing and then use that momentum to finish off the job when your mood has changed from 'down' to 'good'. Creating that fun part results in recognising that the dull parts are an essential way of making the fun part important and relevant. It's still about momentum.

Bite the bullet. Face up to it, and Just Do It. Become a person known for making decisions and taking action! So when I suggest you 'Do It Now', either

- Do it now, like I said: or
- Put it into your planner when you are going to do it.

After all "Well begun is half done". (Mary Poppins)

Appendix C – Running Programme

This is the running programme I used to go from 12-minute to one hour runs in 4 months. You can adapt your start day to whatever suits your circumstances, but be mindful that the numbers are in minutes, not miles!

Running Programme

Week	Sun	Mon	Tue	Wed	Thu	Fri	Sat
1.	15	8	10	8	12	5	12
2.	18	8	12	8	12	8	15
3.	20	8	12	10	12	8	15
4.	20	10	12	10	15	R	15
5.	25	10	15	10	15	R	15
6.	25	10	15	10	15	R	20
7.	30	10	20	15	15	R	20
8.	30	15	20	15	15	R	20
9.	35	15	20	20	15	R	20
10.	35	20	20	20	20	R	25
11.	40	20	20	25	20	R	25
12.	40	20	25	25	20	R	25
13.	45	20	25	30	25	R	25
14.	45	25	25	30	25	R	30
15.	50	25	25	30	25	R	30
16.	50	25	25	30	25	R	30
17.	55	25	20	35	25	R	30
18.	55	30	20	35	30	R	30
19.	50	30	20	35	30	R	30
20.	60	30	20	40	30	R	30
21.	60	30	25	40	30	R	30
22.	60	30	25	45	30	R	30
23.	65	30	25	45	30	R	30
24.	65	35	30	50	40	R	2X20
25.	70	35	30	50	40	R	2X20
26.	70	35	35	50	50	R	2X20
27.	75	35	35	50	50	R	2X20
28.	75	40	45	60	40	R	2X20
29.	80	40	45	60	40	R	2X20
30.	80	40	45	60	40	R	2X25
31.	85	40	50	45	60	R	2X25
32.	85	40	50	45	60	R	2X25
33.	90	40	50	45	60	R	2X25
34.	90	40	50	45	60	R	2X30
35.	95	40	50	45	60	R	2X30
36.	95	40	55	45	60	R	2X30
37.	100	45	55	45	60	R	2X30
38.	100	45	55	45	70	R	2X30
39.	110	45	55	45	70	R	2X30
40.	110	45	60	45	70	R	60
41.	110	45	60	45	70	R	60
42.	120	45	60	45	75	R	60
43.	120	40	60	45	75	R	60
44.	130	40	70	45	80	R	60
45.	140	40	70	45	80	R	60
46.	140	40	75	40	70	R	60
47.	150	30	60	30	70	R	60
48.	120	20	40	30	60	R	40
49.	80	R	30	20	R	5	Race

Appendix D – Miscellaneous Articles on a Three Resolutions Theme

In a book like this it would be impossible to encapsulate every possible idea on discipline, character, competence, service and purpose without realising that new ideas come to mind during every reading session. As such, the author has a blog in which updated concepts and suggestions are detailed.

These blogs also provide examples of applications – and misapplications – of **The Three Resolutions**.

With that in mind, here are some earlier blog entries from that website, http://threeResolutionsguy.com. which continues to provide updates on time management and life leadership perspectives.

"Why Do People Avoid Time Management Training?"

This entry is dedicated to the sceptics (who just need convincing) and the cynics (who think they are right because they have too much *invested* in being right).

The reasons people avoid time management training are:

1.   "I don't need to manage my time."

There are ONLY two kinds of people who do NOT have to manage their time.

There are those who have others manage it for them. They have secretaries or personal assistants to whom they delegate their diary management. Usually 'bosses' in the commercial or public sector who are paid well, and who are therefore 'entitled' to pay someone else to save their expensive time by managing their diaries on their behalf. The trouble is that delegation of your diary management can result in your priorities being undermined by other people – those whose own high level in the hierarchy can powerfully influence the lower level diary managers! Taken to the nth degree, it also gives the personal assistant power over your life and decisions. (We are all familiar with the doctor's receptionist who won't let patients bother their doctor, don't we? 'Nuff said.)

That isn't to say that a trusted, properly briefed and highly competent P.A shouldn't be used but, unless you are really close to them, they won't manage your time as well as you can. Yes, there are situations where they can be used – for example, when you get a call out of the office from someone who wants a brief meeting, you can get them to ask your P.A to slot them in at an opportune moment. In truth, however, being paid more raises the expectation you can do the important planning yourself. Or does it? I don't know, I'm not a manager.

The other people who don't need to manage their time are those who have nothing to manage their time *for.* By that, I mean that they have no sense of purpose in their lives so letting things go by does not offend any plan. These people usually work in supermarkets, stacking the shelves. Everything they do is dictated for them – they have no responsibilities except doing what they are told, then spending their money as quickly as possible.

People like *US* who have multiple responsibilities, objectives in and outside of work, community organisations and charities to serve, kids to 'manage' (lead) and so on *need* to be able to manage ourselves in the context of time if we are not to melt into chaos.

I know of no-one who has only one role. Think of any job and ask yourself if it truly contains a singular responsibility, or if it in fact contains a lot of sub-roles. I know of secretaries who are responsible for organising events (there are professionals who do that, you know), managing their supervisors, maintaining records and overseeing accountabilities of people in other departments. Every police officer has to deal with a plethora of different calls, witnesses, court appearances, meetings and file management. I may have mentioned I have several roles myself and I am 'just' a detective constable.

Real people have to manage their time.

2. "I don't want to be restricted: I like being spontaneous."

You cannot be spontaneous and responsible *unless* you know what tasks and appointments you can be spontaneous around! For the simple reason that I manage my time I find I am more able to assist colleagues with the ad hoc tasks and opportunities that arise, because I get more done in a focused fashion than they do.

Imagine having a managed to-do list that magically disappeared because you'd done everything on it, forgotten nothing and created excellent results *quickly*. The time you save is yours to be spontaneous within.

Of course, if you base your entire life on 'being spontaneous', you will probably find yourself remembering and doing things at the last minute. Or forgetting things and being unable to do them because that minute has already passed. Why put yourself through the stress?

Or I suppose you could rely on buses, trains, planes and other people to 'be spontaneous' and see what a total mess our lives would be. No-brainer?

3. "It's too hard!"

Everything seems to hard the day it is taught. Ralph Waldo Emerson said that what at first seems to be difficult becomes easier as time passes, not because the thing itself became easier, but because our ability to do it improves. I bet your first driving lesson was a hoot, but you are competent now, aren't you? (Don't answer that.)

I use the system described in this book for one simple reason. Because it *is* a system. There is a technique to it from start to finish – many so-called 'systems' are just a loose list of techniques which are useful, but which are disjointed and have to be applied as and when they seem relevant. Secondly, having studied the science of time management for 20 years I can't say I have ever seen a better one. Ever. Save yourself 20 years of study and take my word for it.

I used to compare my investigative skills to a more experienced detective and one of less experience (and application). I decided that the detective could find shortcuts to results; I used a system that got me there; the other colleague tripped over results. What is was trying to describe was how someone with experience *and* knowledge could develop a working practice that got results quickly; I had to follow the routines; and the other one got the odd result but couldn't replicate them because of the luck involved. The detective used to do it my way, but experience had identified short cuts and methods that made parts of the routine redundant for him.

It is the same with the management of time. Use this system, familiarise yourself with and apply it, and your life will improve. Very soon, like the veteran DC you will be able to adapt it to your own circumstances, for example by utilising an electronic version or by designing your own template forms for use in your own areas of work and life.

4. "It takes up too much time in itself."

Failing to plan is planning to fail. Hackneyed? Think about this:

Time spent planning saves time in execution.

Looking ahead at the 'what will happens and the what might happens' allows you to prepare for contingencies in advance.

That's why we businesses have briefings about operations. That's why major criminal investigations succeed. That's why routines, protocols and systems work – because they have been planned in advance.

That doesn't just apply to big things, either. You can look in your diary and see a dental appointment. 'Just turn up', says the non-time manager. The time manager thinks, "I can take some paperwork, a book to read, I can pop round to get some shopping, I can take my diary in with me to arrange the next appointment'.

Point taken?

5.   "Time management is for losers."

The real reason behind this comment is fear that you won't be able to practice it, a fear based on ignorance (as many are) because it really *is* easy once you start applying it.

I never met a true success who didn't use their time in a well-planned fashion. I have met a LOT of people whose lives could have been better, even though they appeared to have succeeded. Yes, they held senior positions, and if that is your whole idea of success then so be it. But they frequently have dodgy marriages, contribute little or nothing outside of work, and will have left nothing when they go – the gap they leave will be filled very easily, take it from me.

True successes aren't just missed because someone else is there instead – they have been truly lost. What kind of 'success' do you want to have? The one that only your family knows about, or the one that is recorded, permanently, in some historical records.

Time management can help you do that, if taken to the extent described in my book – that is beyond technique and towards the principles of effective, values-driven, passionate life *design*. Identifying your values makes it easier to communicate and live them. Realising how important your family is makes you more likely to put them first, ahead of money or career. Realising what your dreams are, and managing yourself and your time to live them, reduces the stresses and depression that you take out on those around you.

For me, time management turned me from "that bloke who sat at that desk" into someone respected, well known, a contributor in his industry with influential friends. You try it.

"If It Wasn't For The People."

I have a tongue-in-cheek saying for my own role in a public service sector, and many readers will sympathise a little (in private) with it. It goes

"If it wasn't for the public this would be a great job."

They call us expecting us to deal with their problem as if it is the only problem we have to address. They see the TV and how things are sorted in half an hour (minus ad breaks) and expect us to do the same. They also seem to think that we don't have time off at weekends and after hours, like they do.

But in absolute fairness, if it wasn't for 'people' life would be a little humdrum. When you think about it –

"Everything we do, we do for someone, because of someone, or with someone."

Consider your own circumstances. In truth, is there anything you do that does not come under one of those headings. Think broadly, because things you think you do on your own usually require either direct or indirect involvement of someone else – perhaps, for example, the inventor of the equipment you are using. (I lose count of people who hate 'personal development' books because they are 'so American': I ask them to give up their computers because they are pretty much American, too. Microsoft and Apple pretty much run the world in computer terms, after all.)

So, realising that all you do is because of, for or with the help of someone, perhaps your attitude towards the interference of 'people' in your life should mellow, just a teeny bit.

Then you can start to Think Win-Win with people, as per Habit 4 of the 7 Habits. That's a whole new challenge! On courses I have attended, when asked what Habit 4 is, participants often shout back 'Win-Win!' and have to be gently corrected because the emphasis is as much on the Think as it is on the Win-Win. Habit 4 is the mindset of the Public Victory; Habit 5 (seek first to understand, then to be understood) is your part in the Technique, and Habit 6 (Synergise) is the combined execution that brings the desired result.

Just entering into a conversation, negotiation or situation with the mindset of mutual satisfaction with an end result makes a massive difference to the interaction between people – even the ones who you don't want to interact with. So here's a question I have used when he sensed the beginning of a dispute (for example with someone who opens with 'the policy is....').

"What is the nature of your concern?"

This requires an answer that comes from behind the initial objection to you getting the result you need. It asks, "If this policy is preventing us from agreeing, what is behind the policy – what caused that policy to come about?" All too often, the policy is designed as a safety blanket to prevent a problem that will not necessarily apply in your own situation, and is therefore changeable 'just this once' because a sense of trust and understanding – resulting from your own approach in Think Win-Win – allows it.

People – treated with respect and understanding they can be soooooo much nicer.......

"Crossing That Bridge."

I am currently summarising the Covey book 'Marriage Family; Gospel and Insights', and in the opening chapter of his half of the book he writes:

'There is a common problem in only focusing on the ideal *(i.e. in focusing on the dream and not the immediate reality – my summary DP)*. A false dichotomy is set up. A dichotomy means either/or. Its fault is that it doesn't reflect the full reality. When people separate the abstract and the concrete, the ideal and the real, many end up frustrated. Although they may be temporarily 'psyched', even inspired, by a description of the ideal they come to see themselves falling terribly short of it; in their mind the distance between the ideal and their own performance is so great that they feel the ideal to be an unreachable goal for them, that in a fundamental way they are incapable of attaining it.'

This shows us why some people ask the question – **"is my ideal 'so' ideal that it is impossible to attain and, if so – why even try?"**

I wonder if that is where I sit. I need to lose 4 stone. I read of athletes and housewives who have achieved this. I know it can be done, and (with all due respect to those who have achieved it) in some cases I am more intelligent than some successful dieters (at least on paper!).

So I set out to diet and exercise. Then an injury occurs, or we go out to a party meal, and suddenly it's too hard a goal, or I can start again tomorrow, or I'm really not that round and I'm carrying it well (bad eyesight helps).

Is the answer to perhaps make an 'ideal' less so, working towards a lesser goal until it is achieved and then 'starting tomorrow' on the next 'ideal' step that is just a little bit closer to the ultimate ideal? This attitude or approach makes that bridge between real and ideal more of a plank or pontoon than the Golden Gate! Baby steps.

I am close to retiring and intend to spend just a little bit of time working towards my ideal before I look for a new paid role. When that space between jobs happens, I will be totally responsible for my own environment, and the working atmosphere with its propensity for convenience foods won't be there as an excuse (reason) any more, and I won't have the 'tired after work' excuse, either. If I start to create the ideal (sorry, best) home environment possible to serve my intention I will be more likely to achieve that goal – my first baby step towards the ultimate ideal, so to speak.

And maybe just being aware of the false dichotomy will better prepare me to address it?

Ultimately, there is an ideal, but reality sits within it. Life can get in the way, or life can be what we do on the way. The latter is the best approach!

"The ONLY Way to Win?

Continuing on the theme of 'the ideal', I am reading an interesting book at the moment called 'The Only Way to Win' by Jim Loehr. The book is looking at how building character drives higher achievement, and an early chapter addresses the question – is high self-esteem a consequence of achievement, or is achievement a consequence of high self-esteem? There is a lot of discussion about having too much self-esteem being as bad, if not worse than having too little because inflated egos need, well, more inflation!

But one relevant quote provided is that of Dr Roy Baumeister, professor of Psychology at Florida State University, who says, "After all these years, I'm sorry to say, my recommendation is to forget about self-esteem and **concentrate more on self-control and self-discipline.**" This is exactly the objective of applying the First Resolution.

The suggestion has often been that self-esteem is either a pre-cursor to achievement (usually good) or a consequence of achievement (occasionally bad). Here's the discovery Loehr made – if achievement is required in order to gain self-esteem, then anyone failing by any degree loses their self-respect. Furthermore, when people get what they seek they frequently become depressed because having achieved it they feel that it was too easy, so creating doubt in themselves that they earned what they have – and so they go seeking more in order to get the self-esteem that eluded them because they decided – *they* decided – that they didn't deserve the esteem their achievement should have provided them!

This relates again to earlier posts – is my goal truly mine? Is my ideal truly ideal? If I DO get it, will I be happy?

Now, referring back to Baumeister's quote and to further utilise the philosophy of Dr Charles R Hobbs, author of TimePower , if instead of using achievement as a measure of self-esteem we use our desire and ability to be in CONTROL of our lives as our 'self-esteem measuring stick', could we be happier in the moment? Could we still seek to achieve but do so more happily, to the degree that provided we remain in control of that striving we stay happy *regardless* of the end result. We live in the now, not in the hope that we will live 'when we get there'.

Loehr used an example of a schoolboy wanting to be a doctor.

"I'll be happy when I get my school exams done with," becomes "I'll be happy when I get my medical degree" becomes "I'll be happy when I finish my doctor training/internship" becomes "I'll be happy when I can be a consultant" etc etc. Such dependence on achievement to assuage one's self-esteem is fraught because one failure along that route means 'the END!', despite the potential each step provides. And in circumstances like that example, we won't be happy until we are far too old – and too tired – to enjoy the success we sought.

Indeed, while we are striving we tend to use what we achieve as we go along to influence everything we do – for example, we spend money in a way that serves each step and doesn't necessarily serve the end in mind; we nurture or stifle relationships that serve/obstruct our goals; and we dress, eat and live 'in the expected way'.

(Don't get me started on how we are taught to avoid stereotyping when we all, ALL OF US willingly comply with stereotypes to get what we want, either consciously or subconsciously. In my country, we say it's easy to spot a conservationist/social worker/Guardian reader, and have you noticed how people being interviewed in the media are often wearing suits but have taken their ties off to look 'media cool'. Well, they're not. I digress.)

Anyway, I asked the question that perhaps every goal-orientated person should ask at the off – "What responsibility or consequence will arise from my success?" Not just the award, prize, wealth or immortality, but what goes with it.

Fame – and the media interest in your private life? Perhaps you seek a Professorship – and the subsequent need to lecture, write, and be approached for authoritative opinion ad nauseam? How about professional status – and the realisation that you will have to earn a living at it 60 hours a week for 50 years? All the time having to spend time with colleagues you don't trust rather than spending time with the family you love? (BTW, earning millions while your kids don't know what you look like is NOT the only way to bring up happy kids. Try earning only £1million and spending time with them instead.)

So – great self-esteem is something you deserve to have NOW. It comes from having great self-discipline and exercising self-control. You being in charge means you recognising and deciding whether the consequences of your dreams are what you expect and want them to be, and to adjusting your sights and plans accordingly. **Make sure the Important Things are YOUR Important Things.**

"Living – Or Being Lived?"

Have you noticed the proliferation of the word 'obviously' when people speak, these days? Have you also noticed, as I have, that the word 'actually' seems to have ebbed away just as quickly as 'obviously' came in?

Yes, these days people use obviously where they used actually (or actual) where they used to use 'erm'.

In my view this is a reflection of the increased pace of our world, in particular our communication capacity (email, text, phones) and the psychological effect of 'conditioning'. Let me explain.

1. Conditioning occurs when, like Pavlov's Dogs, we learn to react in a certain way to a consistent stimulus. When A happens, we automatically do B. This serves us, for example, when we see a door handle. we assume, from conditioned experience, that it will push downwards to open the door. Watch the bemused look when someone fits a handle to move upwards. Conditioning also applies when we hear things, as we adopt the language of those around us most often – don't knock it, that's how you learned to talk as a child. So it is a true principle.

2. Communication has changed, in the sense now that it is more immediate than it ever was. We speak, action is expected. If we text, we expect an immediate response, as we do with email (occasionally). I see people conduct conversations by text – which takes 10 minutes to have a chat which, if conducted on the PHONE, would have taken seconds. Odd.

3. The immediacy of communication, or our *perception* of that immediacy, means when we DO talk to people we expect immediate understanding. At the same time, we do not want to be interrupted so we speak quickly and try not to create gaps which, given the chance, the person we are speaking to will fill with what we call 'interruptions'. We don't want that, so we fill the inadvertent gap. These inadvertent gaps are caused because we are talking faster than we are thinking – for example, Freudian slips and Spoonerisms are caused by doing that – and because we do that we have to fill the gap with something to prevent the other person interrupting. That used to be the word 'erm', but that sounds like we aren't clever. Thus we started using the word 'actual' and its derivatives because it sounds intelligent. But after using it three times in one sentence it doesn't sound clever any more.

Some people stopped using 'actual (etc.) but still needed to sound clever, so 'obviously' was its replacement. I have heard that used 8 times in one telephone call.

If it's obvious, you don't need to use the word or explain why it's obvious. Duh!

Anyway, to address the title – we are all using it simply because instead of thinking for ourselves we are letting other peoples' habits, idiosyncrasies and (dare I say it) lack of verbal skills or intellect to dictate how WE talk, which is in turn a reflection that we comply with other things like fashion, popularity, celebrity and other societal 'norms' because we allow it, consciously or unconsciously. We dress like heroes, we talk like them, we behave like them because it's 'cool' (A 1920s term, which shows just how trendy 'cool' actually isn't.)

Are you being lived, or are you willing enough to be different and a true individual?

"Opinions – Influenced by Falsity?"

On a theme of 'being lived', another question arises. Is the media to be believed?

In the UK, there is a lot of press attention being given to one particular party at the moment, one which is pro-British and which some take to be racist in intent. I am not considering whether it is or is not. Parties, like any other organisation, are made up of people and if they all thought the same they wouldn't need committees, so the occasional nutcase will always come out and say something stupid, or contrary to a popular 'ism'. Again, I do not want to get into that – it's too dangerous.

What I DO intend to get into is this – can we trust the media, and if so, to what extent?

The Press have done some wonderful things – but.

They expose corruption that we should know about, but they sensationalise misconduct that we really shouldn't give a toss about. They keep us informed about the facts, but they also twist and exaggerate using adverbs and adjectives which are theirs, and are not necessarily designed to support the facts as much as they are intended to sell newspapers. They expose the 'surveillance society' and then take pictures of holidaying 'celebs' and focus on their cellulite, or camp outside people's houses harassing them into submission. (All the time demanding private investigators be licenced for doing far less, but that's my focus group and I'll say no more!)

I am amazed by how often, at 6am in the morning, I buy a newspaper that tells me that I (aka 'the public') am outraged by something that I don't know about, yet. So – is that true? Is the public 'outraged', or do they just want us to be so we'll buy their rag?

The BBC is now in the habit of having one journalist report a headline, only to turn to another reporter to interview them – giving us the impression that the latter is an authority on the matter, as opposed to another journalists who has a bit more information than us but is otherwise just as uninformed as us. That air of authority warps our opinions because like it or not, it comes across as authoritative opinion – which it patently is not.

Wouldn't it be wonderful if the papers reported "just the facts, ma'am"? No emotive language, no sensationalist descriptive terminology – just tell what is true and leave us to decide whether we care or not. Perhaps then we'd start living in a world where the opinion of the press was no longer relevant, or that there was at least a clear distinction between the facts and the fluff?

I say all this because whether we like it or not, if we are not properly proactive about deciding whether what we hear is accurate, or not, we will allow ourselves to be influenced by things which are INTENDED BY OTHERS to influence us, not things that SHOULD influence us.

Which will really annoy the advertisers!

(Have you noticed how, despite the media's insistence that their channels are about entertainment and information – all the adverts seem to come on at the same time so you can't avoid them by channel hopping?)

"Self-Preservation Through Unified Living."

Living your values, it is generally accepted in the personal development field, is the best way to ensure high personal self-esteem and life-long happiness. Charles Hobbs and Hyrum Smith both specifically address how living in accordance with your highest universal principles – your own set of genuine, conscience driven rules and standards – is the best way to feel successful, because it is intrinsic (part of you) and not dependent on outside approval, social acceptance or material wealth. Living your values means serenity and peace. And violating them brings anxiety, guilt and even depression.

How do I know this? From experience, that's how.

A couple of days ago I was merrily driving along, using the correct driving principles as taught to me by skilled police drivers, and adhering to the speed limit when a chap drove up behind me so close I couldn't see his headlights. Considering we were in a 30mph limited road which was on the approach to a roundabout this seemed a bit silly, but I didn't bite. I just raised my hand in a circle, separated the finger and thumb, and indicated thereby that perhaps the driver may consider pulling back a tad. He did so, and I gave him the thumbs up. Just as he accelerated hard and overtook so that he was still on the wrong side of the road as we came to the bollard at the roundabout entrance.

Now, if I had been proactive and used the stimulus/response gap to think 'he's a nutter so I'll give him space', things would have been fine. However, in that instant, I chose the 'oh, we'll see who can get to the gap first then, shall we?' reactive technique. As it was, there was just enough – by inches – space so that no collisions occurred and I was able to add a verbal description of the driver through our mutually open car windows before we went I our separate directions.

And for the rest of the day I felt really off.

I felt off because I had failed to act in accordance with my unifying principle 'I demonstrate high levels of skill and patience in driving.' I felt off because I had not considered that circumstances like this lead to potential confrontation and while I am not fearful of 'it', confrontation is such an open ended activity. If I win the immediate confrontation I have no guarantee that it stops when it is over, especially these days when violence and revenge and utter stupidity seem to be the watchword of people whose first response is reactive thuggery, rather than being dragged slowly towards that end. Would I find that he would torch my car, find out where I live and threaten my kinfolk? If there had been a rumble, even if I had won what could the legal consequences have been? Was I prepared for them, did I want or need such inconvenience? And if the road hadn't been wide enough, was I prepared to spend money and time repairing my car because I was reactively miffed?

Over the remainder of the day (and my reaction still irked me at bedtime) it occurred to me that, occasionally, it is not the highest ideals that we find hard to live up to, but the tiny ones. Say we choose to study, and do so diligently towards a professional qualification. It's hard, but it's doable. At the same time we resolve to be patient, and then someone jumps into the front of a queue and we go nuts. In many ways the patience objective is the easiest – easy to understand, easy to see ourselves doing it, easy to define – but the stimulus to challenge it can be too sudden and we have no time to think (correction, we do not take the time to think) and so we fail.

It's a lesson we should all consider to be valuable. We have failed, so next time we won't. It's a demonstration that we are compliant with both the First and Second Resolutions. We discipline ourselves to be patient, deny ourselves the counterfeit sense of righteousness that the offending behaviour can engender within us, and our character shines through (with some competence in patientology).

Next time – just drive off ahead of the tailgater, or let him go. Let him offend and endanger someone else – I am too important to me and to my family and friends to suffer because of my own ego.

As are you.

"Bushido and the Three Resolutions"

Bushido is a Japanese term most would be familiar with, even if they didn't know what it meant (like me). It is the Japanese warrior code and strictly means Military-Knight-Way (Bu-Shi-Do), but here for me was the interesting part. According to Inazo Nitobe's 'Bushido – the Art of Japan', the Bushido knight's code has not been written down except for a few maxims being handed down from mouth to mouth or being noted by some knight. In a similar vein, the terms 'gentleman' and 'genuth' (German) communicate a meaning which may not be formally defined in terms of any Code, but which most would understand nevertheless.

It occurred to me that this is a parallel to the 7 Habits and the **Three Resolutions**. Dr Covey writes of undeniable Principles as being timeless, extrinsic, accepted without question and universal. But some readers of his books criticise him for not being more specific with defining what 'the principles' are. He does mention a few, like truth, integrity and so on, but there is no defined and authoritative list provided – even in the later book ,Principle-Centered Leadership.

So, like Bushido, the principles set out in both books remain, like Bushido, 'understood'. You know what it means but would have to think about how to define it, if asked.

Which is not to say that we can't define them at all – it just means, for me, that we need to define them for ourselves. We do that by reading, experiencing and occasionally just knowing what our truths are going to be. We then live by those rules, in the main. For some, like me and I hope by now, you, we write a personal mission statement, a set of defined values or simple a general 'credo' by which you try to live. You may not manage it 100% but the awareness that you have it, and the awareness of others that you have it, makes it more likely you'll comply.

So, the **Three Resolutions** might mean something different to all of you, but we understand them enough to 'know' what they are and that we should be living in their accordance.

"High Standards - A Cross to Bear?"

When I was allocated a new position in the police service, I was also required to undertake an advanced driving course. Hitherto I had prided myself on being a talented driver, having tried my advanced driving test (failed twice); completed a racing driving course and done a few laps of Brands Hatch, and had a few amusing off-road type experiences. I'd even driven Land Rovers on tank courses. Over the years I'd read widely on advanced driving theory and practice and I felt I was quite skilled, even if my attitude stunk and I occasionally took the odd silly risk.

But in 2001 I went on this course, run by a 'proper' pursuit trained police Grade 1 Instructor, and my eyes were opened wide to new thinking, better observation skills and, one could argue, a higher expectation of what was expected of an advanced driver.

(For the purist I was an 'intermediate' advanced driver – not driving the full-blown Volvo T5s, BMW 535s etc. but a Volvo S40 area car. My take – the road's the same shape and the pedals are in the same order, the rest is pursuit responsibility, familiarity with a slightly faster vehicle and even higher expectations. But traffic officers have a tendency to be a bit anal about their abilities/training so I dare not say all that out loud.)

Anyway, as a result of these higher expectations and a slightly more mature desire to comply with the new training and associated skill levels, I drove to the new system until I got to the point where I couldn't drive the 'old way'. My attitude still stinks a bit but the car control part is much better, as is compliance with protocols like observation skills, lane discipline, indicating, and so on.

The reason my attitude stinks is because I am very much more aware of the s**t skill levels of the 'average' motorist around whom I have to negotiate. The non-signaler, the ones who pull out on roundabouts in your path without indicating or not accelerating swiftly enough NOT to get in the way, the lane-hogger who switches his brain off on arrival in the middle lane and stays there from London to Edinburgh. And the phone user – a***holes whatever excuse they might think justifies potentially fatal consequences. You know the type – in fact, you may be one. (In which case change your attitude or get off my site! :-)

At the same time, not driving related, my 'high' standard of verbal skills and the ability to write using sentences, correct grammar and punctuation means that the inability of others to do so, particularly when some of them are (on paper) cleverer than me – gets on my nerves. And the reading of Stephen Covey and Anthony Robbins on how we can reactively allow our environments to condition us to act in a certain way has made it abundantly clear to me why people use the word 'obviously' seven times a conversation and why teenagers say 'like' a lot; in fact, on holiday I heard a man use the word three times in one sentence – and that was three times in a row in one sentence!

Unfortunately, having (or at least striving to have) higher standards makes it abundantly, **abundantly** clear how low other people's standards have become. Let me be clear – their standards are not necessarily low by intention (although they often are), it's usually because they give **no thought to how they are**

conditioned by their surroundings and the people in them, or they excuse their lowering of standards (driving being a very good and common example) because they aren't being tested or examined any more. The lack of accountability for higher standards results in them being socially permitted to drop their standards to the common level.

Remember the Anthony Robbins experience with the US Marines I mentioned in an earlier blog? In one audio recording he described how he was asked to coach US Marines on leadership and motivation, and in doing so he was told that the men and women present were at the peak of their performance 'lives', and that when they left the Forces their standards slipped. When Robbins tells the story he opines that the reason their standards slip is because the expectations of the veterans' post-service peer groups – new colleagues, friends, communities and society in general – are lower, and so the new standards displayed by those veterans are a reflection of the lowered expectations of the new peer group. In the Marines expectations were very high. Outside, they're more 'whatever works in the moment'.

One of the objectives of application of the First and Second Resolutions is to develop the self-discipline to behave in accordance with your higher values and to become exceptionally competent (expert?) in your chosen field of work – and competence can include competency in 'routine' life skills. To develop a higher sense of personal integrity as you discover what is important to you, to strive to act in accordance with those needs, and to achieve them at the highest possible level.

And that's why it is annoying when I see what goes on around me. I see people capable of better who either don't, or won't, seek to behave at the higher level of competence or character. People who just let life dictate to *them* whether their behaviour is acceptable, convenient, just enough or even dangerous. Instead of taking action to make sure that they dictate to life what *their* standards are and how they will keep acting in their accord.

I'm still trying – are you?

"Mind Your Language"

In his book 'The Seven Habits of Highly Effective People' Stephen Covey recommends   the   following: "For a full day, listen to your language and the language of the people around you. How often do you use and hear reactive phrases such as 'If only', 'I can't' or 'I have to'?" He makes this suggestion following the input (headed 'Listen to Your Language', page 78, standard print).

My take on this is that he is saying that as our attitudes and behaviours flow out of our paradigms (how we see things), we tend to behave as those paradigms dictate. As a result we can blame our behaviours on those paradigms. As our language is one manifestation of our behaviours we can also blame what we say on what we think. "Oh, I'm sorry, I thought....." Analysing even further, then, it is fair to say that what we say suddenly when provoked, angered or otherwise emotionally shoved is what we are thinking in the moment, and that this is therefore an honest thought expressed candidly. The only problem with that assessment is that is that it isn't necessarily so. It's a paradox – we are being honest but we are not stating the truth – because our paradigm is wrong.

Going back along the paradigm- perceive-think-say continuum, this 'honest expression' that we blurt out is based on some prerequisite factors.

First, we may have an accurate paradigm, in which case our perception is better, so our thoughts are aligned with that accuracy and what we say is therefore 'fair comment'. Alternatively, or paradigm is inaccurate, in which case our perception is flawed, so our thoughts are corrupted by that false perception, so what we say is manifestly wrong. Our paradigms can be subject to many influences, one of which is our personal value system. Our values and beliefs affect how we see things (ask any football fan about the average penalty decision), therefore what we see is also affected because we look through our values window at the world. In our example, we are speaking what we believe, but our belief may be based on a false premise and therefore not be true.

So why does Stephen Covey suggest that watching our language make us more proactive?

Surely it is this: if we decide to watch our language and take more care with the words that emerge from our mouths, we take a second or two – seldom any more than that – in which we can re-assess the stimulus that gave us the desire to respond verbally. In that space we can use our self-awareness, imagination and conscience to identify whether our initial paradigm is accurate, and we can use our independent will to reframe, in more exact terms, what it is we truly wish to communicate. Did we hear what we thought we heard? Did we see what we thought we saw? Even if the answer to either question is 'Yes', we can also ask "Did I understand it correctly?" and "Could there be another explanation?"

Each moment that passes as we silently ask any or all of those questions provides a unique opportunity to reconsider what we are going to say, even whether we are going to say anything at all. In taking that moment we can consider whether there is a better way to express what we feel must be expressed; to fully consider the needs of all of those involved in the intended communication, including ourselves and those we love and respect. If by taking that moment we stop ourselves from offending someone, do we not save ourselves from having to apologise? Do we not save ourselves the conscience driven angst that comes from the unintended Freudian slip?

In addition, by reflecting more on what we thought was true and occasionally finding it not to be, do we not find that our understanding improves in all we see or hear?

I think this is why Dr Covey identified how we can use our words as a means to demonstrate and teach how a moment's proactivity can make such a difference to our effectiveness. He is saying that keeping your mouth shut just a little bit longer can allow you to fully reassess what just happened. And then say something – or not say something – in an effort to achieve a better end. And at the same time, that pause empowers our learning and also, by extension, our intellect.

This isn't easy. On the one hand there have been many times when I have said nothing despite being wearied by the inanity of something challenging that has been said, an insult, or a repeated moan. On the other hand, there have been many more time when I've shot off at the mouth and ended up feeling worse, rather than validated, for doing so.

Hyrum W. Smith, co-Vice-President of FranklinCovey, expresses the opinion that our intellect is affected by our vocabulary, because the greater the vocabulary the better we can understand others, and the better we can express ourselves with accuracy. The more words we have, the better we communicate – often by using less of them.

So, Be Proactive. Take a moment to pause and consider what you understand and what words you have available to you, before uttering any at all.

"Am I Competent?"

No, I don't mean me, specifically. It's a question I often asked myself in times of doubt, and I'm sure it's a question you may have asked yourself. It is something I know I've asked myself when a colleague has pulled some masterful piece of work out of his or her bag, a piece of work I either should have considered or could have considered – but didn't.

What *IS* Competence? In my book I define it as "the ability to get things done in accordance with the technology, methodology and ethics of the role being undertaken". That general definition covers a multitude of professions, trades and pastimes. The 'things to be done' are the results expected from the individual that relate to the objectives of the organisation – it may be sales, it may be production, it may be distribution, it could be the provision of any services you can think of. But if you disagree with the definition just apply your own – it's your understanding of competence that is important, and even more so when you apply it to your own work.

The chances are that having obtained a 'job' you either got training, or were expected to already know what it was you were supposed to be doing. Even in that latter situation I'd imagine there was some tempering of what you knew in the sense that it had to be applied to the specific situation in which you found yourself. I know, for example, that after 14 weeks Police training my naïve colleagues and I underwent a Force-level 'local procedure course' where we were enlightened as to "how we do it 'round 'ere", followed by another "how we do it 'round 'ere" inflicted on us when we got to our first station. Then there were to be many other "how we do it 'round 'ere" courses as we were to transfer between stations and departments. I probably inflicted a few rounds of "how we do it 'round 'ere" myself. (What do you mean I still do?)

And on each pf my subsequent HWDIRH courses I probably discovered that either I was not competent in the eyes of new 'trainer' because of the way I HAD been doing it, or the 'trainer' was evidently incompetent because I could see (having got older and wiser) that s/he was incompetent. Such incompetence, by the way, was often the reliance on HWDIRH being set in stone – the ONLY way.

It is clear to me that no matter where you go and whatever you do, there is a 'window' that exists, through which you will be viewed as competent or otherwise, and this is called the 'AYNOBETA WINDOW'.

Someone, somewhere, will always know better than you. It is plain if you are wholly new to a field and are completely uninformed that people will see you through this window, and be right. On such occasions, suck it up, accept the impatience as a sense of urgency that you learn the new things being taught. (Particularly if you've just joined the Marines)

But in progressing along a 'training continuum' where you've already gained some competence in your field, the situation may be a bit different with the other party's AYNOBETA WINDOW. If they DO know better it will be evident the moment that they take the time to explain their thinking and you discover a new perspective. If they DON'T know better, that will become evident the minute they shout you down, refuse to listen to you, or call you an idiot for your failure to succumb to their greatness. Avoid these people like the plague. And don't become one.

A friend of mine suggests that when we disagree with somebody, a great sentence is this: "Ah, you see things differently – tell me more." It's seldom easy to remember to use it, but there it is. Another question to be asked in any difference of opinion is, "What is your underlying concern?" They both send the same message – 'your opinion is important to me and may be correct – tell me more', and it actually invites the respondent to review their own understanding of the situation. This practice may well develop BOTH parties to the conversation.

Competence can be learned and incompetence can be unlearned. And in the great continuum of life, the skills applicable today may no longer work tomorrow and our competence needs to take new possibilities, and the subsequent need for new learning, into account.

We're only competent until something changes, but after that change we are only incompetent as long as we are unable or unwilling to learn the new skill required. Once we take the time to be retrained, or to train ourselves, we resume our journey through competence to expertise. And that is a place many of us would like to be.

"Why (some) Personal Development Advice is Wrong!"

This week I was running along on one of my longer runs listening to my iPod, this time to an audio book called 'The Good Psychopaths Guide to Success' by Kevin Dutton and the SAS veteran Andy McNab. They proposed that the one way to get anything done in this world, the only way, was to decide what you want and then focus on that 100% of your waking hours – okay, perhaps not quite 100%, but certainly to focus 100% on achieving that goal. This was also a suggestion made by the personal development writer and speaker Brian Tracy, who says, *"Decide upon your major definite purpose in life and then organise ALL (my capitals) your activities around it"*, which I took to have the same meaning as that proposed by Dutton and McNab. It seemed sage advice when I heard it from Tracy, so much so that I downloaded a picture of that quote and used it as my smartphone home screen screensaver for a week (before I re-loaded my Personal Mission Statement again).

There is certainly a lot to be said for discovering your fundamental purpose in life and dedicating your time to it, putting your heart and soul into achieving that noble purpose in the hope that it will come to pass. The great successes of our history are often said to have done it 'like that'. And, like I said, it made sense. For a bit.

I say 'for a bit' because I realised that this piece of advice was absolutely fine for a single man or woman, who is responsible and accountable only to themselves for what he or she does, and for whom other people are not necessarily a factor in that success. I don't mean that other people aren't important to them, only that the focus on their singular purpose is so precise that those other people are either with them, or they're not in the circle, so to speak.

For most people, there is a problem with focusing all your time on your passionate purpose and that is – you love, respect, like and need to spend time with other people who are not, necessarily, involved in your noble purpose. They may support you but they aren't part of the great plan. For most of us, those people we love who are not part of the inner circle of The Plan are those in our other inner circle – our family.

I suggest in my (it's coming, honest) book that one example of a noble purpose is that of family. This isn't a mind-blowing discovery for which I take credit, it's the counsel of Dr Covey. He didn't only write about personal success like so many other authors (and I'm surprised how many do focus only on 'you' when I think about all my reading), he always, always included that most important of organisations to which we provide great service, known to all as The Family. (Not the Mob, that's a different family.)

Half of 'The 7 Habits of Highly Effective People' was about relationships. In Principle-Centred Leadership two whole chapters were about family relationships and 'Making Champions of your Children'. ALL of The 7 Habits of Highly Effective Families was about family.

Providing service to others (the Third Resolution) must be part of one's Noble Purpose if it is to succeed. NOT providing a service is unlikely to serve a noble purpose anyway – try not serving your customers in a business. Seriously, though, one organisation, one set of 'customers' that we all should serve – indeed, when we married them or created them we intended to serve them – is Family. For me, great service to others is noble, desirable, and honourable. But how about service to your kith and kin – is it any less noble?

If all you can do in your own circumstances is serve your own family, then that just might be enough. And if you think about most of the true historical greats you see (more often than not) that they had fantastic familial relationships, too.

I guess what I am saying is this – if you can serve your organisation, community to a high level, that's marvellous. But if you have to choose (because of time or circumstance, e.g. the needs of an ill relative) then choose family. Your work will forget you soon after you leave the job. Your community changes and develops. But your family is always there and will always need you. Don't focus all of your time on your Purpose at their expense.

It so nice to think that if you serve family well - you will serve yourself, too.

"Bringing Behaviours into Line with Values – or Bringing Values into Line with Behaviours"

Just musing the other day I considered one of my favourite Hobbs concepts, which is that of Congruity. He describes Congruity as being a core element of successful self-management and used this diagram to show what he meant.

Consider these two Circles. One is representative of how we behave and the other is representative of our personal values, those things and states of being we consider to be important. In this diagram the two circles are quite far apart although there is an overlap. This illustration shows someone whose behaviours are often quite separate from what they believe in.

Hobbs (and Smith and Covey) all agreed that the 'ideal' state of being is when the two Circles wholly overlap, when what we say and what we believe in is completely demonstrated in how we act. When we walk our talk. Hobbs called them 'Unifying Principles' because when what we valued became our behaviour, we were unified. We had integrity. Thus:

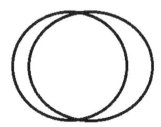

This got me to thinking as I traipsed around London looking at the self-help (ugly term) sections in the better bookshops – which activity comes first, the chicken or the egg? In our efforts to improve, do we first choose Values or behaviour?

I concluded that there are 5 approaches to this concept.

1. We can do nothing about any of it.
2. We can accept the values that we have learned over the years and behave in accordance with those values.
3. We can identify our values, and then ignore them whenever we decide it is convenient to do so.
4. We can identify what our behaviours are and then identify what values our behaviours represent.
5. We can design our lives by making a conscious decision on what our values should be if we are to get what we want in life, and then act in their accord.

Taking each in turn:

1. We can do nothing. Many who decry the self-help drive are those who live in the moment, who give little or no thought to what their values are and who would probably have trouble identifying more than three if they were pressed. This isn't necessarily bad but it isn't the best. But their lives are often dependent upon circumstances rather than driven by intent.
2. We can accept the values that we have learned over the years, and we can behave in accordance with those values. This is probably the most common state of affairs. This is what Covey called 'determinism' in various forms, but the crux of it is that when we live like this we are 'being lived' by our upbringing and by the standards of those with whom we spend our time. This is fine if the people we spend time with are not unprincipled, dishonest, unfaithful, or demonstrate any of the other self-destructive and undisciplined behaviours that we know, in our conscience, will not serve us or anyone else. It may suit you because the people you mix with are disciplined people of great character. If this is so, you can identify your values from theirs, and live accordingly. But then you have still made a choice – see 5, below.
3. We can identify our values, and then ignore them whenever we decide it is convenient to do so. This is a poor way to live, and is possibly one great cause of personal stress and/or guilt – the knowledge that we are *deliberately* not living according to the rules that we actively set for ourselves.

4. We can identify what our behaviours are and *then* identify what values apply. This is the life of the person who can misbehave, err, pre-judge and generally act as he or she feels because whenever challenged they will find an excuse for what they just did. It'll be 'freedom', 'liberalism', 'identity', or 'to put it to the man'. It is willing defiance of authority just for the sake of establishing their independence, while wholly ignoring the interdependence of life. It is the telling of rational lies.

5. We can design our lives by making a conscious decision on what our values should be if we are to get what we want in life, and then act in their accord. This is the only sensible option and the one representative of a higher intellectual approach to living (in my opinion), but it is often the hardest one to carry out. First of all, identifying the values themselves can be difficult because finding the right words with the right meaning can be problematic. Then, assuming we've defined our identified values appropriately, we come up against the obstacles of peer-pressure, societal norms and our own convenience when trying to execute on them.

Hobbs called them Unifying Principles, most others call them Values. One writer called them 'valuables' but I suspect he's one of those who uses different terms for the same things just to seem (annoyingly) different while not *actually* being different, but I digress.

Unifying Principles. To wholly mix up philosophical terms, the objective is to live in accordance with your own identified and defined, timeless, understood, self-evidently true and extrinsically existing 'truths', rather than constantly bob and weave between doing the right thing one minute and having to make excuses the next.

I'm still trying. Are you?

"Make your Right Decisions well in advance."

"Each decision we make is an important decision." Stephen R Covey.

Why is that? It's because what happens immediately after that decision is made will impact not just the activity that results, but the relationships involved. Make a bad decision that affects someone else, and they will undoubtedly judge you, and not your decision, when laying blame on the way they feel – and when deciding what they might do about that feeling.

A bad decision leads to another bad decision, and that later one (and the ones that follow) are wholly outside your Circle of Influence.

Our decisions flow from our paradigms — how we see a problem in the moment influences how we make our decisions.

For that reason it is important that our paradigms are as accurate as they can be, as objective as we can make them, and as principled and aligned with our personal values and mission statement as possible. Decisions made in keeping with principles and our (principle-based) mission statements are made with meaningfully-thought-through foundation, in that we effectively made the decision — in fact, any decision — when we established the way we wish to live and behave. When we drafted and committed to our personal mission statement(s) we had already influenced future decisions, because the root of those fruits had been planted in our very souls.

Another reason to write one, dear reader.

"Trust"

"Personal trustworthiness makes trust possible." Stephen R Covey

This is one of the precepts of the Second Resolution — that one should seek the honour of being trusted, because one has strived to develop the two ingredients of trustworthiness, namely character and competence. The interdependence of the two is covered by analysing those who gave one and not the other.

Do you know someone who does a tremendous job, but who you wouldn't trust with your significant other? Are you familiar with an unbelievably nice bloke, whose car you would avoid climbing into because he just can't drive safely?

We should all try to be people of character — good character, not just 'characters' — who provide excellent results in our employed or voluntary work. That is the objective of the Second Resolution but it also a common-sense approach to life, isn't it?

Although if I was asked to choose, I think I would rather be a person of character who is still capable of learning to be competent, than a highly competent a***hole.

How about you?

"Congruent Conversation – How do you do yours?"

"Integrity means avoiding any communication that is deceptive, full of guile, or beneath the dignity of people." Stephen R Covey

Integrity s more than honesty. While honesty is speaking the truth, integrity means living it. So with that sentence and the above quote in mind I really do 'weep' when I listen to 'celebrities' demanding money off me while avoiding taxes; when I hear politicians say 'the reality of the matter is' before again merely spouting a party line exaggeration which is so blatantly ideological it bears no intellectual merit – FOX News does make me laugh, in that regard.

But the most telling interpretation of the quote for me is this: How often is the deception, guile of sub-dignified disrespect communicated directly to ourselves? How often do you lie to excuse misbehaviour? We learn to do that as children, and then take years 'off' conscience=focused living until one day in our middle age when we suddenly realise that we've been lying to ourselves as much as, if not more than we have lied to other people.

Speak the truth to yourself. You might not like what you hear, but if you act upon it you may never have to lie again.

" Don't just Leave a Legacy – Live One."

"The key to the fire within is our need to leave a legacy." Stephen R Covey

The Third Resolution is the pinnacle of the pyramid* of the three. It is the summit of our intended compliance, the ultimate, principled objective of Three Resolution living. It is the provision of service, and it is the observance of a noble purpose.

We all want to be remembered. Some do it by being arrogant, believing that respect comes from a significance born of the Big 'I AM'. Some do it by focusing their time on the attainment of wealth, and while I do understand that from my bedroom/office and sub-£400 laptop computer, it is not an end in itself.

The best of us do it by believing in something, and by living for it. Sadly, some heroes die for it, too. In a play about Joan of Arc, the writer Maxwell Anderson quoted her as saying, *"I know this now. Every man gives his life for what he believes. Every woman gives her life for what she believes. Sometimes people believe in little or nothing, and so they give their lives to the little or nothing..."*

She goes on

"...One life is all we have, and we live it as we believe in living it and then it's gone. But to surrender who you are and to live without belief is more terrible than dying—even more terrible than dying young."

What do you believe in? Not necessarily to die for, but something that you would stand up for? Something that you would resign from work for, or risk incarceration for if there was a choice of compliance or denial?

(* From an earlier illustration in the 1ˢᵗ Ed..)

"Here we go again, and again, and again. How about you?"

"I am not a product of my circumstances. I am a product of choices*."* Stephen R Covey

It is a matter of some regret that this lesson is not taught in schools, accepted by teenagers, modelled by young adults, nor learned all too often until it is too late. Consequently all too many of us are, in part at least, products of what has gone before.

However, good news!

Every single day, every decision, is an opportunity to re-create the future and thereby the conditions we seek to enjoy. There is hope in that circumstance, but there is equally some dread. There is some dread because in order to make those decisions and to take the actions necessary to act upon them – we have to work really very hard.

In one of his metaphors, Dr Covey wrote how the most effort expended in launching the Apollo missions was expended during the need to break out of the Earth's atmosphere, while 'a baby's breath' was all that was need to release the Eagle module from the Moon. The message was that it is really hard to change ourselves, but the further into 'change' we go, the easier it is. But I think there was more to it, and that was that, certainly, massive effort was needed to break away from what 'was'. But once the work was done, it took little effort to carry on doing it.

I'm still at the place where 'massive effort' is and continues to be called for. I have what a psychiatrist might call 'anger issues' but which I prefer to call 'tolerance issues', in that I have great inability to tolerate some things: poor driving (another attempt to kill me was made last night), poor diction, affected behaviour ('gay' does not have to mean 'camp', any more than 'manly' needs to mean 'hard'), biased press and eternal use of the dramatic media to liberalise us through concentrated bombing.

And I am impatient with my loved ones, less than proactive in terms of exercising my body, and a little lost in terms of 'working', in that retirement isn't bringing much.

But every day is a chance to start again. Including today, including NOW.

(Go!.......)

"Shining a light on something sometimes isn't illuminating."

"A man's character is like a tree, and his reputation like its shadow. The shadow is what we think of it; the tree is the real thing." Abraham Lincoln

Nigel Mansell, former World F1 and Indycar champion, spoke of the time when he left Lotus F1 team and joined Williams F1 as Keke Rosberg's partner. Mansell had suffered from a poor relationship with the Lotus team manager Peter Warr, and on arrival at Williams it was evident that Warr had 'put the poison pen' in with Rosberg. It was a few months into their partnership that Rosberg said to Mansell, "I am sorry. I listened to what was said about you instead of using my own judgement."

I, too, have suffered such back stabbing – many times. As a 'boy' on a pop round I changed drivers to discover that someone I had spent one day with had spread the word I was lazy, only for my new driver to assess me in one day as a hard worker. In the police some people saw my carping as work-avoidance, whereas the more alert saw it as frustration with poor working practices and lauded my actual productivity. My better managers also saw something in me. They all agreed that I had my idiosyncrasies – I just needed managing!

It is easy to assess someone negatively based on the narrow view we have of what's happening, and we forget that what we see is but a snapshot of their whole character, a snapshot based on the circumstances within which we see them perform. But they are people 24 hours a day, while we see them for one or two. We tend to forget that.

Try not to judge people based on how little you actually know. Look for the tree, not the shadow. The shadow is a reflection based not on reality but on the ever-changing position of the light being shone upon it. The light moves, the tree does not.

That's actually quite profound – Lincoln was a clever chap.

"Have you found that person, yet? No, not that one – the other one."

"Our chief want is someone who will inspire us to be what we know we could be." Ralph Waldo Emerson.

Unfortunately, our chief objection is to hearing the truth. And we are also unwilling to openly admit such truth when we hear it, using what both Covey and Hobbs called Rationalisation – rational lies that we use to excuse our failures to act in keeping with our word.

But, oh, the growth when we allow ourselves to hear, admit and act upon such criticism. I remember being taken to task in a work appraisal in 2000 – it's in my diary – at a time when I was fortunate enough to have the appraisal just before I was due to take a couple of days off where I would be alone for long periods of time.

I was able to spend that time considering what was accurate about the appraisal, what was a misunderstanding, and what strengths I had that could overcome the true criticisms. (There are times when I wish I could focus enough to do that again.)

My next appraisal was a reflection of what I learned in those few solitary hours. I also learned that if you get up too soon after anaesthetic, you wake up with a crowd around you.

Who has inspired you? I know that reading Covey's works inspired me, I think that's obvious from the blog. Have you found someone, personally or as the result of an accidental find in a bookshop or library, who made you stop and think, "Wow!", to think enough to make changes and rediscover yourself and the way you could behave to finally, in some small or even magnificent way, achieve your goals? And if not 'goals', perhaps just to live according to what you believe?

If so, let me know.

If not – off to the library........

" There's no 'I' in Team. But there's a 'Me' if you look."

"No matter what accomplishments you made, somebody helped you." Althea Gibson

Which, if you like, is the corollary* of The Third Resolution, because the consequence of serving others is a heightened sense of self-worth that in turn makes us more productive and more creative. This is also a demonstration of how the sixth of the 7 Habits – Synergy – works.

Synergy is the result of creative co-operation, where two or more parties come together to create something that was greater than any one of them could have created alone, and which is even greater than the sum of the parts. To use Covey's own metaphor it is when 1+1=3, 10, or 10,000. It's how Steve Jobs and Steve Wozniak created Apple, and how Bill Gates and Paul Allen created Microsoft.

But possibly the greater example of synergy could be Thomas Edison. He had been working with Nokola Tesla, and both were acknowledged and great innovators in the field of electricity. But while Tesla essentially worked on and pursued his own inventions, Edison utilised teamwork to a more effective degree and eventually registered three times as many patents as Tesla. And to be fair, more people have heard of Edison.

To use the inappropriate cliché phrase 'Chiefs and Indians', those 'Indians' among us will be aware of how many 'Chiefs' have been rewarded, feted and even celebrated for great work. How many Knighthoods, peerages, bonuses and promotions they have won – all on the work done by other people. That said, I must emphasise that not every person so honoured was inappropriately rewarded. Most awards and accolades are deserved.

But let's not forget that even Newton admitted that he was just standing on the shoulders of 'other' giants when he made his discoveries.

There's nothing I like more than a sincere expression of gratitude by one honoured person for the work done by other, anonymous team members. And nothing worse than a blatantly insincere one.

Everything we do is done for, with, or as a result of something done or not done by, somebody else. In the context of this entry, what we achieve is the result of action done in the same way. Nothing happens in a vacuum. There is no response without stimulus. The man who invented the bottle did so not just because he wanted a transparent container in which he could keep liquids, but because there was also a need for others, probably identified by others, for the invention. And he probably didn't invent glass, either – someone else did that and he used their skills to develop his own idea. That's synergy.

And it's the manifestation of The Third Resolution. A service identified and met by someone with the nobility of purpose to do the work necessary to make it happen.

(*It is right, I checked.)

"Look at what I did!" "No. I'm looking at what you ARE!"

"Life is made up not of great sacrifices or duties, but of little things." Sir Humphrey Davy

That said, where do the awards, citations and peerages go?

Those who have read my musings on the **Three Resolutions** know that I promote service at home before seeking the rewards – and accolades – of great service to others. It has been said that the one thing that society cannot survive is the collapse of the family unit, and one thing a child remembers more than

Dad's medals or mum's directorship is the time they spent together, the fun they had, the lessons they learned and the examples that were set. They remember more of who you were, and less of what you did, particularly what you did for others. They focused more on character than deeds.

I suppose it's about balance. No one is suggesting, and nor should they, that people should neglect the 'greater goods' of service to charities. But if you achieve that secondary greatness at the expense of the primary greatness of character, and of service within and towards the family, have you achieved anything meaningful, really?

For example, I have been told of someone who was awarded a national level award for services to the community. Apparently, at a charity function to which she had been invited and fed, they held a raffle. The idea was you put £5 in an envelope with your name on it, and they drew envelopes for prizes. She won a nice prize in the draw, but when they opened her envelope some time later, they found that this paragon of the community on a very nice wage had forgotten to put her money into the envelope. She was never invited back and for those in the know she was always going to be considered with absolute disdain. For £5 she could easily afford.

Her character, the primary source of who we are seen to be, was now flawed for ever in the sight of others. And to be accurate, that one act reflected her character more accurately than anything she said or did afterwards.

Going back to Davy's quote, that little negative 'thing' will, for many, be what she will be remembered for.

This entry started out as a missive on service at the small, yet arguably most important level, but ended as a reflection on how the smallest of character flaws can undermine anything else we do.

"Is your look partially preventing people from seeing you?"

"I base most of my fashion taste on what doesn't itch." Gilda Radner

The world is not allowed to stereotype any more. 'Political Correctness' in its most positive form is the title produced to prevent the hideous 'isms' that exist(ed) in society, but in its slightly over-reaching form its over-interpretation prevents human beings doing what human beings naturally do when presented with an image – make an assessment.

And fashion is a source of judgment, like it or not. I refer mainly to dress-fashion when I write that. The one thing fashion does is identify a person's life choices, bank balance, chosen peer group, occasionally even their sexuality. Admittedly, in a 'cats breathe, I breathe, therefore I am a cat' sense, how a person dresses is not automatically proof of any of those things, but just like sharp teeth used to make Neanderthal Man think twice about an approach from in front, how you dress does send a message. And it is often a stereotype – suits for professionals (except on telly, tie off or else!), linen suits for academics, weird scarves for social worker ladies (and badly stuffed A5 diaries), shirt tails out on Friday night pub visits, pointy shoes for young sales reps, and lately some extremely odd haircuts for men (some too old for them) that MY dad would have thought old-fashioned.

The question I ask of you, dear reader, is – do you follow fashion? Do you in any way follow a 'trend' instead of conforming to a 'norm'? Do you follow 1Direction because of their musical talent or 'cos everyone else does? Do you watch Strictly because YOU dance, or so that you can talk about it in work tomorrow? Do you drive one-armed, wrist on the steering wheel because it looks 'cool'? Do you watch Big Brother and then wear a tiny pork-pie hat to work because the winner did?

Do you say, 'Like' as a gap-word in conversation? Do you swear because Lee Evans did at the O2?

If so, you are a follower, not a leader.

In his book 'Thinking Big', author David Schwartz wrote a small piece about such things, which I quote here. He said,

"In theory, it's pleasant to hear that people should look at a man's intellect, not his clothes. But don't be misled. People do evaluate you on the basis of your appearance. Your appearance is the first basis for evaluation other people have. And first impressions last."

Another quote was directed specifically at young people, where Scwartz quoted someone else who stated, "You can usually spot a wrong kid just by the way he looks. Sure it's unfair, but it's a fact; people judge young people today by their appearance. And one they've tabbed a boy, it's tough to change their minds about him, their attitude towards them. Look at your boy: look at him through your neighbour's eyes, his teacher's eyes. Could the way he looks, the clothes he wears, give them the wrong impression? Are you making sure he looks right, dresses right, everywhere he goes?"

Add speech, attitude, focus, deeds, social circle – and you start the list of what people judge you on.

You can ask society, even legislate society to speak differently, to say they must not judge. But tough – you're making a law that people should overwrite human instincts. Some can, some can't, many won't. I like to think I'm at the 'better' end but the truth is when stereotyping there is a better than 50% chance you're right. You know it's true.

So choose better. You don't have to blindly, slavishly follow anyone or anything. But me mindful that when you do, you are sending a message. Just make sure it's the message you want to send.

"Anything you can do, I MUST do better!"

"When you choose your fields of labour, go where nobody else is willing to go."
Mary Lyon

Is a quote I wish I'd known about years ago. Occasionally, history shows I stepped up to the mark a bit and went a bit further than others may have done. Now and then I exhibited an attitude, some effort and greater knowledge about something that made me look a lot better than perhaps I was, and certainly better than a 'routine' me tended to be.

In 2003 I met a new boss, and he was the epitome of dedication, character and competence. I'd had some great bosses who were enthusiastic, caring, compassionate and who were great to work for, but in some ways this chap was one step above them in many ways. It may be, in the cold light of 'now', that he was only that one step higher up the stairway to perfection than the others, but that's the point.

Tony Robbins speaks of the 'two-percenters', who only have to put out a little more effort, or more considered effort, to be seen as outstanding. Another fellow (Michael Heppell) illustrates this in his books when he supports Robbins' contention that to get outstanding results you only have to be that little bit better at creating them than those around you. Remember – the Olympic Gold Medallist is usually only centimetres ahead of the next guy, but who can remember the guy who came second. (Which is a shame but it illustrates my point nicely.)

Albert E Gray is often quoted when he says, "A successful person has the propensity for doing the things failures don't like to do. They don't like doing them either, necessarily– but their dislike is subordinated to the strength of their purpose." In addition to doing better than the next person, they're also willing to do the things that the next person would rather not do, or delegate to someone else, or defer it to when it suits (in the hope it's never needed).

Thjis manager was exactly like that. He did the work, and he knew his stuff better than anyone I knew. But he also knew better ways of doing it, or how to find the better ways. He was, without question, a master craftsman – and a thoroughly nice bloke.

The Second Resolution is a commitment to being a person of character and a person who is competent. The person who is competent is the guy who comes second. It is the guy with character, with the ability to do more than is called for, for the better reasons, and even when s/he doesn't want to do – it that comes ahead of the rest.

I wish it as me……

"Judge me by MY standards, not yours. I'm not congruent with YOUR beliefs, I'm congruent with MINE."

"Revel in the ordinary." M J Ryan

This isn't a criticism of 'self-help' literature – a term I detest – but the well-motivated hype of some of the books and seminars just doesn't suit a lot of us. We don't all want to be millionaires and we don't all want to be super-fit and we don't all want big houses and big cars. We'd like some of those things, certainly. Our upbringing may have instilled in us the false belief that 'money' and 'stuff' are signs of a life well lived.

Some of us, on the other hand, just want to be 'good people'. Living honestly, without conflict, with extreme levels of inner peace from living with integrity. And above all, without the expectation and even imposition by others that we should care for the things they are passionate about, and that if we don't we are at fault.

Stephen Covey's Circle of Influence and Circle of Concern illustrate my 'desire' for that. In the 'outer' Circle of Concern is pretty much everything we hear about, see, or affects us, even if only tangentially. In the 'inner' Circle of Influence are the things that are in that bigger Circle of Concern, but about which we can do something. Including 'care', as in 'care about'.

So when someone else demands that I care about things that aren't in that Circle of Influence — guess what, my response will be indicative of my disinterest. And that's when the fights start!

(My intent is that I won't let myself get dragged into such debates, but (unfortunately) I am human and if there's one thing that will grab my attention, it is when someone uses enormous generalisations about a group, attacks them with vitriolic language, and then tries to use an academic argument to justify what, once a general 'lumping together' was used to start the attack, is automatically unsupportable simply because of that initial generalisation! For example, as soon as you say 'ALL politicians are corrupt' you cannot then use an academic argument to justify that case because you haven't met them all. It's an academically unsound argument! Nor can you say 'all (opposing party) politicians are corrupt, because your ideological separation is all too specific — and obvious.)

Back to the point. Just because I want to be an ordinary man who occasionally does something great doesn't mean I should be subjected to someone else's hyperactive and enthusiastic counsel to spend hours trying to build big piles of money. As a result, while I am in no way 'affluent' I am 'comfortable' and secure and have no fears. My goal, for now, is to be wholly congruent with my beliefs and values and to encourage others to do the same.

Be congruent. But remember that congruence for you does not mean that I have to believe and value the same things as you. AND in recognising that, we can respect each other's' viewpoints without necessarily adopting them. We can disagree and both be congruent with what we believe, and neither will be less for that unless the generalised attacks begin.

And just 'cos I ain't rich doesn't mean you are better than me, or more successful (by society's standards). Nor does it mean I am better than you because I have neither money nor 'societal success'. But rest assured – being rich doesn't make you successful.

Being congruent does.

"Spontaneity requires planning. Huh?"

"For the happiest life, days should be rigorously planned, nights left open to chance." Mignon McLaughin

I've been very robust in my musings about the inadvertent smothering of time management methods under the deluge of deeper-thought personal development literature. While the latter is an exceptionally important field of research for everyone, I've discovered a surprising dearth of TM input in self-help courses. And those who have recognised my distain for the excessive (although not wholly inappropriate) breadth of writing on Mindfulness won't be surprised to find that I reckon it's not a field that lends itself to planning for the future.

The dearth I mention is surprising because in many such courses, some exceptional input on how to identify your values, set goals, and deal with obstacles and other people (occasionally the same thing) is being undermined by the lack of input on how to manage your time in such a way as to do those very things. One observation made (by the uninformed) is that planning prevents spontaneity 'and I don't want to be restricted'.

At the moment, I am in the process of setting up a formal coaching practice, (see here) in the South Wales and Bristol/Gloucestershire areas in the UK and I am extremely aware of the amount of planning I need to do in order to make sure that it succeeds. I am also aware of just how much mental space it takes up, and how that focus can affect everything else I do. I am passionate about the material, but not so much that I want to destroy my life in an effort to teach it.

That, for many, is a dichotomy – two challenging and mutually exclusive alternative choices. Society and much literature (mainly the former) seems to say that in order to make a business work you must put everything into it, which in turn means by default that you should stop doing anything else. Which is an evidently stupid suggestion if you have responsibilities and accountabilities elsewhere, including wife/husband/partner and family. Like most of us. (What's the point of success if you have no intimate partner with whom to share it? Discuss.)

That's where time management and the McLaughlin quotes come in. if you manage your time you maximise it, and if you do that you can create time for the business and for the other things that make the business worthwhile.

My routine, therefore, is that I spend the 'working week, 9-5 hours with the business in mind, and evenings and weekends free for 'other important' stuff. That's not to say I don't give any time or thought at all to the business outside of those hours – as we are, like life, one indivisible whole, it is inevitable and indeed helpful that thoughts on the business hit me at all sorts of times, as do opportunities. But when the thought it hits me I deal with it, probably by planning any necessary action into an appropriate (weekday) moment. If it must be acted upon immediately, so be it, but that's rare. What I can do with an idea that strikes when no pen or paper is handy (for example) is send myself an email, with sufficient information about this sudden inspiration, from one of two accounts accessible from my smartphone, and plan action when I am later sat at my desk. In the same vein I can do something spontaneously without it affecting my business.

Planning your week in advance permits freedom, it doesn't stifle it. If you have no plan at all, what on earth can you be spontaneous about?

Plan your week, but don't plan to fill it. Make time for you and yours. After work, not in competition with it.

"Take Action – or reap the rewards of inaction."

You MUST execute on your Mission Statement!

The world is full of nearly people. In his book 'How to Be Brilliant', Michael Heppell tells the story of a man we'll call John, who went to school with a friend of his, a good friend, called Richard. As they passed through school Richard was always coming up with weird ideas about projects and always invited John to take part. John was cautious and would initially promise to help but would then find excuses to avoid participation. When they left school Richard would still invite John along, but John would still prevaricate. In the end, Richard Branson became an entrepreneurial billionaire and adventurer. Who is John?

I'm not for one minute suggesting that execution of your plan will make you a billionaire (even though it might). I AM suggesting that inaction will probably keep you where you are, though. And I am assuming that, having purchased or read this book, you don't like that place. But your situation may get even worse.

If you keep money in a drawer under your bed, interest rate rises and inflation mean that over time your money will buy less, so it actually lessens in value. If you put it in a bank, particularly a safe bank, it will grow, at least in keeping with inflation (okay, probably just under). If you speculate wisely you might make that money increase in value, potentially by some high degree. It is the same with this book. If you put it in a bank....

Sorry to be flippant. What I am saying is this – if you stay where you are, in that uncomfortable place you've decided isn't where you want to be, things will get worse. If you're fat and do nothing, you'll get fatter as you get older and it'll have serious health consequences. Are you planning on having a Stennah Stairlift, to driving around the local shops on an invalid carriage motor-scooter, and to having your bum wiped by a nurse as you dribble over the side of the bed? If you have no job and you do nothing, you'll probably freeze to death in your seventies because you have no pension to pay the fuel bills. If you are a person of poor character and do nothing, you will likely live a long lonely life before dying alone and unloved because people know what you truly are. If you don't contribute in some way, even in the meaningful but simple ways suggested, you will be forgotten. If you suffer from all these maladies, you die fat, alone and forgotten after spending a long time in healthcare/nursing home purgatory. That is what will happen if you do nothing about what you've read here. (Scared, yet?)

It may not come to that. You may be part way to being a semi-disciplined, healthy, employed person of good character with some community involvement that benefits others – but you want more or you wouldn't be here, would you?

But you won't get 'more' if you do nothing. 'More' requires effort, learning and contribution. It requires that you stop doing what doesn't serve you, start doing what does, start living with integrity with principles, ensure you're current in working practices valued by employers, and you purposefully provide some kind of service that benefits others I some way.

It requires compliance with the **Three Resolutions**.

"Stop showing off – it really isn't necessary."

"The most important ingredient we put into any relationship is not what we say or what we do, but what we are." Stephen R Covey

And Covey went on to say that when what we portray is the result of our compliance with the Personality Ethic, where compliance with fads, trends and fashions is more important to us than being our best as individuals, then our relationships will suffer.

If I was to say I have a deep distaste for men who are 'camp' to the degree that they are showy, overly expressive, flamboyantly dressed and so on – what would be your immediate response, even accusation? I won't say it out loud, but I'd be willing to put a small bet on it.

What if, having allowed you the time to decide what you think I just said, I then went on to say I also have a deep distaste for overly loud, drunken, self-obsessed iron-pumping men who are overly-masculine just as much as I hate the aforementioned extreme?

The point I am trying to make is this – how can I trust someone who is so extreme on any continuum of showiness? If they are loud, brash, flamboyant and so on – what are they overcompensating for? What is the 'big show' about? Who is hiding behind all that showing off?

One caveat – once you are convinced that what you see IS what they are, then the potential for trust re-emerges. But until then, you can't help wondering whether they are 'like that' all the time, and if not – what might they be like when you need to rely on them? Is the flamboyantly camp man going to turn up in a sober suit when you want him to be entertaining? Is the macho guy going to run away screaming when you need help in a crisis? (Remember that scene in the film Quadrophenia when the uber-Mod hero played by Sting turned out to be a fawning bell-boy?)

One of the things I learned reading personal development literature is about character, and how people can hide behind screens. How people can even take a negative situation like disability, depression, injury and disappointment and turn it into a badge of significance. How people will do anything to feel 'special', even to the point of self-destruction. For me, that kind of behaviour is the essence of 'trendy', 'fashionable' and 'celebrity'. It's very much about pretence, compliance with something outside of the self (whether it be groups or stereotypes) rather than creation of a genuine, substantial, individual and unshakeable character.

(That's why I rant about:

People waving their arms about when they talk because they do it on the telly – which came first? The arm-waving people or the BBC course on how to be an arm-waver?

Use of the word 'cool' by people far too old to be 'in with the kids'. Specifically 30.

Guests on BBC News wearing a suit but no tie – WHY?

Fads – remember loom bands? Gone ALREADY!

One Direction – name one of their songs. Blowed if I can.

Reality TV – because it isn't.

(Rant over.)

My own objective, and one in respect of which I frequently fall short, is to wholly be a person of integrity and good character and entirely trustworthy. I want people to know I am a person of worth by actually becoming a person of worth. Not by pretending to be someone I am not, or by hiding.

As I said, I frequently fall short. But I will never stop trying.

Obedience. Particularly liberating if you're obeying YOU."

"Obedience is different to freedom. But it is not its opposite. You can freely choose to obey."

"First rule of personal development reading: Don't question the text. Let the text ask questions of YOU."

"Your personal mission/vision statement: "A summons to you every morning, a checklist every night."

(Abbott Christopher Jamison)

I've quoted three times this week because I found all three in a single holiday read entitled, "Finding Sanctuary." Notwithstanding the fact that the book is written by a Benedictine monk (that UK TV viewers may know through the programme The Monastery) it is refreshingly short in religious content – so short that I felt able to reflect on the quotes from a secular, personal development perspective.

From a **Three Resolutions** angle, then, look at the three quotes. The first is recognition that just because a framework exists in life or work doesn't mean that you are controlled by it – it means that you have a framework within which you have the freedom to act with conscience. If you are the creator of that framework, then you are obedient only to your own values and standards, and if you are doing a job you chose, then it will be what you make of it. You are free to obey what you choose to obey. If what you choose seems, to others, to be onerous then they may accuse you of blind obedience – but if you have chosen that obedience as a free man – then you demonstrate self-discipline, self-denial and character.

The second quote is a pointed remark aimed at those who see a book and question its content because of some invented or irrelevant reason, like the woman who picked up a book on leadership and glanced at the contents page, dismissively declared, "Huh! Written by a Mormon" and so failed to ask the better question, "Can I learn from what's in it?" Or, as I might have bluntedly asked, "Do you have the intellectual capacity to get over your prejudice and actually read the book to see if religion is even mentioned?" (Smile...) I only respect the opinions on book made by those who've read and understood the content, not those who judge it by its cover alone. (And copying 'The Secret's cover design template doesn't make your book good.) You don't develop or learn or grow by pre-judging something based on a glance, tempting as that often is.

The last quote was the one that made me get out and go running while I was on holidays (hence my absence last week.) It's a doozy. The quote is a profound reminder that once you have a mission statement or a set of unifying principles it's a good idea to remind yourself in the morning what it says – treating is as a 'summons to action/compliance – and then, at the end of that day, review it to check whether or not you lived in congruence with what you have stated you believe. Did you plan your day based on that mission, and have you demonstrated character, provided service, exercised self-discipline and executed on it? Read more. It's empowering.

"But we've always done it that way, you fool!"

"Once we get into routines we feel comfortable. From comfort comes confidence." Judith E. Glaser, author of 'Creating WE'

Nothing confines us more than an imposed requirement to comply with 'the system'. In many ways systems serve us, keep us safe, and provide for the creation of consistent results. A properly considered system is a valuable tool. Or we could all decide, every morning, which side of the road we feel like driving on today.

But blind obedience to a system disallows creativity, stifles innovation, and doesn't allow for the unexpected to be properly challenged. When something arises that is a bit off-the-wall, the system might not work and our slavish adherence won't change that. A new system is needed, or at least a modification. And don't we fight that!

Change is the greatest constant. So fighting change is pointless. On the other hand, applying Aikido to take control of change does have a point. (Eh?)

Aikido is a martial art that doesn't resist attack like the fist- and foot-focused arts; it takes the force used by an attacker and redirects it until we can take over control. For example, as an attacker moves towards us, instead of resisting we step back and take the impetus away from the imposed force and send it where we want it to go until such time as the threat dissipates.

In the same way we can take a proactive step back when a system is challenged, and redirect our thoughts not to resisting the stimulus, but instead to re-identifying it and its likely direction, and then deciding what to do about it so as to achieve a desirable objective. In that stimulus-response gap we can identify whether the system is wholly inappropriate or just needs tweaking.

Which leads me to the repeated realisation that principles apply. They always do. They never change, and they influence the success of a tweaked system more than any other factor.

So the order of events must be:

What is the system for?

What has the new challenge done to affect the system's ability to achieve that original objective?

Where in the system has that happened?

Can the system change in order to achieve the same result? If so – change it. If not – design a whole new system.

And if a new system needs to be designed – do we have to change the way we see the problem? Because just changing what we 'do' might not be enough of an answer. The 'why we do what we do' might be what's changed.

In any event – don't blindly and repeatedly apply the 'old' system and expect it to work. Because it won't.

"Tempus meum prope est in tempore non tuo.*"

"We're stewards over our time, our talents, our resources. Stewardship involves a sense of being accountable to someone or something higher than self." Stephen R Covey

One of 'my' original tenets is that everything we do in life we do for someone, with someone, or as a result of someone else's input. We don't live and work in a vacuum. Stewardship reflects this situation – for our purposes it is defined thus by Wikipedia – "Stewardship is now generally recognized as the acceptance or assignment of responsibility to shepherd and safeguard the valuables of others." Stewardship 'is a trust, in the sense that what we have (talents, time, resources) are not ours to do with as we please, but they belong to others. We therefore have a responsibility to use those things wisely for others.

Accepting for a moment one of my other tenets (that there's nothing wrong with finding 'what's in it for me' in any service or purpose), you and I are therefore stewards, and accountable for the use of our time, talents and resources because they also belong to those we serve.

Even when what we are doing is essentially selfish on the outside (having fun, partying, starting a new business in an effort to make money, going fishing), others are being served by us – they are being paid to provide their services, they are being employed, they are partying with us, etc.) There is no accountability gap. What we do involves others either as servants or the served. Hence the stewardship argument – to do the best we can with what we have, so that others can be served too.

What are you using your time for? Or more precisely, are you using your time to best effect – are you serving, learning, growing, becoming something more than you were a few minutes, days or weeks ago? How about your talents? Are you holding back on the best you could be in the hope that someone will notice what you're hiding and suddenly make you great? How about other resources – are they sitting idle, rusting and deteriorating through lack of use? Remember that the unused car may look nice, but when you try to start it – will it seize? (Cliché moment – a ship is safest in the harbour, but that's not what ships are for.)

At the moment I am at a bit of a hiatus – a number of projects are ongoing and awaiting the moment of execution. Once they start I hope I'll be run off my feet but just now it's almost quiet. So in an effort to utilise my own time I will be reviewing my writings (books!) and seeing how I can improve and recirculate them as a service to those who may just benefit from the assembly of words and the codifying of random thoughts. I'm also reading a novel or two and I've committed to testing myself in one of my hobby areas in an effort to comply with my **Three Resolutions**.

Time's a-wasting, and as it belongs to you I have every intention of using your time wisely. Oh, and thanks for letting me have it.

*My time is your time. According to Google Translate.

" You're being watched. Make sure that what they see is what you ARE."

"Courage is not simply one of the virtues, but the form of every other virtue at the testing point, which means at the pint of highest reality." C S Lewis.

"(Courage is) the greatest of all virtues; because unless a man has that virtue, he has no security for preserving any other." Samuel Johnson

The message is – unless you act in accordance with your values when to do so is most challenging, then you aren't really living in their accord at all.

We all have those moments when we fail: when we are dieting and dip into the fridge*; when we declare we will be patient then race another driver trying to pass us to get to a roundabout first; when we focus upon excellence and then do a 'get by' piece of work; and so on. (Please insert your own examples.)

Life does tend to undermine our good intentions, sometimes. These examples illustrate moments that are arguably forgivable, because the consequences aren't that great and rarely impact upon others. Except that they do.

When you fail to act in accordance with your stated values, people notice. Their comments on your failure range from taking the mick, as in "Ha! I knew you couldn't do it!" which is a visible and almost humorous response, to a more impactive form of noticing – when they see you for what you are and your failure excuses theirs.

When I was 'the police', we swore an oath to treat all without fear or favour, without any form of preferential treatment. But it was often strange how people of note, suspected of crimes, were treated with kid gloves while colleagues were treated with contempt. How Billy Burglar would have his door kicked in while His Excellency the local councillor would not have his house searched if he wasn't in. How Fred the fraudster would be arrested without ceremony while someone who threatened to complain would be 'invited to attend the police station'. How a manager would not change the decision of a previous manager even as he acknowledged that the former decision was wrong.

I admit I am guilty of the former, lesser examples of values dissonance where my word isn't quite kept when the hunger pangs kick in. I am always willing to be wrong. I am willing to be taken to task (politely) when I fail. Every failure that leads to a later success is worth the criticism because it makes me more courageous as time goes by.

And I fervently pray that when the moment comes, and I am truly challenged to act in accordance with my values, that the kind of courage called for by Lewis and Johnson courses through me and I perform exactly as I stated I will.

Hyrum W Smith put it this way – at 7AM you declare you're on a diet. At 1PM you're sat on the second shelf of the fridge devouring everything you can get your hands on.

"How to be like Malawa Yousafzai"

"Integrity is never painless." M. Scott Peck

At the moment we are being bombarded with adverts made by luvvies encouraging us to go and see the inevitable-soon-to-be-on-DVD film about Malala Yousafzai. (*Wow – no MSWord spellcheck: that's how famous she must be*).

I'll admit I am jaded by the ads: not because of the subject matter but by the luvvies, where I'm not sure of the balance between their genuine admiration for her, and their need to feel associated with her for publicity purposes. Cynical? Yes, I know.

But her story does illustrate Peck's quote as topically as I can think of at the moment. Those of us in the personal development field are well versed in telling the stories of Ghandi and Mandela, Lincoln and Joan of Arc. But Malala is a modern – and arguably more 'real' example of integrity being shown while under real danger of intense pain. I say more real because the other stories are historic and based on what we know after these people became acknowledged greats. They achieved magnificence and then we found out how great they were. They had causes which affected millions, but that effect came later, as did their celebrity.

But Malala was 'just' a schoolgirl. She wasn't planning to overthrow an unjust government. She didn't plan to free a country. She wasn't going to do any of those things.

The only thing she was going to – was school.

I might propose the hypothesis that integrity is easy when you have money and power to support and fund it. That would be trite but there would also be an element of reality infused in such a statement. I would find it easier to be 'fit and healthy' if I could afford gym membership, a personal trainer and large helpings of salmon as the mainstay of my diet. I'd find it easier to serve charities if I didn't feel the need to keep the money I have, and to earn some more just to have a decent holiday now and then.

But – and this sounds a bit conceited – I could be more like Malala in one way, because what Malala did we can all do. It didn't take money, it didn't need intellect, and while it took courage it didn't necessarily require 'bravery'.

She believed in her right to be educated. So she went to school. She knew it was trouble but I am willing to bet that she never once thought she'd be killed for doing it. That kind of thing happens to other people, right? Like smokers who won't get cancer, drinkers who won't be alcoholics, and 17-year-old binge eaters who presumably won't ever be 40 with a slower metabolism, it wasn't her who'd be 'the one'.

But that doesn't alter the fact that she wanted to be educated, and so she went out and got educated even though it would have been easier not to run that risk at all.

Integrity sometimes sucks. But what a hole of a world it would be if some of us, indeed most of us, didn't demonstrate some sense of personal integrity now and then. When we are called upon to tell the truth because not doing so would be a surrender to convention or corrupt influence, or cowardice, for example. When going for a long run when it's raining. When challenging a divisive culture in the face of that culture, and the cowards that allow it to thrive.

It might feel like we're risking everything, but unlike Malala we're often only really risking inconvenience. We can at least have that much courage, can't we?

Bibliography

Books I Believe In

The Seven Habits of Highly Effective People *by Stephen R Covey*

Principle-Centred Leadership *by Stephen R Covey*

The 8th Habit *by Stephen R Covey*

First Things First *by Stephen R Covey, A Roger Merrill, Rebecca Merrill*

TimePower *by Charles R Hobbs*

Books I Unreservedly Endorse

The Third Alternative *by Stephen R Covey*

The Success Principles *by Jack Canfield*

Awaken the Giant Within *by Anthony Robbins*

Unlimited Power *by Anthony Robbins*

The Only Way to Win *by Jim Loehr*

The Speed of Trust *by Stephen M R Covey*

What Matters Most *by Hyrum W. Smith*

The 10 Natural Laws of Successful Time and Life Management *by Hyrum W. Smith*

The Power Principle *by Blaine Lee*

Books I Enjoyed

Best Year Yet *by Jenny Ditzler*

Printed in Poland
by Amazon Fulfillment
Poland Sp. z o.o., Wrocław

54943266R00181